MW00442770

A YOUNG PALESTINIAN'S DIARY, 1941–1945

JAMAL AND RANIA DANIEL SERIES
in Contemporary History, Politics, Culture, and Religion of the Levant

A YOUNG PALESTINIAN'S DIARY, 1941–1945

THE LIFE OF SĀMĪ ʿAMR

Translated, Annotated, and with an Introduction by Kimberly Katz

Foreword by Salim Tamari

University of Texas Press Austin

Copyright © 2009 by the University of Texas Press
All rights reserved
Printed in the United States of America
First edition, 2009

Requests for permission to reproduce material from this work should be sent to:
Permissions
University of Texas Press
P.O. Box 7819
Austin, TX 78713-7819
www.utexas.edu/utpress/about/bpermission.html

♾ The paper used in this book meets the minimum requirements of ANSI/NISO Z39.48-1992 (R1997) (Permanence of Paper).

Library of Congress Cataloging-in-Publication Data
'Amr, Sami, 1924–1998.
A young Palestinian's diary, 1941–1945 : the life of Sami 'Amr / translated, annotated, and with an introduction by Kimberly Katz ; foreword by Salim Tamari. — 1st ed.
p. cm. — (Jamal and Rania Daniel series in contemporary history, politics, culture, and religion of the Levant)
Title in Arabic: Mudhakkirati fi hadhahi al-hayat : macrikat al-hayat (My memoirs of this life : the battle of life).
Includes bibliographical references and index.
ISBN 978-0-292-72355-9
1. 'Amr, Sami, 1924–1998—Diaries. 2. Palestine—History—1917–1948—Biography. 3. Palestinian Arabs—Diaries. 4. Palestine—Description and travel. 5. Palestine—Social life and customs—20th century. 6. World War, 1939–1945—Personal narratives, Palestinian. 7. World War, 1939–1945—Palestine. 8. World War, 1939–1945—Jerusalem. 9. Jerusalem—Biography. 10. Hebron—Biography.
I. Katz, Kimberly. II. Title.
DS126.3.A67 2009
956.94'4204092—dc22
[B] 2009004817

To Samīr, who entrusted me with his father's words.

There are only three things that break the soul of an individual: death, poverty, and illness.

—Sāmī ʿAmr, diary entry, 1 September 1942

CONTENTS

FOREWORD | Life in the Margins

Salim Tamari

Sāmī ʿAmr's mandate-era memoirs of his days working for the British in Palestine in the 1940s provides us with a rare intimate window into the world of thousands of Palestinians who flocked from their villages and provincial towns during the crucial years between the two great wars to seek employment opportunities and social advancement in the British Mandate capital of Jerusalem. With village origins in Dūra, one of the most conservative and "tribal" strongholds of Jabal al-Khalīl, Sāmī grew up in the city of Hebron but set out to make his way in life in the city of Jerusalem.

The central theme of this diary of self-discovery is the tortuous search for a Palestinian modernity that is both Arab and Islamic. In this search the author seems to be fighting the ghosts of his own society—what he identifies as the repressive traditionalism of the village and the tribalism of Mt. Hebron. In this he has internalized a Europeanized colonial image of Arab backwardness, along with a view of progress in a model of emancipation that is anchored in adopting a dress code, mannerisms, and a normative code of behavior derived from the European adversary. Yet ʿAmr's view of social emancipation via British rule is conflicted by the author's own experience of the mandate as a repressive colonial apparatus, especially during the various upheavals that accompanied British rule, his brother's imprisonment by the authorities, and—not least—by his perpetual, but frustrated, search for the Perfect Woman.

In seeking employment within the ranks of the British institutions in Palestine and civil service (in Sāmī's case with NAAFI, in his brother's case with the military) ʿAmr was following in the footsteps of his countrymen from the Ottoman period, when thousands of city folks filled the ranks of the civil service, and hundreds of thousands volunteered or were conscripted to fight in the imperial armies of the sultan. Quite a few nationalist figures, like Muḥammad ʿIzzat Darwaza, Saʿdun al-Huṣari, and Rustum Haydār, wrote proudly of their civil and military service in the imperial bureaucracy. They often saw it as an essential schooling in acquiring necessary skills for the nationalist struggle. The same is true of the early employment in the British police, army, and civil service, when thousands of Palestinians, and other Arabs serving in the service of the British and French Mandates, saw this service as a legitimate source of employment which also fulfilled their national duty by preparing the ground for the period of postcolonial independence. In the case of employment in the British armed forces in Palestine, however, the situation began to differ in the thirties and forties in several facets. First the incorporation of the terms of the Balfour Declaration into the British Mandate made it difficult for most Palestinians to believe that their future was similar to the situation in Syria, Lebanon, Iraq, or Transjordan—where local parliaments, representative government, and the rubric of statehoods were being implemented. The Palestinian Arabs were compelled to contest appointments in the public sector, to challenge budget allocations, and to vie for the land itself, as it was being colonized by the Zionist project. Second, the Rebellion of 1936–1939—witnessed by ʿAmr and his family a few years before ʿAmr began writing his diary—had a major impact on every feature of daily life and was a constant reminder to those who chose to serve in the ranks of the colonial state apparatus that theirs was not a neutral or innocent employment.

Kimberly Katz reminds us of the pitfalls of serving the British in this troubled period. In 1936 the British army created the Palestine Battalion of the Buffs to fight Arab rebellion. Its recruits were both Jews and Arabs, the latter mostly of peasant origin. In 1942 that battalion was expanded to prepare for native participation in the struggle against the Axis powers. At its peak, 27,000 Palestinians *volunteered* as official soldiers in the ranks of the British Army. Of those, one-third—about 9,000 soldiers—were Palestinian Arab; the rest were Jewish recruits. As the war operations extended to the Middle East, most notably in North Africa and the Palestinian coast, their numbers increased considerably. What is astounding about these figures is that the number of Palestinian fighters in the colonial forces, if one also includes Arab members of the colonial police force and Criminal Investigation Department (CID), equaled, if not exceeded, the combined forces of resistance groups, including the militias of al-Jihād al-Muqaddas (Husseini leadership), the Qassāmites (followers of Sheikh ʿIzz al-Dīn al-Qassām) and the Arab Salvation Army (al-Qāwuqjī).

It was this army that Sāmī's brother, Saʿdī, joined in the early 1940s, to Sāmī's great embarrassment. It is not clear from the diary, however, whether this embarrassment was caused by his brother's very act of joining the colonial army, by his going AWOL when he was posted to the Egyptian front, or—possibly—by his escape from the increasing danger of having to fight against Rommel's forces in the Libyan desert. The ambivalence in ʿAmr's diary on this issue is intentional. It extends itself not only to his brother's army career and his own service in the NAAFI, but also to his silence, or ambiguity, on the burning issues of the period—in particular the Arab Revolt and the Zionist Question. While displaying a considerable amount of patriotism reflected in his love of the land, and showing concern that high levels of immigration were likely to undermine the possibility of independence for Arab Palestine, ʿAmr chose not to compromise his standing by joining any oppositional movement or by expressing these sentiments in any coherently anticolonial manner.

In my reading of the diary, this ambivalence is not necessarily a mark of cowardice on the part of the writer. (He is certainly openly critical of his own community's traditionalism and "backwardness"—a position which would have required a considerable defiance of his own society.) Nor does it seem to emanate from fear of losing his job. At the heart of ʿAmr's hesitancy seems to lie a quest for a defiant, modernist Palestine which, in his view, required a struggle that transcended Zionism and colonialism. Such a struggle required a radical encounter with the challenges of Western culture, in which the mandate authority was itself an instrument of this modernity. We notice such obsessions on ʿAmr's part by his references to colonial work discipline, dress codes, unveiling, industrial organizing, and modern farming techniques as the appropriate conditions for the uplifting of Palestine. In his fascination with colonial modernity, ʿAmr was not alone—he joins a notable series of writers from this period that include Khalidah Adib (Halide Edip), Khalīl Totah, Khalīl as-Sakakini, and ʿUmar al-Barghoutī. His dilemma lies in his inability to combine an image of emancipated modernity with an anticolonial perspective.

ʿAmr's diary is an important addition to a new genre of biographic narratives of Palestinian and Arab figures that have appeared in the last decade, in which the personal experience of the narrator highlights unexamined features in the social history of the Ottoman and colonial periods. The distinctive feature of these subaltern narratives is that they invariably belong to non-elite groups—thus throwing new light on major transformations in society—and, more importantly, they are informed by conceptual paradigms that render them important tools in understanding the shifts and ruptures that occurred after World War I in the Arab East. Those ruptures include the nature of urban modernity in the Middle East, the manner in which the state and the colonial civil service constituted a basic instrument of socialization in the public sphere, and the redefinition of the relations between men and women who increasingly sought employment in the public sector.

Kimberly Katz was able, through her skillful editing and framing of this diary, to steer through this tortuous route of ʿAmr's self-reflections without passing judgment on his motivations or his political predicament. In doing so she has provided us with an interpretation of the diary in the context of his time, permitting the reader to appreciate why he wrote these utterances, and their meaning for the postwar generation.

PREFACE AND ACKNOWLEDGMENTS

This book emerges out of a chance meeting I had with the diarist's eldest son, Samīr ʿAmr, and his wife on an airplane en route to Jordan in 1999. The few words I exchanged with a flight attendant in Arabic precipitated the opportunity to work on this rare diary, as Samīr's interest in my Arabic-language abilities led to a conversation on the airplane and then to many more by email, over the course of several years, about the history and politics of Palestine and the Palestinian-Israeli conflict. It was about five years before Samīr and I met again, in ʿAmman, when he invited me for mansef with his family, at which time he showed me his father's World War II–era diary and asked my professional opinion on its historical value. Consumed with completing a book about Jerusalem during the 1948–1967 period, I looked briefly at the handwritten manuscript, which had been preserved well for sixty years, and recognized that it was of great value to the twentieth-century history of Palestine, beyond the familial value it held for Sāmī's descendants. Delighted with the rare source, I enthusiastically accepted his offer to work on his father's diary.

Not able to begin working on it then, I had the diary transcribed into an electronic format without being fully aware of the complexities that such a transcription would entail. Sāmīyya Khalaf, a Jordanian master's student at the time, transcribed the handwritten manuscript to a typed format in Arabic that would be more manageable for me to translate and study. She could not have known that the page-by-page typing of Sāmī's entries, as requested, would bring about confusion when I later came to translate the diary into English. I engaged in a word-by-word check between the typed transcription and the handwritten manuscript to ensure that nothing had been inadvertently omitted. Even to the native speaker and reader, Arabic handwritten manuscripts are complicated, and some passages ultimately required textual analysis and an occasional check with Samīr to verify what Sāmī had written to be able to accurately translate it.

This historical source expanded my interest in the history of Palestine, as it opened up the subset of self-literature and included research on autobiographies and memoirs in addition to diaries. Historical research on these literary genres covers different geographical regions and historical periods, requiring comparative consideration to contextualize Sāmī's diary. Two colleagues at Towson University, Rita Costa-Gomes and Wendy Lower, significantly aided this aspect of the project by sharing their expertise in the related literature of medieval European and modern Central European history, respectively. Their comments and suggestions vastly improved the Introduction and especially the historiographical section.

Indeed, many of my colleagues at Towson University's Department of History deserve my appreciation, as they read and discussed an earlier version of the Introduction during a fall 2007 history faculty seminar. Many useful comments came out of that discussion, and while some have made their way into the text and others have not, the conversation was extremely productive. Thanks to Karen Oslund both for her thorough comments and for allowing me to present my work to the faculty despite its excessive length for such a seminar. Nicole Dombrowski went through the earlier version with a fine-tooth comb, an editing job that greatly improved both the clarity and structure of the Introduction and one for which I am most grateful. Pat Romero graciously offered comments on the Introduction and has consistently encouraged my research since my arrival at Towson. Robert Rook read the entire Introduction twice and served as a constant source of encouragement for the project. Kelly Gray offered a refresher course on constructing the index. Paporn Thebpanya of the Department of Geography did a wonderful job creating the maps and the genealogy table. Jennifer Ballengee, specializing in classics, commented at the eleventh hour on an entry that will remind the reader of the long history of exchange of words and feelings in the Mediterranean region. Terry Cooney, the dean of the College of Liberal Arts, offered considerable support in facilitating a public presentation of diaries and history writing at Towson University, at which a discussion of Sāmī's diary along with a World War II European Jewish diary allowed the public an introduction into the less common nature of diaries as a historical source and to Sāmī's particular and unusual diary. All of these colleagues, along with Emily Daugherty and others who helped in various ways, have my sincere appreciation.

I received considerable student input to this project for which I am grateful and with which I am pleased. During the spring semester 2007, my students in History 340, History of the Israeli-Palestinian Conflict, read an unpublished, early translation of the diary for a class project. Sāmī's thoughts in the diary resonated quite well with most of the students in that course, as they too, like Sāmī did in the 1940s, struggle with how to complete their education and find the right jobs and life partners. Their papers on the diary enhanced my own thinking on a number of issues, just as they identified places in the translation where the language needed improvement. Hadear Abdou, Rebecca Keaton, Talaal Pharoan, Christine Brooks, and Graham Richardson offered a special engagement with the text as they presented artistic and oral presentations on Sāmī's diary at the Eighth Annual Towson University Student Research Exposition. Hadear, Rebecca, and Talaal also deserve credit for pointing out the strong meaning behind the sentence quoted in the above epigraph, which expresses Sāmī's existence and resistance. In addition to participating in the artwork and explaining the history of early-twentieth-century welding to me, Rebecca gave invaluable help in the final stages of the book's preparation by looking up citations and sources when I was out of the country for an extended period during the book's final preparation. Jesse Colvin, a 2006 graduate of Duke University, made a surprise but welcome offer to do research in summer 2007 that improved the bibliography.

Friends and colleagues in the field of Middle Eastern studies also have proven most helpful as I worked on the diary. Rochelle Davis has been truly indispensable as she read some of my earliest writings on the manuscript and served as a constant reference for details on pre-1948 Palestine and for sources on autobiographical literature. She has been unfailing in her assistance and her friendship, always taking a late-night call to answer a couple of questions or checking sources and providing scanned articles for materials that I could not obtain. Salim Tamari looked at selections of the manuscript prior to my working on it and gave me several suggestions for organizing the Introduction; he also provided Palestinian diary sources for the historiographical section. He read early drafts of the Introduction and continually encouraged me throughout the project. Benjamin Hary gave me a crash course in Arabic transcription, for which I am most appreciative. Livia Alexander provided useful suggestions with regard to the films Sāmī mentions in the diary. I would also like to thank the anonymous readers of the manuscript, whose comments and suggestions improved the text. Despite everyone's gracious help, I alone remain responsible for any remaining errors.

Friends outside of academia, too numerous to mention, offered substantial assistance in various ways, and I thank them collectively. I must mention in particular my deep appreciation for those who helped in reviewing the text of the diary as well as my translation of it into English. ʿĀīda Naffāʿ Albīnā and her family hosted me in their Jerusalem home as I traveled back and forth to Hebron to interview members of Sāmī's family. ʿĀīda sat with me, reading through the entire Arabic manuscript in its original form, discussing the diary's chronological reorganization. She made those afternoon and evening work sessions lively and entertaining as she reminisced about Palestinian history through Sāmī's writings, which allowed me to see the text through different eyes. This experience occurred again as Elias Shomali and his wife, May, originally of Bayt Saḥūr and now of Towson, Maryland, welcomed me into their home to review my translations. Elias read the entire Arabic manuscript, occasionally checking the original handwritten manuscript against the English translation that I had done. He strengthened my translation in many places. Elias and May both enjoyed hearing the recordings of their own country by a man a generation or two older than they. This again made me see the manuscript in a new light and reinforced the value of self-literature.

Thanks are also due to the Palestinian American Research Center (PARC) for its support of my research in Palestine and Jordan during winter 2005–2006. The library at the American Center for Oriental Research (ACOR) and its staff provided a good environment to work on the text, while the center served as a temporary home in Jordan during the weeks of meeting with Suhayla, Sāmī's widow. Sāmīyya Khalaf deserves many thanks for the hard work of transcribing the entire manuscript from its handwritten original to an Arabic electronic format. Jim Burr, Humanities Editor at the University of Texas Press, Leslie Tingle, Tana Silva, and the rest of the editorial team were a pleasure to work with, as was Nancy Bryan in the Marketing Department. I thank them for all assistance offered.

To ensure that I did not misunderstand any of Sāmī's writings, from the original transcription to the final translation, Sāmī's eldest son, Samīr, reviewed it from the first word to the last in the final stages of preparation. He made poignant suggestions of meaning in the entries, just as he explained grammatical constructions and paleographic points in his father's diary. Without Samīr's enthusiastic interest, along with his patience in reviewing the translation and answering what must have seemed like endless questions, this book would not have reached publication. I appreciate his, and everyone's, assistance, for without it, the diary's translation would not have reached this level of clarity, and the annotations would not be as richly detailed.

I am grateful to members of Sāmī's family for granting me interviews and otherwise assisting and encouraging me in this project. Among these were Suhayla in ʿAmman and Sāmī's youngest sister, Ruqayya, in Hebron. Suhayla, who passed away one year after my interviews with her, and Ruqayya were most generous with their time and delighted me with their warmth and kindness. Sāmī's extended family members, including Layla al-Ḥammūrī and Mufīd al-Ḥammūrī and his wife, Imān, facilitated my research in Hebron and hosted a wonderful lunch of *qidri,* a local dish that Sāmī mentions in the diary, at the conclusion of my research there.

Finally, my deepest appreciation and love are reserved for my parents and my sister, who never cease to find ways to support my scholarly pursuits.

NOTE ON TRANSLATION, TRANSCRIPTION, AND USAGE

Every effort has been made in the diary's translation both to maintain the flavor of the Arabic original and to make it accessible to the reader of English. Thus, while many of the cultural expressions have been retained, some phrases have been changed to make them clearer in English by using familiar idiomatic English expressions rather than direct translations. In some cases, the literal translation has been provided in a footnote for the reader to get the essence of Sāmī's writing.

Since Sāmī wrote in a British-produced notebook for his personal writing in Arabic, from right to left, his diary begins backward to the English reader, on page 92, and finishes on page 27 of the pages preprinted with numbers. It was an ordered system, if in reverse to writing left to right in English, and came in quite handy for entries that Sāmī had not dated. Sāmī initially skipped the second side of several pages and later went back to fill them in, sometimes by continuing long passages without repeating the date or indicating that it was a continuation from another page.

Someone reading it from beginning to end, whether in Arabic or translated into English, without the benefit of reorganization, would find confusion in the text and would not be able to follow along chronologically. The reorganization of the diary into its form in this volume preserves Sāmī's gradual recording of his life's events and his observations, although the order is different than if one were to pick up the original diary and begin reading it from beginning to end. Those entries that Sāmī had not dated are herein placed contextually when possible, while some follow the original sequence. If some seemed wildly out of chronological context, such entries have been placed where they seemed most appropriate chronologically.

Both the diary and selected quotations and names in the Introduction bear a thorough transcription. That may be cumbersome to the beginning student in Middle Eastern studies and the lay reader but will undoubtedly satisfy those in the profession as well as those with an interest in cross-cultural studies, as it indicates the scholarly and cultural significance of the Arabic language. There are some problems with this decision, and although I have gone ahead with it in spite of the problems, the reader should be aware that indeed

Sāmī's written language reflects the tension between colloquial and Modern Standard Arabic (MSA). Although at times he deviated from MSA, reflecting the colloquial (as in the poems he wrote), insufficient knowledge of MSA, or inconsistent usage such as in *hā*ʾ and *tā*ʾ *marbūta,* at other times he closely followed it, for example, بئر السبع, denoting the *hamza* above the *yā*ʾ.

Language purists will find inconsistencies in the transcriptions, as I tried to remain faithful to Sāmī's language usage, which shifted between the standard and the colloquial. In another important example, Sāmī was inconsistent in his usage of the definite article *al,* and I have followed his usage. When he used the definite article, I kept it; when he omitted it, I left it out. My transcriptions are consistent in that they follow a standardized system for Sāmī's MSA usage, while following a system of internal consistency for Sāmī's colloquial usage, as a standardized transcription system for colloquial Arabic is rather varied. In the Introduction and some annotations, and further complicating the transcriptions throughout this book, there are several references to published works with Arabic transcriptions in the titles or quotations from those works, some of which do not follow standard transcription systems or have been published without transcription (including authors' names)—in other words, they have been Anglicized. In those cases, I have kept them as they appear in published form, but that means they appear differently than transcriptions that I have undertaken in this work. This is part of the exercise of translation and transcription, complicated by the fact that some authors either omit or limit transcriptions for various reasons. I have also preserved original punctuation from the diary to the extent feasible.

For names of people and places that are commonly used in English or names of people who have published in English under a particular spelling, I have chosen to use the transcription of what has made it into common usage, as, for example, with the name Abdullah or the title "Effendi." Still, there are problems with transcribing such a text that is partly in Modern Standard Arabic and partly in Palestinian colloquial dialect. When Sāmī wrote names, including that of his future wife, Suhayla, it is unclear whether he was using the spoken pronunciation or Modern Standard Arabic. Her name transcribed, according to a pronunciation in spoken Arabic, would probably be rendered "Suheela." The transcription of the standard Arabic of this name is "Suhayla." I have chosen the transcription of MSA for two reasons: first, I sought consistency throughout the text; second, I do not know his actual pronunciation, and by using the standard Arabic, the transcription is clear.

Although Sāmī writes the dates as year/month/day, read from right to left (for example 42/8/24 or marking the full year 1941/5/6), I have chosen to translate dates as 24 August 1942 or 6 May 1941 for clarity and consistency and to follow conventional standardization for writing dates in academic works. The diarist at times spells out the name of the month in Arabic above the date, so in some cases entries appear to have double dates.

There is no capitalization in Arabic; in this work I have capitalized proper nouns as in English usage. Sāmī regularly used the titles *as-Sayyid* (Mr.) and *as-Sayyida* (Mrs.) followed by the first name of someone. This is a common way to refer to people in Arabic, although in English it is not common at all to use such titles with only first names. For reference, *ibn* means "the son of," while Umm Aldū means "the mother of Aldo," and Abū Sawwān "the father of Sawwān," common ways in Arabic to refer to people. In some cases they appear as *as-Sayyida* Umm Aldū and *as-Sayyid* Abū Sawwān. I have left such usage as is.

Sāmī calls on God often in his diary to reform someone (a brother or cousin) who has strayed from the right path, to thank Him for bringing good fortune, and to recognize frequently and in demonstrative fashion that it is God alone who is capable of delivering anything to the faithful and that God is to be feared. For Sāmī, God is always present and to be thanked for His blessings and His mercy, something that fifteenth-century Egyptian scholar Jalāl ad-Dīn as-Suyūtī found ever-present in Arabic-language autobiographical literature. Readers of English may not be accustomed to this, but I have nevertheless chosen to retain all such expressions in the diary's translation. They are pervasive in Arabic, and to omit them would have been to belie a culturally accurate translation. While peppering the speech of secular Arabic speakers as well, in this particular case, such usage reflects Sāmī's personal beliefs.

Finally, I have employed frequent interchanging of the terms "Palestinian Arabs," "Arabs," and "Palestinians." Sāmī makes references to "Arabs" in Palestine to mean the Arab population of Palestine. To distinguish Palestinian Arabs from Jews and to clarify that Sāmī is writing in the diary about the Arabs specifically of Palestine and their unique situation, I have often employed both "Palestinian Arabs" and "Palestinians" in my references to this population. I refer to Jews in Palestine either by that expression or by "the Jews," "the Zionists," or "Zionist Jews" to remind the reader that it was the Zionist movement that concerned Sāmī when he wrote about the growing conflict.

Sāmī wrote about other interactions he had with Jews, and those individuals are identified simply as "Jews," indicating that his comments about them were from outside a political context.

Historical documents and newspapers bear full citations only in the pertinent footnotes. All other sources have short citations in the footnotes and full citations in the bibliography.

A YOUNG PALESTINIAN'S DIARY, 1941–1945

PART 1

HISTORY AND HISTORIOGRAPHY OF THE DIARY

The Diarist and His Times

The title of Sāmī ʿAmr's diary, *My Memoirs of This Life* (*Mudhakkirātī fī hadhahī al-ḥayāt*), bears a subtitle that sums up how this young Palestinian diarist viewed his life: "The Battle of Life" (*Maʿrikat al-ḥayāt*). Written with emotion and political candor, mature awareness and naiveté, Sāmī's diary entries present the broader context of the life of this young man from Hebron, a life challenged by a traditional social environment at a time of great change during the British Mandate for Palestine (1920–1948).[1] Writing with no regularity over four years during World War II, Sāmī penned his thoughts, reflections, observations, and analysis of his life in his late teens and early twenties, a life stage filled with change and challenge for people regardless of origin.

Sāmī's writings convey how deeply he loved his family and his hometown, yet he clearly felt restricted by the social and familial structures in which he lived. He wrote about his professional ambitions, although he was keenly aware that his limited education constrained his upward mobility. The diary records his hopes and aspirations, his loves and heartbreaks, his career opportunities and difficulties, and his relations with neighbors, family, and friends. This web of relations is further complicated against the backdrop of World War II, which followed on the heels of the Arab Revolt of 1936–1939. The revolt was the most vocal and violent Palestinian resistance to British rule in their country—a rule that had directly increased Jewish colonization of Palestine. In one entry, Sāmī makes a prediction about what would happen to the Arabs if the Jews continued their settlement and economic activity.[2] The situation between Arabs and Jews in Palestine compelled Sāmī to proclaim

1. Britain maintained a military administration over Palestine from 1917 with its conquest of the country and its ouster of the Ottoman rulers. Britain received the mandate in 1920, which was formally approved by the Council of the League of Nations in July 1922; by September of that year Transjordan was separated from the Palestine mandate, thus separating Transjordan from the terms of the Balfour Declaration of 1917. By September 1923, the mandate officially came into force.

2. Sāmī consistently refers to Jews, but there is no doubt that he means Zionist Jews from European countries who came because of persecution but also because of the ideology of a nationalist movement that Zionism represented for mainly European Jews in the late nineteenth and early twentieth centuries, a time of growing nationalist consciousness in Europe. In this introduction, I use "the Jews" and "the Zionists" interchangeably, although Sāmī did not use the words "Zionist" or "Zionism." That he did not use these words simply reflects a lack of sophistication regarding nationalist terminology.

his existence through the diary and in it the existence of fellow Palestinians, their presence in Palestine clouded by more than two decades of British rule and increasing Jewish immigration into Palestine and blurred by the war.

His premonition regarding the settlement and economic activities of Jews in the country five years prior to the actual Zionist military takeover of Palestine, coupled with life under the British Mandate, shaped Sāmī's understanding of his social, political, and economic environment. In 1948, three years after Sāmī stopped writing his diary, Zionist leaders in Palestine declared an independent state of Israel. This declaration brought to an end the British Mandate and set into motion the circumstances that led to the creation of a Jewish state in Palestine and the enduring Palestinian refugee problem.[3]

Sāmī's writings offer almost nothing of his life prior to his diary entry on 30 April 1941. He makes no reference to the major events of his childhood, he offers no explanation for the political structure of his country, and he criticizes the Arab political leadership in Palestine very little in his entries. As a result, it is hard to imagine that he engaged in strategic writing intended for a broad public. This young man contemplated contemporary events through a discussion of situations closer to his heart and to his home: how to find the key to his future through work and love. Along the way, his entries offer rich detail about people, some of whom we will likely never know any more than what Sāmī mentions fleetingly in his diary. Nevertheless, we learn a great deal about him and the experiences of those around him—bosses, co-workers, family members. Sāmī's diary allows the reader to imagine, indeed to develop a mental picture of, this young man's life. Through Sāmī's discussions of employment and economics, loyalty and love, we also learn of larger topics of the day, prominently war and justice.

Sāmī's Early Years in Palestine Under British Mandate

By the time of Sāmī's birth in July 1924, Palestine had experienced three years of British military administration (1917–1920) and the beginning of the British Mandate that would last until 1948. The country of Sāmī's early years struggled to recover from the devastation caused by World War I. Moreover, the majority indigenous Arab population painfully adjusted to life under the British Mandate. The period in Palestine from Sāmī's birth until he began writing his diary in 1941 brought remarkable political, demographic, and eco-

3. Morris, *The Birth of the Palestinian Refugee Problem Revisited.*

nomic change. When he was four and five years old, the Arabs of Palestine sought the support of the British to prevent Jews from buying the Wailing Wall in Jerusalem or changing the centuries-old status of Jewish rights at the wall, a site Muslims also consider holy. The incident began small in September 1928 when Jewish worshippers brought items for prayer to the Wailing Wall that Muslims deemed to exceed the norm established during the Ottoman period. Upon Muslim complaint, the British police took action, and Jews responded strongly with protest, demonstration, strike, and mob action. The incident became quite politicized on both sides and led to more demonstrations and recriminations over the next year. Demonstrations in August 1929 ultimately led to violence and the death of 133 Jews and at least 116 Palestinian Arabs.[4]

Again, it is not likely that Sāmī understood or even knew about the conflict at age five nor of the violence that resulted from such disputes. The 1929 Wailing Wall incident did not make it into Sāmī's diary. Only nine years old in 1933, Sāmī undoubtedly knew nothing of Hitler seizing power in Germany or of fascism's creep across Europe that forced Jewish emigration. Many European Jewish refugees sought residence, legally and illegally, in Palestine, some of them having been refused entry into the United States or Western Europe. When Palestinians came together in 1936, primarily in the countryside, to revolt against Zionist colonization and British rule in Palestine, twelve-year-old Sāmī may have known about trouble in his country. ʿAwdat al-Ashhab of Hebron, a few years older than Sāmī, mentions his participation in the Arab Revolt of 1936–1939 in his 1999 memoir, *Mudhakkirāt ʿAwdat al-Ashhab.* Still, the on-and-off violence of 1936–1939 does not appear in any of Sāmī's diary entries.[5]

The years of the mandate leading up to World War II served as the formative years of Sāmī's youth in a personal as well as a political sense. In 1929 Sāmī's father died at the age of fifty-three from complications of diabetes, leaving his widow with five children ages three to thirteen—including five-

4. Philip Mattar discusses this and earlier historiography on the incident and al-Ḥajj Amīn al-Ḥusaynī's role in it in his book *The Mufti of Jerusalem;* see especially Chapter 3. British investigation through the Shaw Commission, Mattar notes in that book, "determined that the Zionist demonstration of August 15 [1929] was the immediate cause of the violence, and blamed Arab and Zionist extremist groups" (48).

5. For more on how Palestinians remember this period of the mandate see Swedenburg, *Memories of Revolt.*

year-old Sāmī and his younger sister, Ruqayya—still to raise. Soon after that loss, Sāmī began his education in Hebron. Some ten years later, at about age sixteen, he completed the seventh grade and a year or so after that moved to Jerusalem to begin his working life at the age of seventeen. At this time he began writing his diary; the first entry is dated 30 April 1941. In his diary Sāmī primarily addresses issues of personal life, but while in Jerusalem, Sāmī developed a growing awareness of politics, from World War II to the conflict developing in Palestine between Arabs and Jews to office and labor politics related to his work. Though the British Mandate authority does not take center stage in Sāmī's diary entries, the city of Jerusalem, the capital of British administration in Palestine, serves as a backdrop of anxiety and uncertainty through his residential relocations, absence of family, and dissatisfaction with employment. By contrast, the city of Hebron appears in his writings as the object of Sāmī's rootedness and yearning.

Hebron and the History of the ʿAmr Family

Geopolitical History of the ʿAmr Family

Likely in the seventeenth century members of the ʿAmr family from Karak took the Hebron mountains through force and made the village of Dūra the family's base in Palestine, while a branch of the family remained in Karak.[6] Sāmī's paternal grandfather, Yaḥyā ibn ʿAbd ar-Raḥmān, presumably was born and grew up in the village of Dūra near the town of Hebron. By the time Sāmī was growing up, his family lived in Hebron itself (Appendix 1). Sāmī's father, Saʿīd ibn Yaḥyā, worked as a tax collector for the Ottoman government. Sāmī's eldest son, Samīr, recalled that his paternal grandfather was indeed literate.[7] Many of the extended family had come to live in the city, but they maintained strong ties to Dūra, just as many of their fellow Palestinians who made the shift to urban life retained connections with the villages of their forebears.

Upon the arrival of Islam in Palestine in the seventh century, Hebron was a modest village whose district association varied with the change of its rulers

6. This came up during conversations with family members in Hebron in December 2005.

7. Samīr knew very little about Sāmī's grandfather Yaḥyā ibn ʿAbd ar-Raḥmān but believed that he had a basic education and could read. There are no family documents penned by either Sāmī's father, Saʿīd, or his grandfather Yaḥyā; email from Samīr, 10 August 2007. There are frequent references to Sāmī's eldest son, Samīr ʿAmr (henceforth Samīr), both here and in the diary's annotations, as he served as an important source for clarification and oral historical accounts of his father's life.

and whose holy places became significant for Muslims. In the Hebron volume of his multivolume study of the historical geography of Palestine, Muṣṭafā Dabbāgh identifies Canaanite and Roman associations in Hebron. For Palestinians and Hebronites, before, during, and after Sāmī's writing, the city bears the distinction of housing al-Ḥaram al-Ibrāhīmī, the sanctuary of patriarch Abraham (Ibrāhīm in Arabic), who is mentioned in the Qur'ān, although Hebron is not.[8] Dabbāgh notes that the city was part of the *jund filasṭīn* (*jund* is a regional district, and *filasṭīn* is the Arabic name for Palestine), but after the Crusades it became part of the district of Gaza. Until 1948, Palestinians understood the boundaries and associations of Hebron with other villages and cities much as Dabbāgh describes them: "The boundaries of Hebron . . . [are] from the north Jerusalem and Ramla, from the East, the Dead Sea, from the south B'ir as-Sabʿ [Beersheba] and from the west Gaza and [the city of] B'ir as-Sabʿ." People moved fluidly from place to place,[9] as Sāmī describes in diary entries about his own trips to those towns. Today's political complications arising from the creation of the state of Israel and Israel's occupation of the West Bank have changed the place of Hebron in the geographical, social, political, and economic fabric of Arab Palestine. Today, Hebron's inhabitants can enter Jerusalem or B'ir as-Sabʿ, previously accessible neighboring towns, only with great difficulty (Map 1).

In 1909, approximately fifteen years before Sāmī ʿAmr's birth, the Ottoman administrative district of Hebron encompassed thirty-five villages and 109 farming estates connected to the villages. The province of Dūra, which takes its name from the village, had 70 farming estates linked to it. By April 1945, at approximately the same time Sāmī stopped writing in his diary, statistics put Hebron's population at 89,650 inhabitants, the overwhelming majority of them Muslims. Dūra, the largest of the villages in the Hebron district, had a population of 9,700 in 1945.[10]

Although Dūra, and soon after Hebron, served as the initial ʿAmr family home in Palestine from which they maintained local rule during the Otto-

8. The Arabic name for the city, al-Khalīl, reflects Muslims' regard for Abraham/Ibrāhīm as "the Friend" (al-Khalīl) of God. Jews and Christians revere Hebron for its association with the same historical figure, the patriarch Abraham of the Bible; Dabbāgh, *Bilādunā filasṭīn*, 45–50. The Qur'ān, 2:125, also associates Abraham with Mecca, the site of Muslim pilgrimage.

9. Dabbāgh, *Bilādunā filasṭīn*, 12.

10. Ibid. Dabbāgh derived this from the *Statistical Abstract of Palestine* for 1940 (published c. 1940), 1943 (1944), and 1944–1945, published in Jerusalem in 1946.

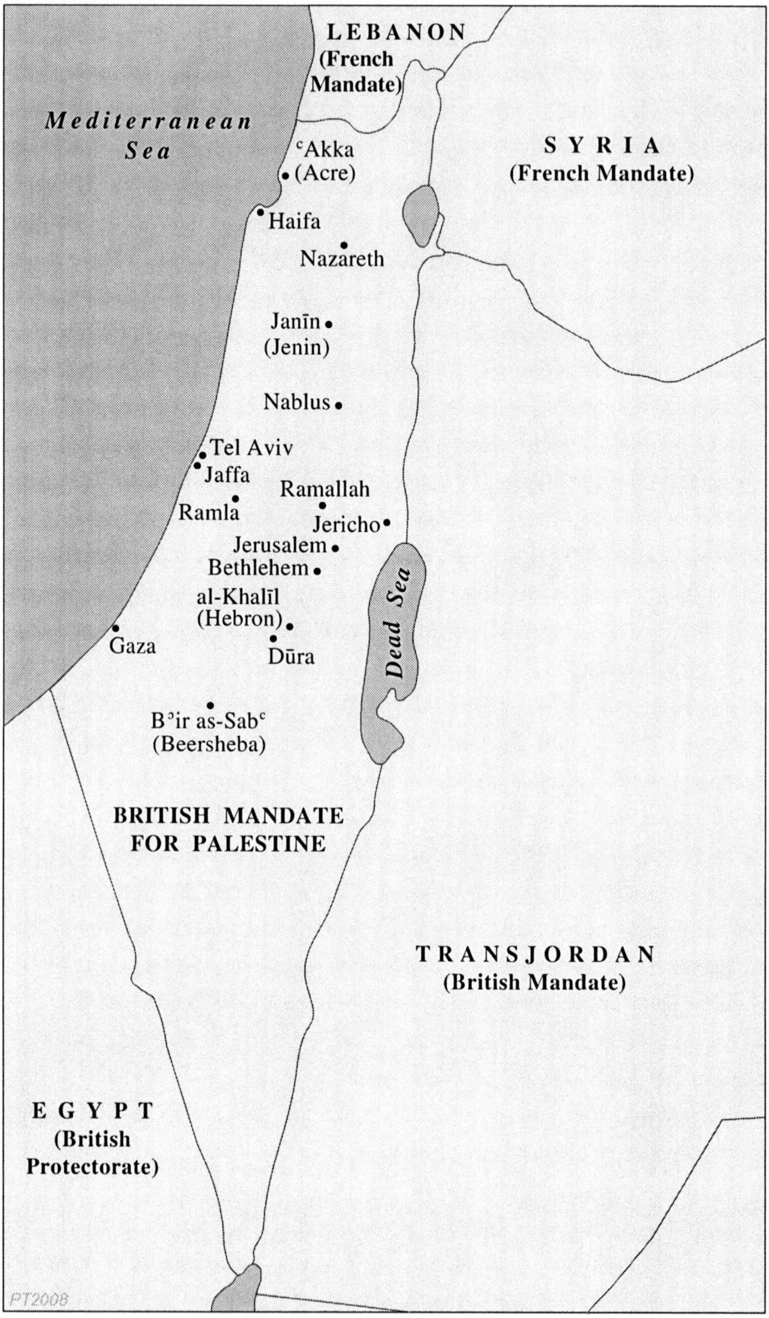

Map 1. Palestine Under British Mandate. Courtesy of Paporn Thebpanya, Towson University Department of Geography.

man period, Sāmī's family has many branches that all trace their origins to ancestors from Karak, in today's Jordan.[11] Family members say their earliest ancestors came from the Arabian Peninsula. Dabbāgh confirms that claim, tracing their roots to the Qaḥṭānīyya.[12] By the end of the nineteenth century, members of the House of ʿAmr who first settled from Karak in the village of Dūra had managed to consolidate landholdings all the way to the borders of the district of Bʾir as-Sabʿ and rule territory in the district of Hebron. During the period of Egyptian rule in Palestine in the 1830s, Ibrāhīm Pasha, the son of Egypt's ruler, saw to the removal of ʿAbd ar-Raḥmān ibn ʿĪsa (Sāmī's great-grandfather) from his post as ruler in Hebron. ʿAbd ar-Raḥmān ibn ʿĪsa succeeded, however, in gaining the post of *qāʾimaqām* (administrative district head) of Hebron after the departure of Ibrāhīm Pasha and the Egyptian overlords in 1840.[13] Dabbāgh notes that this post did not last long, as by 1859 ʿAbd ar-Raḥmān ibn ʿĪsa resumed fomenting trouble against the Ottoman government, which captured him and his brother Salāma probably by 1860 and installed a Turkish *qāʾimaqām* in Hebron, bringing to an end rule by the ʿAmr family in Hebron though not its familial ties and association with the place.[14]

ʿAmr Family Composition and Identification with Hebron

Sāmī was the fifth of his father's six children, all born in Hebron and all mentioned in his diary (Appendix 1). The eldest, a girl named Yusrā, was not the child of Sāmī's mother, Zahīya ʿUthmān al-Budayrī, but Sāmī's half-sister remained an active part of his life. Sāmī's mother's family, the al-Budayrīs, a well-known Jerusalemite family, factored significantly into Sāmī's life. Widowed with young children, Sāmī's mother, it seems, relied on her brother,

11. For more on the branches of the ʿAmr family that remained in Karak and others that went to Palestine and other parts of Jordan see ʿAmr al-ʿAmla, *ʿAshīrat Āl al-ʿAmla "al-ʿAmr."* His work is a family history that includes ethnography, geography, genealogy, and family customs as well as family participation in the nationalist activities of the modern period.

12. Dabbāgh, *Bilādunā filasṭīn,* 189. Tim Mackintosh-Smith discusses Qaḥṭān, the legendary ancestor of the Qaḥṭānīyya, the South Arabians, in his travel narrative, *Yemen: The Unknown Arabia.* Some family members mentioned to me that they believed that the family came originally from the Arabian Peninsula, although they did not specify where in the peninsula.

13. For more on the Egyptian period in Palestine in the nineteenth century see Shamir, "Egyptian Rule (1832–1840)." For an important and slightly different reading of the Egyptian period in Palestine see Doumani's *Rediscovering Palestine,* especially 44–48.

14. Dabbāgh, *Bilādunā filasṭīn,* 118–121, 189–190. See also Abu-Bakr, *Qaḍaʾ al-Khalīl, 1864–1917.*

Jamāl al-Budayrī, as he and his daughters, Hind and Faṭṭūmah (nickname for Faṭima), appear in several diary entries.[15] Sāmī and his mother continued to live in the city of Hebron until he was seventeen years old. Sāmī's half-sister, two full sisters, and oldest brother, Asʿad, had married by then and left the family home. His brother Saʿdī, who never married, seems to have moved to Jerusalem already for work, and Sāmī followed him there.

Colonial conditions across the globe, wartime exigencies, and slowly accelerating industrialization all fostered economic instability in traditional economies that depended on agriculture. Though agriculture remained important, the twentieth century highlights the rise in migration due to economic instability predicated in part on changes in the agricultural realm. Employment was unpredictable and led many in Palestine, as in most parts of the world, to move frequently for employment. Though not a farmer, Sāmī shared the migratory experience with many young men from rural Palestine as he moved from his home in Hebron to Jerusalem at age seventeen to find work. He took a job in an organization affiliated with the British government—the Navy, Army, and Air Force Institute (NAAFI)—initially as an errand boy and later as a clerk.

Sāmī's mother remained in Hebron, while his siblings and in-laws moved around Palestine for employment opportunities or their own family reasons. His eldest brother, Asʿad, worked as a schoolteacher and moved with teaching assignments in different villages. Yusrā, Sāmī's half-sister, married a man whose work in the government's Department of Forestry took their family north to the town of Nablus. The husband of Sāmī's youngest sister, Ruqayya, lived for a period in Tulkarem and in ʿAnabtā, where he worked as a surveyor for the government.[16] Nablus and ʿAnabtā, along with Jaffa, where members of the al-Budayrī side of Sāmī's family lived, served as focal points for a trip that Sāmī took during his annual leave from work in 1942 and which he describes in poignant detail.[17] Sāmī frequently came "home" to his mother's residence

15. Jamāl was not her oldest brother, but Sāmī's mother relied on him more as she saw him more. Their mother had gone to live with Jamāl rather than with their older brother, ʿĀṭif, because it seems that ʿĀṭif's wife did not get along with her mother-in-law very well; interview with Sāmī's widow, Suhayla ʿAmr, henceforth Suhayla, 16 January 2006.

16. Ruqayya said her husband moved around quite a bit while working as a surveyor but would come back to Hebron every weekend; interview with Ruqayya ʿAmr, henceforth Ruqayya, 23 December 2005.

17. Entry dated 29 May 1942.

in Hebron on weekends away from his work, whether he was in Jerusalem or in Ramla.

The change of rule from Ottoman to British after World War I and the death of Sāmī's father in 1929 led to changing circumstances in the fortunes and livelihood of the family and thus in the mode of employment that Sāmī and his brothers sought. Sāmī's entries suggest that his father might have acquired some wealth. According to Sāmī's sister Ruqayya, their father, Saʿīd ibn Yaḥyā, had been quite content with his position as an Ottoman official and had three horsemen with him to do his job. He lost his job with the arrival of the British when he refused to cooperate with them, at which point the family wealth began to decline. As an official, Saʿīd ibn Yaḥyā had a good salary; as an unemployed opponent of the new rulers, he did not find work and began to sell what he had in order to provide for his family. When he died, Ruqayya noted, their mother sold off land owned by the family to make ends meet. Ruqayya added that her mother would sell her jewelry at the time of the Muslim feasts to provide for the family. This was a very difficult financial period for the ʿAmr family.[18]

In an Arab family unit, a child is considered orphaned when his or her father, the male head of the family, the breadwinner, dies. In this patriarchal society, Arab Christians and Muslims see the fatherless child as no longer having a protector and provider, something Sāmī clearly felt and expressed in his diary. The religion of Islam encourages generosity and kindness to orphans so that children who have lost their fathers and perhaps their mothers do not sink into poverty.

While not impoverished, as the family had owned land and shops, it is clear that this branch of the ʿAmr family suffered hard times from 1929 onward with the death of Sāmī's father. The decision by Sāmī's family to forbid him to study in Haifa may have been due to the war; it is more likely that the family simply could not afford to send him to study. As he writes at the outset of the diary, his only choice was to work. Entries in which Sāmī complains about not having money are followed by entries describing his brother's decision to sell off shops in Hebron or cut trees from their land in the Hebron area. He does not mention actually selling the land, but it seems that his brother Asʿad had difficulty at the registration office in receiving payment for the sale of the trees. Administrative details encumbered the sale and landed Asʿad a

18. Interview with Ruqayya, 23 December 2005.

night in jail over the matter.[19] Although he received some money, Sāmī notes that the sale was initiated to take care of their brother Saʿdī resulting from his incarceration for going AWOL, absent without leave, from the British military, a situation that caused Sāmī great anguish. Such sales were overshadowed by the inflation that had hit Palestine as a result of World War II, as Sāmī realized when commenting that the banknotes he received were not worth much.[20] While in one case they sold assets to obtain needed funds to take care of Saʿdī, at other times it was for undefined reasons. At one point, however, the sales provided Sāmī with the money he needed to marry.

The subjects of girls, love, infatuation, and refraining from sexual activity pervaded Sāmī's thoughts and animate his diary pages. He records his love for or attraction to several girls, but the one he married came from the ʿAmr family. Suhayla, his eventual bride, was the daughter of Sāmī's older cousin Abdullah Bashīr and lived in Hebron.[21] Family interviews revealed that considerable cousin marriage took place among members of the ʿAmr family. This is a common practice in many parts of the world that has historical ties to the preservation of a family's wealth. The couple lived in Hebron after they married, as Sāmī had again changed jobs to begin their marital life in their hometown. Sāmī's mother later came to live with Sāmī and Suhayla until her death in 1975.

Leaving Hebron

Many branches of the ʿAmr family remain in Hebron, but Sāmī's line dispersed, voluntarily at first, to take employment opportunities with the Jordanian government in the early 1960s. The British Mandate office that Sāmī joined in 1945 became part of the Jordanian Ministry of Interior after 1948.

19. Entry dated 27 April 1942. Sāmī does not specify, but perhaps the tree cutting was registered because the British government or military needed wood during the war.

20. See entry dated 18 September 1943. The entry is a summary of months of events, with some events repeated. It is difficult to know if the first sale of cut trees in April 1942 is the same one that he refers to in September 1943 or if the brothers had to continue to cut and sell trees to get money.

21. Suhayla was thus Sāmī's first cousin once removed. Out of respect for his much older cousin who became his father-in-law, and according to custom, Sāmī refers to Abdullah Bashīr (Abdullah ibn Bashīr) as "my uncle" (*ʿammī*) throughout the diary. Abdullah Bashīr was far wealthier than Sāmī's branch of the family, and Sāmī's siblings initially pressured him to marry Suhayla, not wanting him (and the family perhaps) to miss the opportunity presented by such a union.

Sāmī rose to the position of chief clerk in the Hebron office in 1958. In 1960, he was transferred to the Jordanian ministry in ʿAmman and became chief clerk of the entire Ministry of Interior in ʿAmman in 1963 or 1964. In an email dated 22 January 2006 Samīr relates the following about the family's history during that period:

> My father was groomed to have a good administrative position at the Ministry of Interior. In 1964, he was sent to the American University of Beirut (AUB) for one full year to study government and administration, and obtained a diploma. In 1966 he was sent to the University of Birmingham in the UK for six months to study "Government de-centralization." He had a rotation in Cardiff, Wales to see how this was applied in practice.
>
> In 1966 he was appointed assistant to the Governor of ʿAmman. In 1969, a former Director of the Jordanian Intelligence Department (al-Mukhābarāt) was appointed as the new Minister of Interior at a period of intense political instability with upheavals and confrontations in Jordan between the Jordanian Government and its Army on the one hand and the PLO [Palestine Liberation Organization] fighters and their leadership on the other. The new Minister brought his own team to be in charge of sensitive posts at the Ministry of Interior including Governors and Assistant Governors. Sāmī's position was terminated, and he was placed on early retirement at the age of 45. His early retirement from Government service was a blessing in disguise. He went into the real estate business and made a little fortune there.
>
> Following the confrontations between the PLO and the Jordanian Government and its Army, which culminated in the so-called "Black September," the Jordanian Government regained total control. Sāmī was asked in 1971 to rejoin the Government, back to his previous post. However, he declined the offer and remained in his new career as a real estate agent.
>
> He built his villa [in ʿAmman] . . . and built the building where I have an apartment and where my sisters, my brother Zuhayr, and my mother live now. He gave each one of us an apartment and kept one for himself, which is used by my mother now. [Suhayla died in January 2007, a year after Samīr sent this email.]

The regional conflict would again penetrate the life of Sāmī's family, limiting his choice of home and work. He had been working for the Jordanian Ministry of Interior in ʿAmman and maintaining the house in Hebron although he and Suhayla and the first four of their seven children lived in ʿAmman as of 1960.[22] Sāmī built the house in Hebron in a most defiant manner, aware of

22. Sāmī and Suhayla's children's names and birth years are as follows: Samīr (1948), Amāl (1950), Samīra (1953), Zuhayr (1956), Fayrūz (1960), Rīm (1962), Ibrāhīm (1966).

Figure 1. Sāmī and family at his home in Hebron, circa 1949. Courtesy of Samīr ʿAmr.

the problems in the country. He wanted his house there, and if the Jews came and took over the city in a violent fashion, then Sāmī was prepared to die on his own base of cement and blocks of stone.[23] His family was not permitted to return to their Hebron home after Israel's capture of the West Bank in 1967. Sāmī's house, the one he built for his bride and their young family, remains standing, empty, in the center of Hebron, to this day (Figure 1).[24]

British Rule in Palestine, 1917–1948

Colonial Rule, Jewish Immigration, and Palestinian Resistance

The British Mandate period marks Britain's determination to solidify its geopolitical interests in the Mediterranean and Red Seas. While in the diary Sāmī does not define the origins of his family's hardships in Palestine's colonial context, the promises, agreements, and military and diplomatic maneuvers that occurred prior to Sāmī's birth crystallized during the mandate period and

23. Correspondence from Samīr, 29 January 2008.

24. Sāmī and his mother appear in the photo on top of the kitchen of his father's house, built circa 1915, with Sāmī's niece Suʿad (the daughter of his eldest brother, Asʿad) between them. Sāmī's wife, Suhayla, is standing on the veranda of the house that Sāmī built in 1948 on the roof of his father's house. Next to her is Sāmī's nephew (the son of Sāmī's half-sister, Yusrā), who is holding Samīr (barely a year old).

endured to shape his family's affective and economic relations throughout his adult life. The British Mandate brought the most dramatic shift in the history of the country since the Crusades, when European Christians took political control of Palestine through military means. World War I provided the unique circumstances that allowed the British takeover, as countries and governments across the globe were drawn into the war to preserve their interests; in the early twentieth century, a period of high imperialism, these interests for some governments included the taking of territory.

For much of the post–World War I period, Palestinian Arabs were recovering from the horrors of war, adjusting to the end of four hundred years of Muslim Ottoman rule, and resisting the Christian British rule that replaced it as well as resisting the Zionist Jewish colonization of Palestine that the Balfour Declaration of 1917 made possible. The British Mandate was a pervasive form of colonial administration; as it is too extensive to summarize here, what follows is an overview of the political context that gave rise to Britain's mandate for Palestine along with details on aspects of British rule that affected Sāmī and about which he wrote in his diary.

Not represented at the World War I peace conferences, Palestine's Arab population fell under a British Mandate at the conclusion of the postwar settlements. In 1919, U.S. President Woodrow Wilson sought to ascertain the wishes of the inhabitants of the Levant (Syria, Lebanon, Palestine, and Transjordan of the mandate period) and Mesopotamia (Iraq of the mandate period) regarding a postwar settlement. Though the British and French articulated such a concern, they refused to name any delegates to the commission that would travel to the region to query local leaders and inhabitants. Authored by two Wilson appointees, Henry Churchill King and Charles R. Crane, the King-Crane Commission Report of 1919 has been largely ignored in histories of Palestine of the early twentieth century. The report is based on King and Crane's forty-two days spent traveling the region surveying inhabitants regarding their preferences for the territories' administration after the war.

Contradictory in places yet poignant in its certainty regarding the Zionist project in Palestine, the commissioners' report called for a "serious modification of the extreme Zionist program for Palestine of unlimited immigration of Jews, looking finally to making Palestine distinctly a Jewish State."[25] The

25. Howard, *The King-Crane Commission,* 349. See further analysis of the commission and report in Gelvin, "The Ironic Legacy of the King-Crane Commission."

commissioners were acutely aware of anti-Zionist sentiment in Palestine and Syria based on their queries and confirmed by British officers with whom they spoke. The commissioners did not believe "that the Zionist program could be carried out except by force of arms" against the indigenous Palestinian Arab population.[26] With the United States not yet a major Middle Eastern player, the British and the French ignored the commission's report. The United States did not support the report in terms that led to active U.S. involvement in the region, thus leaving it firmly under British and French mandates.[27]

So contrary was the King-Crane Commission Report to the objectives of European powers at the peace conference that they did not even publish and distribute it in Europe before the Palestine mandate was finalized. Its delayed publication robbed the Palestinians of efforts to document evidence in their favor that might have been circulated among those deciding the fate of the region (Map 2). Due to the onset of illness, President Wilson likely never read the report. As a result, the report remained confidential, although British and French officials probably had extracts of it. Their failure to send participating commissioners to the Inter-Allied Commission left it an all-American effort, and the British and French had thus received the report as hostile. With Wilson unable to even read it, the report was buried for three years—too late to possibly aid the local population in the peace settlement.[28] With the peace settlement arranged at Versailles in 1919, reinforced at San Remo in 1920, and finalized by the League of Nations in 1922, British Mandate rule with its incorporation of the Balfour Declaration, which provided a "national home for Jews in Palestine," imposed on Palestine a sharp break from centuries of Ottoman rule and the onset of European colonial rule.

In more than two and a half decades of British rule in Palestine, the country experienced an increase from 9.7 percent to 35.1 percent in the proportion of the Jewish population,[29] the creation of a Jewish Agency to manage Jewish

26. Howard, *King-Crane Commission,* 351.

27. Klieman, *Foundations of British Policy in the Arab World,* 36–39.

28. Khouri, *The Arab-Israeli Dilemma,* 13. Howard adds, "There were rumors that both the French Government and the Zionist Organization, and perhaps the British Government, had brought pressure on the American Commission in Paris and the Department of State in Washington to suppress the Report" (*King-Crane Commission,* 259–260).

29. From 1919, the year of the Versailles peace conference, until 1946, just one year after Sāmī stopped writing, the Jewish population in Palestine increased from 57,000 to 608,225 (Chapple, "Jewish Land Settlement in Palestine," written in 1964 but first published in 1987, in W. Khalidi, *From Haven to Conquest*).

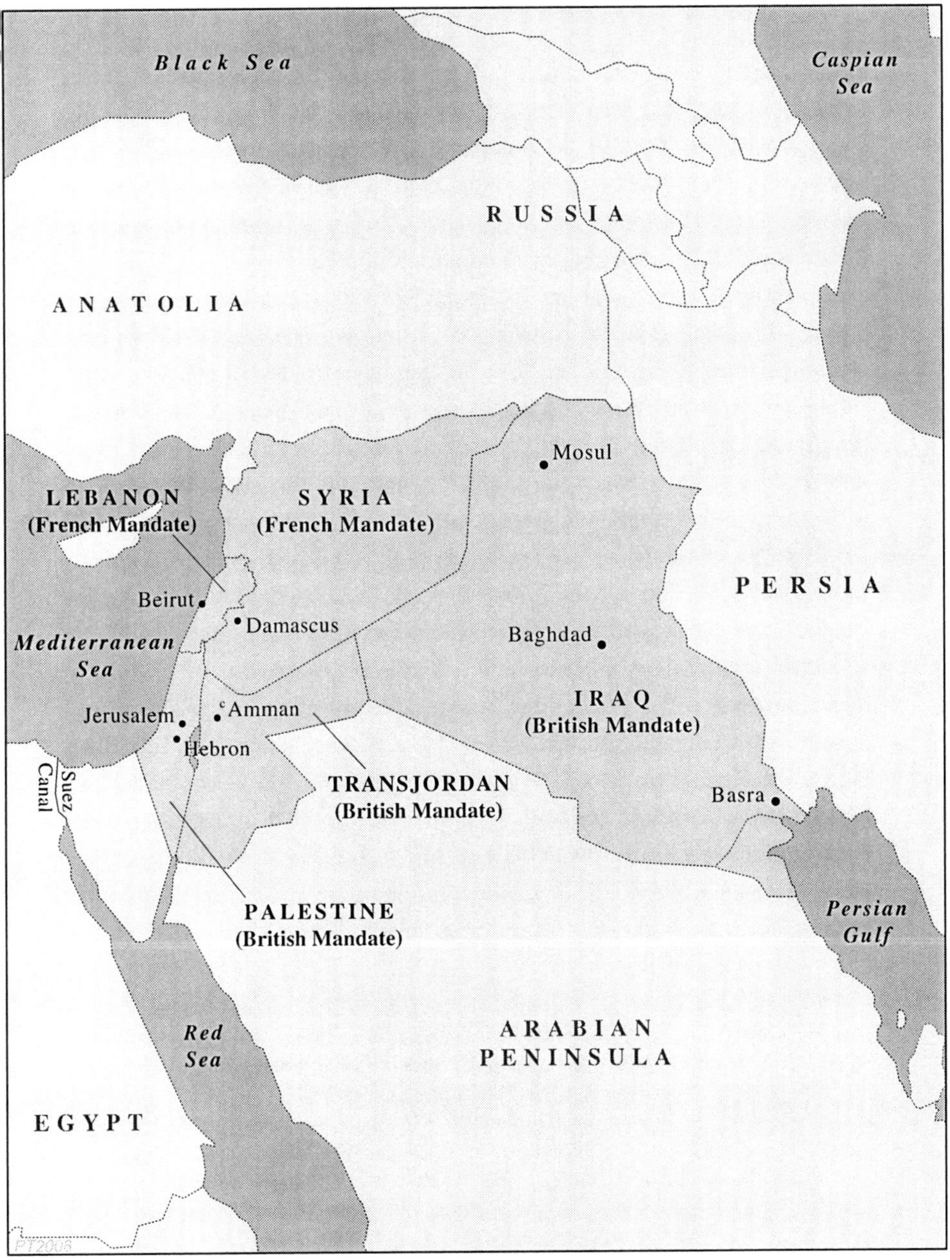

Map 2. Post–World War I Mandate Systems. Courtesy of Paporn Thebpanya, Towson University Department of Geography.

affairs, and growing Palestinian resistance to Zionist colonization and the British Mandate that made it possible. Palestinian Arab nationalists sought a path toward an independent Arab state in Palestine but disagreed on how to deal with the British to achieve this, especially given the successes of the Zionist movement in creating independent Jewish institutions and swaying British political decision making in London.[30]

After the Dreyfus Affair of 1894 exposed widespread anti-Semitism in France, Jews felt constant persecution in Europe. Swayed by nineteenth-century notions of nationalism, Theodor Herzl came to lead a political movement of Zionists that ultimately sought to populate Palestine with Jews, seeing the country as their ancient ancestral land. Indeed, Jews had already begun immigrating to Palestine in the 1880s. Though initially Jewish immigration to Palestine was for religious reasons and small in scope, the pace of Jewish immigration increased in the first decade of the twentieth century. Both persecuted Jews and ideological Jews—those subscribing to Zionist ideology—sought to escape often difficult circumstances in their home countries.

Zionist immigration to Palestine received sanction from the British government as early as 1917. The Balfour Declaration's promise of a Jewish national home in Palestine emerged without any kind of consultation with Palestine's indigenous Arab population.[31] Having dismissed the 1919 King-Crane Commission Report outright, the British government admitted in the 1939 Anglo-Arab Committee's report that at the time of the post–World War I peace settlement, "His Majesty's Government were not free to dispose of Palestine without regard for the wishes and interests of the inhabitants of Palestine."[32]

30. On the issue of changing Palestinian positions, for example, al-Ḥajj Amīn al-Ḥusaynī, who would become a central figure in the nationalist opposition to the British, cooperated with the British until the mid-1930s. On Palestinian social structure from the nineteenth century onward see *Encyclopedia of the Palestinians,* s.v. "Society."

31. The text of the Balfour Declaration appears in nearly every study on this period of mandate history. See Hurewitz, *Diplomacy in the Near and Middle East.*

32. Quoted in Hurewitz, *The Struggle for Palestine,* 100. This is excerpted from the Anglo-Arab Committee's report in Britain, Parliamentary Papers, 1938–1939, Command Paper 5974. In the late 1930s, the British reassessed the Husayn-McMahon correspondence of 1915 in which the British made postwar territorial promises to the Arabs led by Sharif Husayn of Mecca that omitted Palestine. In the Anglo-Arab Committee report, the British concluded that the language determining the territory to be included in a post–World War I Arab kingdom indeed identified Palestine as part of the proposed kingdom. Still, they maintained the clause of the original correspondence that exempted territories not said to be "purely Arab" and claimed that Palestine could not be said to be purely Arab. However, the British con-

The political consciousness of a post–World War I generation of Palestinians coalesced during the mandate period over how to approach the two-pronged problem of British rule and Zionist colonization in Palestine. During the first decade of the mandate, Palestinian leaders organized through the Arab Executive to persuade the British authorities to abandon their pro-Zionist policy and simultaneously to seek Palestinian self-government. As the decades of the mandate passed, with petitions and delegations having failed, differences emerged among Palestinians over how to sway the British to the Palestinian position. While some came to see total opposition and violent protest as the way to convince the British to end their support for Zionist immigration, other Palestinians believed that they needed to work the levers of power to influence British policy in their favor. While the latter impression prevailed among Palestinians by 1927, a year when Jewish emigration exceeded immigration, by 1928 Palestinians' fears returned with increased Jewish immigration and Jewish economic activity in the country.

By the late 1920s and early 1930s, Palestinians convened various congresses (women's and youth congresses, farmers' congresses, and an all-Palestine congress) to express their political opposition to Britain's policies in Palestine. Palestinian delegations traveled to London to influence Britain's Palestine policy, all to no avail. In the 1930s, Palestinians' political expression grew through the rise of several political parties, which increased alongside the escalation in Jewish immigration following Hitler's rise to power. The parties that emerged differed ultimately only in approach, agreeing on their objection to Zionist colonization of their country and lack of Palestinian self-determination. By the end of the 1930s, violent opposition to Britain's policies expanded outside of the urban environment as national committees emerged in nearly all towns to coordinate a strike that began in 1936.

Responding to the 1936–1939 Arab Revolt that resulted from the strike, the British either arrested or exiled much of the Palestinian leadership, none of which diminished Palestinian nationalist sentiment. Nevertheless, during World War II, Palestine's Arab population could do little to overcome divisions among the remaining leadership and forge a common front while Britain banned political activity in the country.[33] By 1939, exacerbated by war

---

ceded that Britain did not have the right to give Palestine away as happened through Jewish settlement during the mandate period based on the Balfour Declaration.

33. Much of this political discussion is based on *Encyclopedia of the Palestinians*, s.v. "Pales-

in Europe, the British were in no position to rectify the historical situation. World War I promises and postwar settlements ultimately allowed for the Jewish takeover of much of Palestine in 1948 upon the British departure and the concomitant expulsion of hundreds of thousands of indigenous Arabs. A commonly cited figure of those who left is 750,000, which the United Nations reported in 1949. Some Palestinians were expelled, while others fled as a result of war. The debate over flight by or expulsion of Palestinians is at the heart of both the academic and political discourse of the Israeli-Palestinian conflict.[34]

Media and Literacy

British administrators wavered over how to implement the mandate and the entire colonial policy in Palestine, and their uncertainty ensured the emergence of a conflict that persists until this day.[35] Those British administrators on the ground in Palestine were tasked with the job of implementing first and foremost Britain's colonial interests; some saw the serious contradiction in the Balfour Declaration that allowed for the Jewish takeover of Palestine at the expense of the Palestinian Arab population's homes, lands, and self-determination. Sāmī writes about growing conflict in a diary entry dated 15 March 1943 and may have understood even earlier, as other Palestinians did.[36] Sāmī never mentions in his diary where he gained his knowledge of the war or local politics, but one might assume that radio and newspapers played a role in his education.[37]

---

tine Mandate (1922–1948)." For sources on Palestinian factions during this period see Hurewitz, *The Struggle for Palestine;* Khalaf, *Politics in Palestine;* R. Khalidi, *The Iron Cage;* Lesch, *Arab Politics in Palestine, 1917–1939;* and Muslih, *The Origins of Palestinian Nationalism.*

34. Ilan Pappe cites this figure from the United Nations' "Final Report of the Economic Survey Mission" of 28 December 1949. He lays out a succinct presentation of the Israeli and Arab scholarly accounts of the number of refugees that emerged from the war in *The Making of the Arab-Israeli Conflict, 1947–1951;* see Chapter 3, especially 96 and 284n23.

35. For more on British accounts, including wavering positions toward British policies, see Sherman, *Mandate Days.* Other such accounts, along with support for British policies, can be found in his bibliography.

36. Palestinian memoirs and oral histories listed in the bibliography confirm that others anticipated the Zionist takeover that British policies fostered.

37. Some, like ʿAwdat al-Ashhab, got their political education in prison. Sāmī never served in prison, but it is possible that when Sāmī worked in the military camp near Ramla he met and talked with prisoners there about various subjects including politics.

Broadcasts on Radio Palestine came to the country by 1936, and receivers were marketed in Palestine the year before, when radio broadcasts from Cairo began, the schedules for which appeared in Palestinian newspapers.[38] In Jaffa in 1942 the British set up the Near East (*Sharq al-Adnā*) Broadcasting Station, which ran only programs in Arabic for the local population and the surrounding countries.[39] In their interviews with ʿAlqām, Palestinians recalled that the British brought radios, probably during World War II, to village leaders or those with spacious *muḍāfas* (reception rooms) to enable large numbers of people to hear the broadcasts from London and later from Radio Palestine.[40] One interviewee said the British brought radio sets to every village but would only let the people hear government news, "only what the British wanted, otherwise why did they bring them?"[41] Interviewer ʿAlqām describes this as part of a policy of conciliation in which British Mandate authorities gave Palestinians some kind of benefit as a way to implement their own policies.

The time-honored tradition continued in Palestine of a literate individual sharing the news from newspapers with townspeople or villagers by reading to them. People knew what was written even if they did not read it themselves.[42] As literacy rates rose in the country, however unevenly, newspapers may have served as an increasingly important source of information about the country and beyond. In *The Struggle for Palestine,* J. C. Hurewitz notes that newspapers became a tool for recruitment in Palestine for the British army in the early 1940s in a stepped-up recruitment campaign that likely targeted villagers and the urban poor.

Sāmī does not mention in the diary whether he read newspapers or listened to the radio. His reading material, he notes, was mostly books and magazines or journals. The latter might have been imported or local. In his *Reading Palestine,* Ayalon lists the variety of imported journals from Arab and other sources that arrived in Palestine during the decades of the mandate. Ayalon says that one way to determine reading habits of individuals is to look at their private diaries. Sāmī writes demonstratively that he loved to read. Even when

38. Ayalon, *Reading Palestine,* 9. ʿArif al-ʿArif notes that in 1936 there were 20,500 radios in Palestine and 58,000 by 1947; see his *al-Mufaṣṣal,* 443–444.

39. Hurewitz, *Struggle for Palestine,* 118.

40. ʿAlqām defines *muḍāfa* as "a central place in the life of an individual within a clan or family, socially speaking"; *al-Intidāb al-bariṭānī,* 43.

41. Ibid., 71.

42. Ayalon, *Reading Palestine,* 159.

it harmed his vision and his friends told him not to read so much, Sāmī writes that he ignored their advice and continued to read nightly, yet he does not tell us what he was reading.[43]

Palestinian Arabs had an indigenous reading tradition, although literacy continued as the domain of the elite. With the spread of mass education under British rule, though uneven, more young people acquired literacy. Sāmī completed the education that was available to him, but when his family hit hard times, it seemed that Sāmī might be cut off from enhancing his knowledge. The opposite was the case, as Sāmī seemed to get his hands on ample reading material despite not being able to continue a formal education. Sāmī's entries do not tell the story of how he obtained his reading material, yet his limited descriptions of reading call for examination, for they may help explain or at least provide context for understanding Sāmī's writing trajectory during World War II.

In *Reading Palestine,* Ayalon examines changes in literacy, modes of reading, and typologies of texts during the transitional period from late Ottoman Palestine to British Mandate Palestine. Ayalon's study offers some clues as to how Sāmī might have procured reading material. The educated elite undoubtedly had the means to purchase reading material, sometimes even by special order from abroad, and to subscribe to journals when they first began to appear in Palestine at the beginning of the twentieth century.[44] Sāmī may not have had disposable funds for subscriptions and thus may have turned to local venues to purchase reading material.

In his classic work on Jerusalem, *al-Mufaṣṣal fī taʾrīkh al-Quds,* prominent Palestinian historian ʿArif al-ʿArif provides statistics on bookshops and the like that Sāmī could have encountered while living in that city. Whether Sāmī purchased books and, if so, how many are open questions, but al-ʿArif states that there were seventy-nine bookshops in Jerusalem selling books, eight of them owned by Muslims (fifty-five by Jews and sixteen by Christians), and fourteen book warehouses (probably distributors), one of them owned by a Muslim (ten by Jews, three by Christians). Al-ʿArif notes eleven reading rooms in Jerusalem, four owned by Muslims (three by Jews, four by Christians), in addition to printers, typesetters, bookbinders, and paper makers.[45]

43. Diary entry dated 18 September 1943.

44. See Ayalon, *Reading Palestine,* especially Chapter 2, for more on texts imported into Palestine during the first half of the twentieth century.

45. al-ʿArif, *al-Mufaṣṣal,* 472.

Al-ʿArif does not mention book prices other than to say that books were inexpensive and abundant, whether originally in Arabic or translated from other languages.[46] Still, Sāmī complains in his diary about his low salary, wartime inflation, and the high price of food and other goods, making it difficult to understand how he managed to develop a small personal collection of books. Samīr recalls, however, that by the time he was a young boy in the 1950s, his father owned books from the 1930s, so indeed Sāmī apparently managed to buy some. Sāmī often mentions going to the movie theater in his diary, so, one gathers from the diary, once he got to Jerusalem Sāmī took part in the bourgeois lifestyle of the rising Arab middle class that took shape after World War I.[47]

Sāmī might have bought a few books, but he also could have taken advantage of the burgeoning opportunities in Palestine, particularly in the urban areas and especially Jerusalem, for borrowing books from people he knew, from libraries, or from literary clubs, though he does not mention that he attended such places. He mentions reading journals or magazines (*majallāt*), but he does not mention whether he subscribed to any. Based on all of this, we can assume that Sāmī bought a book every now and then when his financial situation allowed.[48] Sāmī seemed to read voraciously and obviously liked to write as well. His keeping of the diary signifies him as an individual who valued the written word.

Samīr recalled that his father remained an avid reader when Samīr was growing up. Samīr said he and his siblings were the only ones in their neighborhood of Hebron whose father would buy books and journals. In correspondence from 14 May 2007, Samīr adds, "When I was a child, he [Sāmī] would buy me kids' magazines, and I used to bind them and loan them to the kids whose families would not buy them. To allocate money from his low salary

46. Ibid., 451–452.

47. Davis, "Growth of the Western Communities." Salim Tamari discusses the post–World War I bourgeois environment that Wāṣif Jawhariyya enjoyed; see his introduction in the second volume of the Jawhariyya diary that Issam Nassar and he edited, *al-Quds al-intidābiyya,* especially page 16. Sherene Seikaly discusses the middle class, commodities, and consumption in her "Meatless Days."

48. A random scan of newspaper advertisements of the time in the Palestinian daily *Filasṭīn* shows that books sold were written by local authors and those elsewhere in the Arab world; they were written in Arabic and translated from other languages. They could cost as little as 20 *mils* if published locally or as much as 500 *mils* or more if translated and published outside of Palestine.

to buy books and journals was something exceptional in al-Khalīl [Hebron] in the 1950s." Having enjoyed reading so much and having found such great comfort in it, Sāmī bestowed his love for reading on his children. All seven finished high school, and at least three earned university and advanced degrees. They went far beyond the personal reading that formed Sāmī's education beyond his seventh-grade level, although that was a sound education for the 1930s in Hebron.

Education

When the British reworked the curriculum in Palestine from that of the Ottoman system, they maintained existing courses that had been revised as a result of the Young Turks' revolt in 1908. The new Ottoman curriculum in place when the British took control of Palestine included Qur'ān, Turkish, history, geography, and arithmetic. That was the bulk of the curriculum, which worked along fairly secular lines and came also to include hygiene, object lessons, physical training, domestic science, and music. The British changed the curriculum minimally, to replace Turkish with Arabic and to introduce English from the fourth year.

The uncertain years from the British military administration (1917–1920) to civil administration (begun in 1920) led to uncertainty over a final curriculum, as tension existed among the British over the goals of education. Tibawi lists the subjects in the British curriculum in Palestine to include "religion (Muslim or Christian), Arabic, arithmetic, hygiene, history and geography together, nature study, elements of agriculture, physical training, drawing, manual training, and practical agriculture."[49] However, it took some time before textbooks were produced in Palestine to cover these subjects.

During the mandate period, Palestinian Arabs completed a standard education through the fourth or fifth grade.[50] Emphasizing elementary over secondary education, British Mandate officials in charge of education expanded the former Ottoman system only at the elementary level. In some of the larger towns, elementary schools had a four-year or a five-year curriculum followed

49. Tibawi, *Arab Education in Mandatory Palestine,* 80. This is a classic work on the educational system in Palestine under British Mandate.

50. Jews had an entirely separate educational system from that of Palestinians. Some Christian and Muslim students attended Christian missionary schools in Palestine.

by a “higher elementary cycle” or an intermediate cycle of two years, as was the case in Hebron.[51]

Those children whose geographical and financial circumstances allowed it continued on to the seventh grade, and Sāmī was among these students. Struggling to further his education, Sāmī evidenced a consciousness that without educational opportunities Palestinians faced challenges of advancing in society. Educational policy affected rural policy, both of which stemmed from decisions about colonial policy that ultimately sought to limit nationalist sentiments and ideology among Palestinians who might challenge British rule in the country and the Jewish national home project facilitated by the British.

While the curriculum had clearly moved in a secular direction under British rule, some aspects of a more traditional education remained, including, importantly, absorbing the Muslim religious schools into the Department of Education. Although post–World War I Palestinian historiography criticizes the Ottoman (four-hundred-year!) rule over Palestine as a period of backwardness due to Ottoman policies, the Ottomans initiated a process of modernization as part of the mid-nineteenth-century *tanẓīmāt* (reform policies) that stretched to the realm of education.[52]

Government education at the elementary level in the district of Hebron began in the nineteenth century, toward the end of the Ottoman period. The Ottoman government established the first primary schools in the Hebron area in 1882, with four opening over the next dozen years. In addition to the Rāshidiyya school in the city of Hebron, schools also opened in the villages of Bayt Jibrīn, Bayt ʿAtāb, and Dūra.[53]

Approximately ten years into the British Mandate, ten elementary schools for boys existed in villages in the greater Hebron region. By 1936–1937, there were eighteen village schools in the district, and the highest level—through the fifth grade—functioned only at the school in the ʿAmr family village of Dūra, according to Muṣṭafā Dabbāgh. During the 1937–1938 school year, the

51. Tibawi, *Arab Education in Mandatory Palestine.*

52. In his article on Palestinian educator Khalīl as-Sakākīnī’s diary, Palestinian historian Adel Mannāʿ remarks that the Arab nationalist account of this period reflects ideology over critical analysis and should be rectified in future scholarship; see Mannāʿ’s “Between Jerusalem and Damascus.” Palestinian sociologist Salim Tamari also calls for more critical scholarship on Ottoman Palestine in his introduction to the memoirs of Wāṣif Jawhariyya, edited by Nassar and Tamari.

53. Dabbāgh, *Bilādunā filasṭīn,* 35, 129.

British government created the first girls school in the countryside of Hebron, also in Dūra. By this time, twenty government elementary schools for boys existed in the Hebron district, with one school for boys in the city and one school for girls in the city; this number remained until the 1942–1943 school year. During that year, the government added a sixth grade to the schools in three of the villages, including Dūra.[54]

The English language, according to Tibawi, was offered in the fourth year of elementary school, and with Sāmī having completed the town school course, he would have studied English formally for four years. Problems with adding English into the curriculum in Palestine ranged in scope, much as they did in all colonial contexts. English-language textbooks offered topics of unfamiliar social and historical meaning.[55]

The goal of introducing English into the curriculum lay somewhere between providing too much and too little education to indigenous populations to suit British colonial objectives. Tibawi recognizes in his study on Arab education in mandate Palestine that "two years of English were useful at least for boys who hoped to find employment in workshops or canteens in British military camps or as messenger boys in government departments."[56] Sāmī worked in just such jobs once he finished school and moved to Jerusalem. There is no doubt that Sāmī used English in these jobs and later for his welding job, where the entrance exam was an oral exam in English. Sāmī probably finished school in 1940, as Samīr said his father spent about a year working in Hebron to support his mother before moving to Jerusalem in 1941 to find other work.

Samīr said Sāmī was probably sixteen when he completed his formal schooling, something not at all unusual for Palestinians during this period.[57]

54. Ibid., 35–36, 188. Tibawi offers some comparison of the late Ottoman period with the British Mandate period in *Arab Education in Mandatory Palestine* (270): in 1914–1915, there were 98 government schools throughout Palestine, and ten years later there were 315. Writers differ over the grade levels offered in Hebron. Compare ʿAwdat al-Ashhab's account in his memoir (Chapter 1) of his completing the fifth grade in Hebron with Muṣṭafā Dabbāgh's explanation (139) of fourth grade being the highest for pupils in Hebron, the latter likely being a simple mistake. What we know about Sāmī's level of education matches what al-Ashhab says about his primary level. See also Tibawi, *Arab Education in Mandatory Palestine,* 42–43.

55. Examples include *Gulliver's Travels, Robinson Crusoe, Treasure Island,* and *Ivanhoe;* Tibawi, *Arab Education in Mandatory Palestine,* 84.

56. Ibid., 86. For more on the curriculum in Palestine see especially Tibawi's Chapter 3.

57. Correspondence with Samīr, 2 February 2007. See note 5 in the diary for a fuller explanation of grade levels.

Available instruction varied in quality as well as length. In his *Shay᾿ min al-dhākira,* Maḥmūd al-Qāḍi recounts his own village schooling experience, noting that the teacher was not committed to teaching but rather preferred visiting people in the village. This dampened the students' motivation for school. Al-Qāḍi says that instead of studying, he and his brother "often worked in [their father's] shop during [the] father's absence . . . Sometimes we accompanied the shepherd to help him guard the sheep from wolves."[58] Fruit picking, digging for irrigation, and other jobs required of sons by their families led to high rates of truancy and sometimes led the authorities to close schools due to prolonged low attendance.[59]

The lack of funds to pay for the necessary school items such as uniforms and writing instruments likewise discouraged parents from sending their children to school.[60] Pupils whose families relied on their children to work on the family farm, for example, might not have been able to spare their children's labor long enough for them to attend school on a regular basis. Circumstances differed among families and from the villages to the towns, but many students had erratic school attendance during this period. Economic realities force one to consider the impact that educational attainment and agricultural success might have on each other.

58. Al-Qāḍi, *Shay᾿ min adh-dhākira,* 13. This excerpt of al-Qāḍi's writing, translated into English, explaining the challenges young Palestinians faced in completing their schooling during the British Mandate period appears in Ayalon, *Reading Palestine,* 36.

59. Ayalon refers to a number of personal accounts of childhood schooling in his study on literacy in Palestine.

60. Contrast this with Davis' critique of the mandate's Department of Education program for expanding village education and providing universal education in Palestine, drawn on Tibawi's *Arab Education,* among other studies. She states that the government's department "has traditionally taken much credit for the expansion of education in Palestine. However, the rural education expansion was predicated on the villages providing the building and the equipment for schools. The government was to provide the teacher and his/her salary. The statistical evidence reveals an amazing commitment by the villagers towards education," a remarkable discovery considering the large number of children whose applications for schooling were denied. Drawing on data from *A Survey of Palestine Prepared for the Anglo-American Committee of Inquiry,* Davis notes, for example, that in 1932, rural public schools accepted 3,766 students from 6,555 applicants, while town public schools opened their doors to only 1,702 students from 3,738 applicants. Education in mandate Palestine, particularly in villages, remains largely understudied; Davis, "Commemorating Education," 200–201n21; for data on students admitted, see 201n26.

Agriculture, Land Claims, and Urbanization

The British did not intend assimilation for Palestinians. Instead, they simply sought to avoid the mistakes of the past (in India and Egypt) whereby British institutions created an educated elite class in the colonies. Too much education might take people from the land and bring them into the cities, creating a variety of urban problems such as unemployment and the possible increase of antigovernment political activity while decreasing the necessary agricultural production. The British in Palestine sought a kind of colonial rule that allowed for autonomy of the local population, but they ended up with a much more interventionist policy that had a greater impact than they intended on the political, social, and economic realms in Palestinian society.

Historian Ilan Pappe notes that this policy was meant to foster "limited modernization" in the country.[61] In two primary realms, namely agriculture and the economy, Pappe elucidates British policy: the British sought to improve "rural life with the help of existing local tradition so as to avoid the dangerous leap forward [in Palestine] that had produced anti-British nationalism in Egypt and India."[62] British officials guided their policies on the basis of their experiences in those two colonized regions. A. L. Tibawi notes a report that argued that British officials making education policy saw rural Palestine as comparable to rural India and chose to replicate Indian policies in Palestine. In fact, he adds, that report merely confirmed existing British practice that based early educational policy in Palestine on the Ottoman policy and a borrowed Egyptian system. Nevertheless, the first British officer appointed to work on education in Palestine cut his teeth in the Indian civil service. The next two who followed, the "military educationists," Tibawi remarks, were army majors who worked in Egypt, Sudan, and Iraq before coming to Palestine.[63] British policies for change in Palestinian education were limited and thus curtailed Palestinian professional and political advancement, including in the realm of agriculture. Taken together they limited Palestinian economic prospects.

Mandate officials found local elites to deliver their often unwanted policies who mediated, as representatives of their villages, between the villages and the mandate government.[64] The British turned to the *mukhtār* (village head),

61. Pappe, *History of Palestine,* 74.

62. Ibid.

63. Tibawi, *Arab Education in Mandatory Palestine,* 23ff.

64. By contrast some Palestinians worked through the development of institutions such

a nineteenth-century position created by the Ottoman government to replace the leadership of the *shaykh*. The British maintained the village *mukhtār* position as it was under the Ottomans for the first two decades of the mandate. By the 1930s, the British Mandate government in Palestine reconfigured the *mukhtār*'s status and financial remuneration to bring these local leaders fully into the bureaucracy. The *mukhtār* began receiving a government salary.[65] Promoting rapid urbanization in Palestine might well bring large-scale migration into the cities from the villages, something the British opposed, and thus they worked to sustain village structure through colonial policy and rule through local elites.

Against this backdrop, Zionists intent on laying claim to land in Palestine had internally conflicted views of agriculture but firmly moved in the direction of production for the international market. To do that, they imported the necessary equipment for mechanized farming, which differed from the more traditional agricultural practices of the indigenous Palestinian Arab population. Alan George notes that Sir John Hope Simpson, author of the Hope Simpson Report of 1930 addressing the socioeconomic conditions in the country, agreed with the Zionist claim that only by their "intensive methods of cultivation" could Palestine support their continually increasing immigration.[66] The implementation of such practices fostered the Zionist mythology of a stronger claim to sovereignty in Palestine than the Palestinians had because the Zionists had "exploited its agricultural potential more efficiently than the Palestinians could have done."[67]

Before and throughout the mandate period, Zionist claims to an uninhabited and uncultivated Palestine served a central purpose: to disconnect the indigenous Arab population from the land and thus facilitate calls for Jews to repopulate their ancient homeland, in large part through redemption of the land. Deconstructing this myth, George notes that "in the Arab sector of Palestinian agriculture, all that could be brought into cultivation was already being farmed by the early 1930s."[68] With this Zionist myth about the emptiness of nineteenth- and twentieth-century Palestine persisting into the twenty-first

---

as chambers of commerce to try to influence British policy in Palestine; Seikaly, "Meatless Days," 198n103.

65. Miller, *Government and Society in Rural Palestine,* 55.

66. George, "'Making the Desert Bloom,'" 92.

67. Ibid., 89.

68. Ibid., 98.

century, it is easy to understand Sāmī's concern about the state of Arab agriculture during the late mandate period.

It is difficult to pinpoint where Sāmī derived his information about agriculture beyond the family land and the trees that, he notes, they had to cut and sell. Perhaps he also read newspapers or heard about it during visits to Hebron, where villagers may have talked about difficulties on the land when they came to the city. Sāmī lamented the state of the villagers themselves. In his diary, he offers ideas for improving village life and the sale of village agricultural production.[69]

Palestinian memorial books written starting in the 1980s give evidence of the adaptation that Palestinians made in agricultural practice to keep pace, such as purchasing tractors, to improve work efficiency and production.[70] Oral histories also have brought Palestinian voices to the fore, explaining the extent to which British policy impeded Palestinian agriculture, such as through heavy taxation or determining which crops would be planted (citrus) and which forbidden (tobacco).[71] During their interviews with Nabīl ʿAlqām, Palestinians recalled these and other British policies as means to force Arabs to seek work in the cities for higher wages, reinforcing the tensions in British policy in Palestine discussed above. They recalled Arab migration to the city as part of the British policy of support for Zionist land takeover and full implementation of the Jewish national home policy set forth in the 1917 British-issued Balfour Declaration and added into the mandate.[72]

Labor historian Zachary Lockman clarifies the industrial side of British policies in mandate Palestine, a contrast to the views of a policy emphasizing agriculture. He notes that "tens of thousands of Arabs and Jews found employment in new and newly expanded factories and workshops, and in the scores of British and Allied military bases, repair, maintenance, and storage facilities, and other installations which sprouted the length and breadth of the country."[73] Indeed, by World War II many headed to cities for work, and the

69. He writes about this in an undated entry titled "If I Were an Arab Leader," which seems to fall best in October 1943.

70. For more on Palestinian village memorial books see Rochelle Davis, "Mapping the Past."

71. This is particularly true for the World War II period; Seikaly, "Meatless Days."

72. ʿAlqām, *al-Intidāb al-bariṭānī,* 59–61.

73. Lockman, *Comrades and Enemies,* 267.

British developed other new sites of industrialization for their war effort that lured farmworkers off the land.

British Military and Government Jobs

The British presence had become entrenched in the first two decades of the mandate. By the spring of 1941, Germany's Vichy French allies had taken over Lebanon and Syria, which in part spurred the British to seek large infusions of recruits. The Palestinian coastline had been bombed by Germany's Italian allies, and the Palestinian people undoubtedly felt the impact.

Hurewitz mentions February 1942 as the start of an active campaign of recruitment of Arabs into the British army. The propaganda tied Arab military participation to the prospective postwar peace settlement, but Hurewitz notes in a negative tone that "a barometer of the prevailing Arab attitude toward the war was the number of Arab enlistees in the British armed forces."[74] Some 27,000 Palestinians, including Arabs and Jews, volunteered for British military service by the end of 1942, but of that number only one-third, about 9,000, were Arabs.[75] Walid Khalidi also writes about Palestinian Arab soldiers in his *Before Their Diaspora,* but in an entirely different tone. Next to a photo of Palestinian soldiers marching in a parade in 1941 in Nablus, where the recruiting center was, he writes: "In spite of their bitterness at the brutality of the British suppression of their [1936–1939] rebellion, about nine thousand Palestinians volunteered during World War II for service in the British forces against the Axis powers."[76] In March 1943, an article in *The Times* of London about Palestinian recruits in the armed forces explains the circumstances requiring more manpower. As the war spread geographically, more recruits were needed to handle the lengthening lines of communications and a shortage of imports that in turn intensified the need for local production, primarily in the agricultural and industrial sectors.[77]

Sāmī's diary entries on his brother Saʿdī's experience invite new research on the role of Palestinian Arabs in the British military and related employment during the mandate period, as limited scholarly works focus on that

74. Hurewitz, *The Struggle for Palestine,* 119.

75. Ibid.

76. Khalidi, *Before Their Diaspora,* 245.

77. "Jewish War Effort: Palestinian Recruits in the Armed Forces," *The Times,* 4 March 1943, 5, column F.

issue, and the little that does is conflicted by tone and perspective, as seen above.[78] A rare example of this topic receiving substantial treatment appears in Nabīl ʿAlqām's interviews with Palestinians that focus on the mandate period. The interviewees discussed the military mobilization of Arabs as one aimed at villagers and the poor, those whose situations improved from the small salaries they received from the military. While their financial situations improved, they found the work, it seems, highly unsatisfying, as most served only in guarding positions, while British officers served in supervisory positions. Other Palestinians served in positions of *aḥwāl,* described as the registration of those who exited and returned or the registration of weapons, or in positions of *taḥqīq,* investigations of theft. Interviewees recalled that the start of World War II opened the way for Arab military involvement in the areas of guarding and repair work as well as fighting on the front, although mutual distrust existed between the two sides, Palestinian and British. Some spoke of escaping from the British military, going AWOL, while others wondered, decades later, why they went in the first place.[79]

One might consider what was happening in the region that could propel a young man to go to war. In Sāmī's diary it remains unclear why Saʿdī joined the British military by November 1941, even before the February 1942 recruitment campaign. Sāmī himself never served in the military, but by the end of 1943 he did go to work in the industrial sector, from which the military benefited. His family, having lost financial resources and perhaps concerned about the war, had prevented Sāmī's pursuit of technical training in Haifa, an area that experienced war firsthand. But Sāmī's move to Jerusalem for work from his family home in Hebron opened up a world of experiences as he began to work for the British government in different jobs during the four years that he wrote his diary. He had daily interactions with mandate officials, male

78. Ronald Davis writes in "Jewish Military Recruitment in Palestine" about Jewish recruits serving with British military forces in World War II. Davis frames his article at the outset on the creation of a Palestine battalion of the Buffs, the East Kent Regiment that had been stationed in Palestine in response to the Arab Revolt that began in 1936. During World War II, the battalion was to have parity between Palestine's Arabs and Jews. Within it, however, Arabs and Jews comprised separate companies. Davis cites several interesting tables of statistics about Arab and Jewish enlistment in this piece, based on British War Office reports found within the British Foreign Office papers, but the emphasis is on Jewish, not Arab, recruits.

79. ʿAlqām, *al-Intidāb al-bariṭānī,* 62–66.

and female co-workers, and foreigners from Britain and elsewhere among the diverse groups of people living in the capital of British Mandate Palestine, all of which he discusses in the pages of his diary.

Sāmī's introduction to working for the British government came with his job at the NAAFI, as his skills in English helped him land a job first as an errand boy (*murāsil*) and later as a clerk (*kātib*). Mandate offices formed the government of Palestine, and the British opened a branch of the home-based institution in Palestine for the benefit of those who served in the British armed forces. The NAAFI office was in the Jerusalem neighborhood called al-Baqʿa (Map 3). The NAAFI provided British servicemen with recreational services and familiar British goods in Palestine and throughout the world. Though the British military had offered canteen services for each branch of the military for quite some time, the NAAFI emerged as a way to bring them under a unified system.

Britain's Secretary of State for War in 1920, Winston Churchill, who served as Secretary of State for the Colonies when the League of Nations finalized Britain's mandate over Palestine in 1922, created a committee to advise on the formation of a canteen system to serve Britain's armed forces during peacetime. The NAAFI came into being as a not-for-profit association as a result of the recommendations of Churchill's investigatory committee, with a founding date of 1 January 1921. According to the official history of the NAAFI that appeared on the seventy-fifth commemoration of the organization, the NAAFI was established in Palestine in 1935.

Sāmī began work there in 1941, just as he was beginning to write his diary. His next job also came in the context of British military efforts, as he sought acceptance into a technical school in Jerusalem where he learned the craft of welding. After completing the course, he worked as a welder making metal gallon drums, some of which he saw as part of a British military outpost in the Bʾir as-Sabʿ district when he and family members traveled there for a wedding.

The British military and the British Mandate were one and the same for Sāmī in his diary, as indeed they must have been for all Arabs in Palestine during this period. The topic of the military became most urgent to Sāmī when his older brother Saʿdī decided to join the British military; our knowledge of what Saʿdī's work as a soldier entailed is absent, as Saʿdī did not leave memoirs and Sāmī's diary does not mention the actual work his brother did as a soldier. Other jobs existed for Palestinians throughout the civilian and mili-

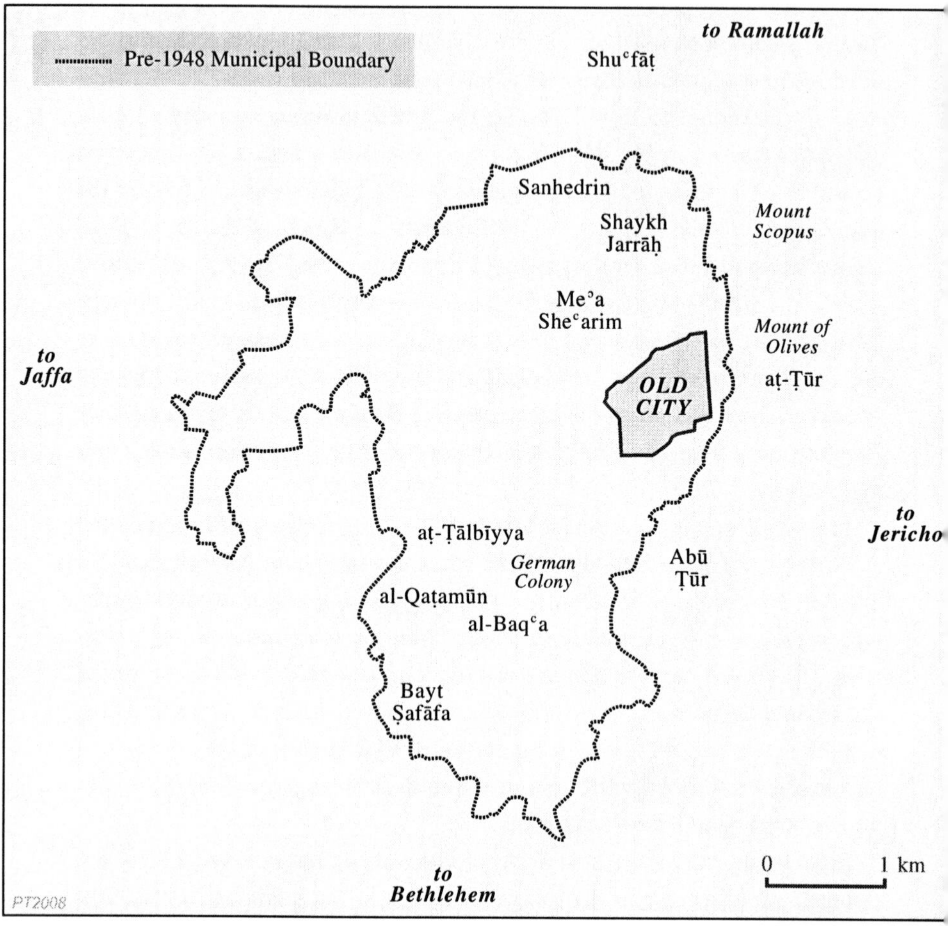

Map 3. Jerusalem During British Mandate. Courtesy of Paporn Thebpanya, Towson University Department of Geography.

tary apparatus in British Mandate Palestine, but Sāmī does not mention these, either. Samīr provided information about such jobs when identifying some of the people his father mentions in the diary. As described earlier, one of Sāmī's brothers-in-law worked as a surveyor for the government and another in the Department of Forestry.

Historiography and Themes of the Diary

Influences on and Preservation of the Diary

Historical source material can turn up in the most interesting of places, often in archives. Old documents become the treasure of families whose elders pass them down from one generation to the next. Diaries, as part of the family treasure, provide a link between generations, particularly after the diarist has passed away. Sāmī ʿAmr's diary has become part of the ʿAmr family's documentary treasures and appears in published form here for the first time. The family's decision to share the personal thoughts, historical observations, and life challenges of their now departed Sāmī provides students and scholars of history with a powerful contribution. For Palestinian history, particularly toward the end of the British Mandate during World War II, his diary adds a youthful and little-known perspective to the available and growing self-literature by Palestinians.

The onset of British rule in Palestine in 1917 brought with it all sorts of change. In the case of writing, Palestinians sometimes found themselves buying and writing in notebooks labeled in English bearing a printed page-numbering system that began with the number 1. The notebooks opened on the left and accommodated writing from left to right. Indeed, this is the kind of notebooks Sāmī used in school, as Tibawi notes: "Script copy books and exercise books used in classes, were according to standards produced in England."[80] However, Arabic and other Semitic languages are written from right to left. As Sāmī wrote in Arabic, notebooks that opened and were numbered from the right side would have served his writing better.

While we have Sāmī's diary to read, we have little to help us determine what might have prompted him to write it in the first place. Textbooks in Palestine during the period of Sāmī's education came from Egypt, and through them students became familiar with such literary giants as Taha Ḥusayn, Aḥmad Ḥasan az-Zayyat, and Jūrjī Zaydān. Palestinians only began to produce their own textbooks in the 1940s,[81] and by then Sāmī already had completed the seventh grade and relocated to Jerusalem. While it does not appear likely that Sāmī read a diary in school, the published diaries from the period of Sāmī's writing and throughout the mandate period show that many in Pal-

80. Tibawi, *Arab Education in Mandatory Palestine,* 84.
81. Abu Ghazaleh, "Arab Cultural Nationalism in Palestine," 40.

estine were keeping diaries, among them Palestinian Arabs (as were Arabs in other countries), British officials, and Zionist Jews.[82] Other literary influences entered Palestine in the form of journals and magazines, primarily from Egypt but also from Lebanon, and Sāmī himself appreciated those influences. When asked what his father might have read during the years that he wrote his diary, Samīr responded:

> I think he was reading the books of [Muṣṭafā Luṭfī] al-Manfalūtī, who used very descriptive language and took ideas from famous Western authors, making stories full of passion and emotion. Also, he read translations of famous authors. These were common in the 1930s and 1940s and were sold cheap, made of yellow, low-quality paper. He loved particularly the Russian authors, especially Leo Tolstoy, whom he admired greatly. I once heard him talking about Dostoevsky: *The Brothers Karamazov* and *Crime and Punishment.* I am not sure if he read them when he was young in the early 1940s, but I assume that he might have. He might have read Taha Ḥusayn and sympathized with him for his childhood poverty and blindness. He did not like [ʿAbbās Maḥmūd] al-ʿAqqad very much. Probably he read Aḥmad Amīn and Aḥmad Ḥasan az-Zayyat in those early days. He read *Majallāt al-Hilāl,* issued by Jūrjī Zaydān from Egypt. I saw when I was a child a few issues of a journal called *al-Muqtaṭaf* edited by Yaʿqūb Sarrūf, a Lebanese (like Zaydān) living in Egypt, which was the hub of Arab culture and book publication in those days. It dated to the 1930s, so I assume that he got these issues when he was writing his *mudhakkirāt* [diary].[83]

Challenged by poverty and blindness, Taha Ḥusayn, a well-known Egyptian literary figure of the early twentieth century, wrote about his life experiences. Sāmī possibly encountered his work in excerpts from his autobiography, *al-Ayyām,* at school, and it is easy to see how the subjects that Ḥusayn covers affected Sāmī and his writing.[84] The subjects of reading and education factor

82. Prominent Palestinian educator Khalīl as-Sakākīnī kept a diary, six volumes of which have been published. Arthur Ruppin, the mastermind of Jewish settlement in Palestine under the British Mandate, kept a diary and wrote an autobiography; these and his letters have been published in English as a single volume. Britain's first High Commissioner in British Mandate Palestine, Herbert Samuel, published his memoirs in 1945, but lower-level British officials in Palestine also published their writings from the period; see for example Courtney's *Palestine Policeman.*

83. Correspondence from Samīr, 14 May 2007.

84. In her analysis of Taha Ḥusayn's *al-Ayyām,* Fedwa Malti-Douglas translated the title to *Battle Days,* suggestive of the struggle of life, a sentiment Sāmī makes clear on the first page of his diary; see her *Blindness and Autobiography.* Taha Ḥusayn's three-volume autobiography appeared under the title *al-Ayyām* (The Days); volumes 1 and 2 were published in Arabic in

significantly into Ḥusayn's autobiography, and he takes up issues related to tradition and modernity.

Friction undoubtedly occurred in Egypt between supporters of traditional religious education versus secular education, and while that was not Sāmī's issue in Palestine, nevertheless he too faced the challenges of modernity and contemplated them in his diary. Sāmī, like Ḥusayn, expresses sympathy toward the downtrodden and oppressed; he complains in one entry about poverty and hunger among Palestinians and the inaction of the government to alleviate such suffering. Sāmī's writing shows the influence of exposure to imported reading material—journals and newspapers from abroad, mainly from Cairo and Beirut—as well as to local writing and translated Western works. As he sought literary knowledge, he bought a blank notebook, wrote a title, signed his name to it, and thus began writings that traverse the critical, final four years of World War II.

There seems little doubt that Sāmī's diary provided a source of companionship for him, as he often wrote about his troubles or his complicated feelings toward family members and young women. Diarists write for different purposes: Jewish diarists writing during World War II, Holocaust scholars note, wanted future readers to know of their existence during a time of extermination, and military leaders penned their thoughts often to chronicle their successes. Other diarists seek to understand themselves and their intimates better through an introspective process of writing about their actions and communications. Frequently people write diaries to work through personal issues. In his article "The Practice of the Private Journal," Philippe Lejeune examines his own experience with keeping a journal and the experiences of a sample of individuals who have done the same. He argues that the diary is "associated with ideas of anguish and lack of direction . . . [such a practice is] a very immediate form of writing and [is] marked by distress."[85] Sāmī peppered the pages of his diary with anguish about his health and uncertainty about his feelings toward girls and his brother, Saʿdī, as much as he expressed the lack of direction about his future.

Unlike other examples of World War II diaries, especially by Jewish diarists in Nazi Europe, Sāmī's diary suggests no desire on his part to save it for future

---

1929 and volume 3 in 1973. Volume 1 was first published in English in 1932, volume 2 in 1943, and volume 3 in 1976. All three volumes appeared in one book in 1997 under the title *The Days: His Autobiography in Three Parts.*

85. In Langford and West, *Marginal Voices, Marginal Forms,* 185.

publication. Still, one look at the first page of the manuscript following the cover and title page offers some thoughts for contemplation about what Sāmī might have intended for his diary at some future date. At the top of that page, there is marginalia, written in the second person, about the presentation of the manuscript, undoubtedly a later addition. The script and the context suggest two scenarios: one is that someone else wrote a line at the top of the first page making a suggestion to Sāmī about how he should present the work if it were to be published. Another is that Sāmī wrote the line himself years later (considering the paleographical difference) as a note to himself in the second person on how to present the manuscript. A second bit of marginalia, at the top of the side margin, offers an explanation that this was not a "story" but rather a book of memoirs or reminiscences (*mudhakkirāt*).[86] Most likely Sāmī later came to see that his diary had value but that future readers should know that it reflected "real life" and was not some kind of fictional account. It is unclear when Sāmī looked at his diary, perhaps twenty or fifty years later, and realized that he still had it and decided to pass it on to his son Samīr, who affirmed that his father hoped that the diary would be published.

Despite the political turmoil during Sāmī's early life, he is an example of a Palestinian man who nurtured the life of the heart and fed his soul with reflection and contemplation. Some of Sāmī's diary might be seen as embarrassing, as he recounts his coming of age, his awareness of his emotional and sexual feelings toward girls, and his need to remind himself of his faith in God and how he must resist any temptation. He describes attempts by an older Italian woman, his landlady, to seduce him. All of these subjects might be seen as best kept for personal or family consumption rather than for a general readership. As Sāmī clearly, in his later years, wanted his diary to be published, one can only discern that he recognized that his earlier ideas, thoughts, observations, and reflections mattered.

By the time he died in December 1998, Sāmī had lived through the loss of Palestine to the Zionists in 1948; the takeover by the Hashemite Kingdom of that part of Palestine that came to be known as the West Bank (of Jordan), which in part precipitated Sāmī's move to the East Bank of Jordan in 1962; and Israel's occupation of the West Bank, including his hometown of Hebron, in 1967. One may surmise that he felt a strong sense of identification with the

86. Indeed, the writings are not recollections, as Sāmī wrote them by and large at the time they happened. The marginalia are annotated further in the diary in notes 1 and 2.

Palestinian collective and had reached the conclusion that one way to make a contribution to Palestinians' living memory was to make his voice heard, to add it to the historical record. It is with that consideration that this diary has been published.

When wondering why Sāmī wrote his diary, one can see all of these factors playing a role. Not only does the diary open with the title "The Battle of Life," but the first entry begins with the phrase "The struggle began," leaving the reader with a clear understanding of why he wrote his entries.[87] Much of what Sāmī wrote expresses the challenges he faced. The diary allowed him the opportunity to share his thoughts with a confidant, as he often referred to the diary as "my friend." Sāmī's separation from his family after he moved to Jerusalem undoubtedly created loneliness and feelings of isolation. His frequent references to the diary as a "friend" suggest that he needed to find someone in whom he could confide and seek solace, with whom he could share his innermost thoughts to work through the incidents, feelings, and complicated relationships in his life as he tried to find his path forward. The loneliness he must have felt comes through when he writes about being unable to talk to his brother who lived with him and not having people around him to turn to in time of need or help him when he fell ill. His challenges evince personal circumstances, work-related issues, and life under the British Mandate during wartime conditions. He worked out these feelings in the diary.

Islamic, Palestinian, and World War II Diaries

The Diary in Islamic Historiography

The Western reader of Sāmī's diary might think that his keeping a journal marked by dates and describing feelings, observations, and historical events follows from his lifelong exposure to the West, as he lived under the British Mandate for the first twenty-four years of his life. Considering the diary genre through a Western historiographical lens raises issues about the nature of written expression and the sentiments that authors divulge in their diaries. The Western literary tradition, however, does not encapsulate the genre historically. By examining other traditions, namely the Islamic historiographical tradition and forms of Arabic literary self-expression, one can dissolve the boundaries of diary writing and place Sāmī's diary into various historiographical and literary traditions.

87. These two titles come from the first page of the diary.

In his short essay on the diary within Islamic historiography, George Makdisi argues that the diary emerged forcefully in Europe within the changed historical world of the Renaissance and its emphasis on individualism, in contrast to the sense of communalism that marked the Middle Ages.[88] He states that Europe had to wait for the sense of "individualism and self-awareness," which in part differentiates medieval Europe from the Renaissance, for the personal diary to appear as a distinct form of writing, separate from the daily writing of public records. Scholars of the medieval period in European history challenge the notion that those who lived in that period had no sense of individualism, thus raising questions about expressive forms in different historical periods in the European context, a topic that medieval and Renaissance historians are better prepared to tackle than this author.

Makdisi may be correct in his claim that the earliest extant Western diary that is emotionally self-reflective comes from the early to mid-fifteenth century. Still, that understanding may be limited if one maintains a restrictive interpretation of what the diary is. Diaries in Europe prior to the Renaissance were written by travelers and monks, but they took a slightly different form, much as they did in the early Islamic period that Makdisi discusses. A broader view of travelers' and monks' accounts shows more fluidity in understanding the personal writings found in medieval manuscripts.[89] By chronologically recording the events of travel or by writing dated letters of daily life, travelers and monks left details of the places they visited and the thoughts they had at the time, as so often happens in modern diaries. It is beyond the scope of this work to belabor this point, but it sets the stage for a wide view of the literature of self-expression.

Makdisi's argument best provides for an indigenous tradition from which scholars can draw when examining the writings of Muslims and Arabs in later periods as they penned their individual thoughts and reflections on the societies in which they lived. When examining the place of the diary in Islam,

88. Makdisi, "The Diary in Islamic Historiography." This discussion of the diary in European historiography is based on his short introduction to that article, but early modern European historians agree on this point. Jürgen Schlaeger, for example, says that "the tradition of self-exploration in diaries and autobiographies [was] a tradition that had begun in the late sixteenth century"; "Self-Exploration in Early Modern English Diaries," 22.

89. For more on this debate see Constable, *Letters and Letter-Collections;* C. Morris, *The Discovery of the Individual, 1050–1200;* Rubenstein, "Biography and Autobiography in the Middle Ages"; Zumthor, "The Medieval Travel Narrative."

Makdisi notes that "in striking contrast to the West, Islam developed the diary very early in its history, earlier than has heretofore been known."[90] Examining in particular the eleventh-century diary of ibn Banna, Makdisi's work makes a strong case for Islam's historiographical tradition of diary writing separate from the European one.

Indeed, while he accepts some European historians' distinction of historical eras in determining what a diary is, Makdisi argues for a broad literary view of the diary in Islamic manuscripts. The diary tradition in Islam, he says, informed the writing of history by Muslims, whether the writings focused on world history or the history of cities, the history of scholars or biographical dictionaries, or other historical biographies. Because so few examples remain, Makdisi states, diaries by early Muslims probably were not intended to be published; the information in them was appropriately added into scholarly works. Yet the Islamic science of *ḥadīth* criticism, in which knowledge of individual life histories was crucial, provided the foundation for the writing of diaries while also serving its main purpose of authenticating the Traditions (*ḥadīth*) of the Prophet.

Sāmī's diary obviously does not look exactly like the diaries of the early Islamic period to which Makdisi refers, as no literary tradition is static in any culture. Like the earlier Muslim diaries, however, Sāmī's diary serves the distinct purpose of informing the writing of history, in this case of Palestinian history during the late British Mandate period. Linking Sāmī's diary to what Makdisi might call the Islamic historiographical tradition also serves to place it firmly within what Reynolds et al. define as the Arabic "self" literary genre in *Interpreting the Self: Autobiography in the Arabic Literary Tradition,* albeit in a slightly expanded list of types of writing.

Long thought in Western historiography to be solely a Western creation, the autobiography has a long tradition in Arabic-language writing (by Muslims, Christians, and Jews) that was well established by the twelfth century, although examples exist from the ninth century.[91] There have not been, until very recently, comprehensive studies of the cumulative autobiographical tradition among scholars who analyze Arabic writings. In *Interpreting the Self,* editor Dwight Reynolds and a collaborative team of authors address the historiographical imbalance by theorizing about and exploring some 150 Arabic

90. Makdisi, "The Diary in Islamic Historiography," 173.
91. Reynolds, *Interpreting the Self,* 2.

autobiographical texts written over the course of 1,000 years; the volume gives readers a sense of how Arabic writers wrote about themselves. A rare collaborative writing effort, the book offers a stunning examination of an obviously overlooked aspect of non-Western literature and prompts a rethinking of how scholars, especially Western scholars writing about the Western literary tradition, have compared and privileged the Western world by diminishing the literary and historical value of non-Western, in this case Arabic, writings.[92]

Arabic autobiographies share the narrative construction of writing about oneself with the genres of memoirs and diaries. Autobiographers express the events of their lives, although not in strict linear fashion. In the course of their writings, they pass on knowledge of their *aḥwāl* or *aṭwār* (circumstances or states) to reflect life as a lived combination of changing conditions.[93] Autobiographers in the Arabic traditions have written specifically of their geographic origins, genealogy, travels, scholarly work, employment, controversies in their lives, and comments on legal opinions, among other subjects, "presenting a comprehensive portrait" of their lives.[94]

While stimulating in many ways for examining self-literature, *Interpreting the Self* omits a discussion of diaries in the Arabic literary tradition. The authors instead focus on the Arabic genres of *sīra/sīra dhātīyya* (biography/self-biography) and *tarjama li-nafsīhī/tarjama shakhsīyya* (interpretation of oneself/personal biographical notice).[95] Nevertheless, there seems to be an obvious relationship to these types of writings, and a comparison of what these authors found in earlier Arabic autobiographies with what is found in Sāmī's diary may provide a link to different "self" genres within the Arabic literary tradition.

Reynolds opens the introduction to *Interpreting the Self* by explaining how fifteenth-century Egyptian scholar Jalāl ad-Dīn as-Suyūtī situated his autobi-

92. Incidentally, Reynolds and collaborators raise the question of looking to other non-Western cultural contexts, including the Chinese and Japanese, to expand the notion of a starting point for particular genres or phenomena beyond that of the Western experience (31–32).

93. Ibid., 4.

94. Ibid., 5. See Reynolds' introduction for a thorough discussion of the Arabic autobiography.

95. The terminology and definitions are those used in Reynolds, *Interpreting the Self.*

ography within an existing and "recognized tradition of Arabic autobiographical writing."[96] As-Suyūtī focuses on three elements that autobiographers have addressed: highlighting God's bounty; describing their life circumstances for the sake of others (to perhaps emulate their good works); and leaving an account for the benefit of later historians or chroniclers.[97] Despite its authors' acceptance of a broad definition of "first-person literature or self-narratives," *Interpreting the Self* has a "guiding criterion . . . for deeming a text an autobiography . . . that the text present itself as a description or summation of the author's life, or a major portion thereof, as viewed retrospectively from a particular point in time."[98]

Sāmī's diary shares all three of as-Suyūtī's characteristics listed above for autobiographical literature. His work, however, is not written retrospectively, and the form and structure of his writings differ. Sāmī does not summarize his life; rather, his diary offers a more "in the moment" depiction of his life. There is no cumulative element to Sāmī's entries, and in a number of cases, there is even repetition. This might be a natural recurrence, as the issues he faced did not simply disappear the moment that he penned them in his diary. The repetition also might suggest that he forgot that he had already mentioned a particular topic or situation or perhaps that he did not reread his diary very often. His entries open up his life and address the events, feelings, circumstances, and changing conditions that illustrate Arabic self-writing. And while it provides the Western reader with the opportunity to cross literary and cultural boundaries, Sāmī's diary makes a significant contribution to the history of Arabic self-literature, to Palestinian and Arab history, and to the history of the British Mandate in Palestine.

Perhaps Sāmī might have been clearer using the Arabic word *yawmīyyāt* rather than *mudhakkirāt* (memoirs or reminiscences), for what his diary is, as it derives from the word *yawm,* meaning "day"; a *yawmīyyāt* is a daily, or at least a dated, set of writings. Still, Sāmī's diary offers an immediate problem in that it is clear that he did not write on a day-by-day basis. Further, it is not clear that he always wrote on the day that things happened to him and pro-

96. Ibid., 1.

97. Ibid. Reynolds includes a translated excerpt of this from as-Suyūtī's autobiography, *at-Taḥadduth bi-niʿmat Allah* (Speaking of God's Bounty).

98. Ibid., 9.

voked him to write.[99] Surely if one looks at the range of literary features that appear in this short diary, evident in the lack of uniform stylistic structure to his entries, one might raise the charge that this is not a diary at all but rather some other form of writing. The reader will find that the entries, some dated and some not, take the form of letters, poetry, polemics, speeches, complaints, and other styles of writing. While Sāmī's diary exceeds the structure of what might be considered a classic Western diary (if there is such a thing) that describes the thoughts and feelings of the author, it is clear that he wrote his diary in a confident Arabic form of writing about the self.

Sāmī's use of poetry, his own and that of a famous historical figure, reflects centuries and centuries of emotive poetic expression in the Arabic literary and oral tradition. He does not simply say, "Where is the girl I will marry?" Instead, Sāmī writes a poem that begins, "I wonder who she is! The one I will live with forever," and we know immediately that he is talking about love and marital companionship. Rather than state that he wants children, he names them in that same poem: "I will call one of them Samīr, the second Zuhayr, and the third Amāl, they all love me and call me Daddy."[100] Indeed these would become the names of three of Sāmī's seven children. Although Reynolds does not specify the diary in his definition, nor do the authors discuss it in *Interpreting the Self,* Arabic self-literature is clearly broad enough to include the diary. What the Western reader must avoid is reliance on the Western understanding of the diary as the only understanding of the diary within the genre of self-literature.

Scholars of diaries already have begun to see diaries as a complex literary form that blends more than one kind of writing style, calling such diaries "hybrid texts" that absorb earlier and various forms of writing.[101] The variety of forms in Sāmī's writings, indications in some entries that he wrote his thoughts on scrap paper and then transcribed them (with the possibility, of course, of some editing in the copied entries),[102] and entries recounting numerous events and feelings after not writing for an undetermined stretch of time—all encourage a broad definition of "diary." Nevertheless, one can be certain when reading it that it generally does not have the flavor and tone of a memoir, in which the writer returns to reflect on earlier periods of life,

99. See especially the first entry, 30 April 1941, and diary note 8.

100. Entry dated 25 March 1943.

101. Garbarini, *Numbered Days: Diaries and the Holocaust,* 17.

102. See especially entry dated 18 September 1942 and diary note 93.

although Sāmī occasionally wrote summary entries covering events of the previous weeks or months.

That Sāmī wrote dates above most of the entries, however, brings us to the conclusion that he intended it as a diary format but did not write in it on a regular basis. The young diarist seems instead to have written when he wanted to express himself or when he had the time. None of this detracts from the obvious benefits to our historical knowledge of the period and the individual. Indeed, the many tantalizing details from the life of a young Muslim Palestinian Arab makes one wonder whether Sāmī thought about the potential for someday publishing the diary.

Sāmī's Diary in the Context of Palestinian History and Historiography

The word *mudhakkirāt* in Modern Standard Arabic to mean memoirs seems almost interchangeable with the more recent term *yawmīyyāt* (diary, as described above). Their usage calls for consideration of Sāmī's diary in the context of Palestinian writings contemporary with his own.[103] Salim Tamari uses both *mudhakkirāt* and *yawmīyyāt* in his published works on the writings of Wāṣif Jawhariyya, who lived and wrote about life in Palestine during the late Ottoman period and the British Mandate period.[104] In an English-language article on the Jawhariyya memoirs, Tamari makes clear that the musician referred to events that would have been impossible for him to have written about at the time they happened, nor could he have remembered them by the time he knew how to write. For example, Wāṣif mentioned events that his father wrote about in his own diary. Not exactly clear as to how Wāṣif included the recollections of his father in his own memoirs, Tamari concludes that Wāṣif's memoirs present "a juxtaposed layering of two succinct generational narratives, a diary within a diary, that guides us skillfully from the mid-century of the Tanzimat period to the commencement of World War I."[105] In his introduction to the second volume of the Jawhariyya memoirs that Issam Nassar and Tamari edited, however, Tamari emphasizes the rare opportunity

103. A very thorough and useful resource is Nassar and Tamari, *Dirāsāt fī-t-taʾrīkh al-ijtimāʿī li-bilād ash-shām*, especially Chapter 3.

104. See Tamari's "Jerusalem's Ottoman Modernity." Issam Nassar and Tamari edited Jawhariyya's memoirs/diaries in two volumes: the first, Ottoman Jerusalem, *al-Quds al-ʿuthmānīyya fī-l-mudhakkirāt al-Jawhariyya,* and the second, under British Mandate, *al-Quds al-intidābiyya fī-l-mudhakkirāt al-Jawhariyya.*

105. Tamari, "Jerusalem's Ottoman Modernity," 12–13.

that Wāṣif's writing gives us to peer into the lives of Jerusalem's elites, some of whom acted as Wāṣif's patrons, as well as into this transition period from Ottoman to British Mandate Jerusalem in an ironic and lighthearted yet poignant manner.

A historical sociologist by training, Salim Tamari turned to a "diary" quest to probe more closely the social workings of individuals who make up a society. His *ʿĀm al-jarād* presents the diary of a World War I soldier, Iḥsān Ḥasan at-Turjumān, an Arab Jerusalemite who served in the Ottoman military headquarters in Jerusalem. With a recognizably middle-class background, at-Turjumān's own life was "short and uneventful, having served as a clerk in the Logistics Department (*Manzil*), and briefly as a foot soldier in Nablus and Hebron."[106] Tamari notes that at-Turjumān's "observations on the manner in which the succession of military events impacted his relationship to his city and his nation are without parallel."[107]

Like Wāṣif but unlike Sāmī, Iḥsān at-Turjumān had close connections with important Arab figures in Jerusalem; he counted none other than the eminent Khalīl as-Sakākīnī as his friend as well as his teacher, a piece of evidence that Tamari traces back to both Iḥsān's diary and to as-Sakākīnī's.[108] While these two men both had access and connections, it is the routine and the everyday—the stuff of diaries—that make their writings interesting. Such common instances, the mundane, weave the material for the fabric of any society.

If, as Tamari notes, diaries can expose a quotidian aspect that gets subsumed within the nationalist discourse,[109] Sāmī's diary complements those of Wāṣif Jawhariyya and Iḥsān at-Turjumān in offering a different perspective. In highlighting the uniquely ordinary details of a foot soldier in his book on at-Turjumān's diary, Tamari recalls that "almost every chronicle that we [have] inherited from the [late Ottoman to British Mandate] period was authored by a political leader (ʿAwni ʿAbd al-Hādī, Muḥammad ʿIzzat Darwaza, and Rustum Haydār), a military commander (Fawzī al-Qāwuqjī), or an intellectual (as-Sakākīnī, Najātī Sidqī)."[110]

106. "Year of the Locust," 2. "Year of the Locust: The Great War and the Erasure of Palestine's Ottoman Past" is an unpublished draft in English. The published Arabic diary appeared in 2008 and was unavailable at the time of writing; Tamari provided the translated draft.

107. Ibid.

108. Ibid., 10.

109. Ibid., 2.

110. Ibid., 12. See ʿAbd al-Hādī, *Mudhakkirāt ʿAwni ʿAbd al-Hādī;* Darwaza, *Mudhakkirāt;*

Sāmī's diary emerges into a limited but growing body of Palestinian writings to offer a view of the very typical, the particularly ordinary life of a young man trying to make his way in the world. This adds the human dimension to our understanding of history, as Issam Nassar concludes, in part, about Wāṣif Jawhariyya's writing in the second book of the latter's memoirs.[111] Within twenty years after his father's death, Sāmī and his siblings were forced to dispose of the family's wealth, selling shops (from which they probably had received some rent) and olive trees (for wood) and affecting their inheritance. He had to manage his own way; he struggled to get an education, find a career path, and work through his emotions before settling on a bride and life partner. While all of this was challenging enough, the British Empire that ruled his country was mired in World War II. None of this was particularly unique; what is unique is the nature of Sāmī's diary, of his writing about life in a way that allows us to see his humanity, how he faced difficult issues and wrote about them.

The writing of twentieth-century Palestinian history has long been overwhelmed by political and nationalist perspectives, but personal accounts subject the narratives to broader consideration. Sāmī's entries show his political and intellectual development, but only at their very beginning. For example, while Sāmī writes about joining a workers movement, he does not enter into details about socialist ideology and workers' rights or mention the Soviet Union or communism, unlike his contemporary ʿAwdat al-Ashhab. The latter, whose memoirs are part of the Bir Zeit oral history book series on Palestinian society, was a fellow Hebronite born a few years before Sāmī; he discusses in great detail, for example, how he learned about workers' rights, particularly while in prison in Acre.[112]

In his diary, Sāmī does not criticize imperialism or the British Mandate for their roles in permitting the Jewish takeover of Palestine. Sāmī's diary contrasts with Nabīl ʿAlqām's oral historical account of the same period about

---

Haydār, *Mudhakkirāt Rustum Haydār;* al-Qāwuqjī, *Mudhakkirāt Fawzī al-Qāwuqjī;* Sidqī, *Mudhakkirāt Najātī Sidqī;* for more on as-Sakākīnī's diary see note 82 above. All are memoirs except Rustum Haydār's work, which was a diary. ʿAwni ʿAbd al-Hādī had kept a diary, but it was burned; his daughter reconstructed it.

111. Tamari and Nassar, *al-Quds al-intidābīyya,* 646.

112. *Mudhakkirāt ʿAwdat al-Ashhab.* The subjects of communism, workers' rights, and a workers' rights movement in Palestine for Arabs are discussed over three chapters (26–63) as the young ʿAwda learned about and became active in the movement. Since this was the focus of his working life, the reader will find it covered throughout his memoirs.

the root causes of the problem in a book published in 2002 called *al-Intidāb al-bariṭānī fī dhākirat ash-shaʿb al-filasṭīnī* (The British Mandate in the Memories of the Palestinian People). Although he mentions it only once in his diary, Sāmī saw that Jewish settlement and Jewish economic activities posed the biggest problem for the Palestinians in their country. ʿAlqām's interviewees specifically spoke about the British authorities as the essence of the problem for Palestinians. The former did not happen without the latter, so this is not a contradiction between Sāmī's words and those of Palestinians interviewed decades later about the subject; the contrast presents an opportunity to consider the difference between Sāmī's writing in the moment, reacting to what he saw happening around him, and the interviewees' responses to questions about the subject at least forty years after the fact. This is not to dispute their memories; it is merely to raise the challenges historians face when examining various sources of modern history.

The availability of historical sources directly reflects the political situation that unfolded following the onset of British rule in 1917, first as a military administration and then in 1920 as a civil administration. The League of Nations awarded Britain a mandate for this former territory of the Ottoman Empire, and the mandate took final form in 1922. The decades of British imperial rule in Palestine that would give birth to the state of Israel, which resulted in the Palestinian refugee problem, affected the creation of state institutions that preserve a people's historical record. Scholars have discussed sources, archives, and state structures (or the lack of them) that have limited the preservation or creation of archives, the traditional bane of the historian's professional work, as being most profound in the Palestinian case.[113] The absence of a state has meant that the "official" record is scattered at best, or absent at worst.[114]

113. Several important articles have addressed Palestinian historiography. T. Khalidi's focus in "Palestinian Historiography" is scholarship on the mandate period. Doumani, in "Rediscovering Ottoman Palestine," covers works on the Ottoman period, although he includes a comprehensive overview of the writing of Palestinian history in the modern period. See also Porath, "Palestinian Historiography," and Abu-Ghazaleh, "Arab Cultural Nationalism in Palestine."

114. This is the point that ʿAli al-Jarbāwī makes in his introduction to the memoirs of Amīn al-Khaṭīb, born in Jerusalem in 1926, two years after Sāmī's birth. Al-Khaṭīb's memoirs are also part of the oral history project at Bir Zeit University's Center for the Study and Documentation of Palestinian Society in the West Bank, a series produced to add the Palestinian view of history into the existing and varying historical discourse; the series includes

The Palestine Research Center in Beirut had long maintained records of Palestinian life in documents and images, but the center suffered considerably due to Israeli warfare in Lebanon and Lebanese internal fighting.[115] The destruction of a people's historical record limits our ability to write a more broadly conceived historical account, a situation particularly problematic for Palestine, which has been subject to constant warfare, both external and internal.

Palestinian scholars have long published from their own collection of records or personal accounts, but such work is available mainly in Arabic, and thus what is available in the West, perceived to be the "official" history of British Mandate Palestine, derives mainly from British and Zionist archives and scholars.[116] Though Palestinians in their chronicles have challenged for decades Zionist narratives of the pre-state history and the Israeli state's creation, those works are little read in the West, which has cultivated its own Judeo-Christian vision of Palestine, from the nineteenth century, one that reflected a biblical (only) view of local Palestinian, Muslim, or Arab influences.[117]

Writings of Uncertainty and Upheaval

Diaries can serve as a form of self-awareness of an individual, of his place in society or in the world, or as a mark of resistance to perceived destruction or displacement. In the case of Sāmī's diary, we gain a strong sense of the individual ensconced in the broader context of life under British imperial rule and Zionist colonization of Palestine. Diaries that emerge under circumstances of oppression, broadly speaking, be it military occupation, imperial rule, or settler colonization of one's country, cannot necessarily be generalized. The historical specificity and circumstances in which a diarist writes must be taken into consideration. World War II was a global catastrophe, but the experiences of European Jews surely differed from those of non-Jewish Germans, which in

---

memories of personal life stories and of the events of the period about which interviewees spoke. Al-Khaṭīb's memoir, *Tadhakkurāt Amīn al-Khaṭīb,* is the second book in a series of at least eight volumes, called *Ṣafahāt min adh-dhākira al-filasṭīniyya* (Pages from Palestinian Memory).

115. Jiryis and Qallab, "The Palestine Research Center."

116. For the works of Palestinian authors see the numerous studies mentioned in the historiographical essays cited in note 113 above.

117. This bias has been studied in history, politics, literature, and culture. See for example Christison, *Perceptions of Palestine;* Little, *American Orientalism;* McAlister, *Epic Encounters;* and Obenzinger, *American Palestine.*

turn differed from those of Palestinian Arabs. Yet the effects of the European genocide of Jews and other groups in Europe, along with wide-scale displacement, had great ramifications across the globe.

Palestine was relatively quiet during World War II after the British squarely put down the 1936–1939 Arab Revolt, in part through excessive violence and collective punishment and in part by exiling Palestinian leaders. Still, Britain did maintain military camps in the country, and these became more widespread during the war, as ʿAwdat al-Ashhab notes in his memoirs.[118] Arabs in Palestine participated in and were affected by the British military effort even if they did not join the army, as was the case with Sāmī when he became a welder making gallon drums. Al-Ashhab remarks that prisoners were sent to work in the military camps as well as to build them.[119] Palestinians including Sāmī and Wāṣif Jawhariyya have written about significant price inflation in the country and a black market but not about shortages of food.[120] The war had its impact on Britain's overall colonial policy and hastened the end of the mandate; what ensued was the dispossession and displacement of Palestine's Arab population with the Zionist takeover of more than three-fourths of British Mandate Palestine.

The human toll of war across cultures and borders, whether immediately perishing (as happened among European Jews) or experiencing related but perhaps delayed effects of upheaval and loss (as occurred among Palestine's Arab population), led many to bear witness to what they saw and felt. They sought self-expression in written form to make sense, to cope, and in many cases, to preserve and document for the future their experiences, which ranged from genocidal murder to guilt to depicting a way of life and a culture, along with the personal feelings of love and disappointment. In her examination of dozens of diaries of Holocaust victims, Alexandra Garbarini found that those who would soon perish in the Nazi genocide of European Jewry (among other groups) wrote as a way "to make meaning of events that seemed incomprehensible."[121] The diaries "gave voice to their authors' personalities but also articulated the expectations and values of the cultures to which they

118. *Mudhakkirāt ʿAwdat al-Ashhab,* 41.

119. Ibid., 29.

120. The black market undoubtedly made some goods unavailable to certain segments of the population; see the entry dated 10 March 1942. Suhayla recalled that some staples were very rarely found; interview, 16 January 2006. See also Seikaly, "Meatless Days."

121. Garbarini, *Numbered Days,* xi.

belonged," as in other European-penned diaries.[122] French scholar Michèle Leleu notes that "more than any other, the Second World War favored the blossoming of diaries of revolt. French and Germans sought in them a relief from the oppression of their consciences."[123]

One can see in some of Sāmī's diary entries that he too was trying to make sense of the imponderable. In one almost prophetic entry, dated 15 March 1943, Sāmī is acutely aware of the dangers looming for the Arabs of Palestine; later events would bear this out in the expulsion and flight of 750,000 Palestinian Arabs, huge numbers of whom have remained in the squalid conditions of the refugee camps.[124] Sāmī's criticisms of his boss, his dissatisfaction at work, his awareness of the Zionist colonization of his country—and perhaps his inability to prevent it—may have fostered his inward turn, which manifested itself in writing a diary.

If the reasons a person starts writing a diary are not clear, the reasons a person continues to keep a diary are also not clear, particularly as those reasons can change over the course of writing a diary. Sāmī's diary entries move chronologically, covering the external (the war, schooling, the office where he worked) and the internal or the personal (love interests, family matters, emotional crises, as well as pondering the deeper meaning of life and how to live it). Still, through all of this, the war raging across the globe remains evident. One might not consider this specifically a "war diary," but the war's impact affected everything he did, whether it was his job or exploring the landscape vistas when traveling throughout the country. Above all, Sāmī's diary makes him an active subject in history.

The diary, though sometimes viewed as marginalized, is in fact a complex piece of writing, offering historical insight and creative style to the historian and the reader of literature.[125] When considering the diary as a historical text, the scholar is bound only by the demands of historical curiosity and thus may delve into the diary—not simply accepting it as a retracing of historical events—as a multifaceted text that stretches the boundaries of historical literature beyond the official or standard narrative. In their volume on diaries from the eighteenth through the twentieth centuries, editors Langford and West suggest that the diary should be read as "'momentary insights', a glimpse

122. Ibid., 2.

123. Leleu, *Les journaux intimes,* quoted in translation in Garbarini, *Numbered Days,* 2.

124. Pappe, *The Making of the Arab-Israeli Conflict.*

125. Langford and West, *Marginal Voices, Marginal Forms,* 8.

of history as it is experienced by those caught in its midst . . . [or] writing from within the immediacy of events."[126]

While they provide rich material highlighting a particular geographical space and a particular historical time, diarists are in no position to analyze their own work, as they do not have the benefit of historical distance. One should not take this to mean that historical events mentioned in a diary are not valuable or are necessarily unreliable, as the diarist is not a stranger to the historical events, while a later reader might be. Diaries clearly have historical specificity. However, Langford and West note,

> [t]he diary, as an uncertain genre uneasily balanced between literary and historical writing, between the spontaneity of reportage and the reflectiveness of the crafted text, between selfhood and events, between subjectivity and objectivity, between the private and the public, constantly disturbs attempts to summarise its characteristics within formalized boundaries.[127]

Diarists are not contemporary historians, but their writings offer thoughts and feelings as well as perceptions and reportage "of a particular moment" and serve, as they did in the earliest Islamic historiographical tradition, as a source for writing history. To contextualize Sāmī's writing into the broad field of modern Middle Eastern history, readers will want to consider examining his diary through a lens that offers a healthy "balance between representation and reality, between meaning and experience, and between text and context."[128]

Sāmī's diary may easily be read as the product of a pluralistic society and differences in rural and urban populations. Jerusalem during World War II, when he lived and wrote in his diary there, had a populace deeply mixed in culture—religion and language, for example—ethnicity, geographic origins, and other demographic aspects, all within overlays of assorted political, economic, and legal systems. Muslims, Jews, and Christians lived and worked in the city; a British Christian power ruled over the indigenous Arab population, which included members of all three of those religious groups; and growth of a European Zionist Jewish immigrant population was facilitated by the British rule in Palestine.

126. Ibid., 12.

127. Ibid., 8.

128. Gershoni, Erdem, and Woköck, *Histories of the Modern Middle East,* 282. The quote is from "The Return of the Concrete," Gershoni and Woköck's conclusion to the collection of articles.

The mandate government often drew its officers and staff from those who had served in British-ruled India, Egypt, or Africa, and their colonial administrative backgrounds affected policy in Palestine. Foreign governments had established consulates in Jerusalem since the mid-nineteenth century that brought significant change for various religious and national groups living in the city, as those groups received protection or benefits from the consuls of major powers vying for influence in the region. The remnants of Ottoman rule were evident, as the legal system in Palestine incorporated aspects of Ottoman law.[129] The Turkish language, the official language of Ottoman government but spoken by few Palestinian Arabs, gave way under the mandate. English, Arabic, and Hebrew all became official languages in Palestine under the British.

Themes in the Diary of Sāmī ʿAmr

Sāmī's diary is rich in family history and family struggles, as Sāmī put his thoughts and feelings on paper about his family relations as well as relations he observed among other people. Movement appears as an important theme in the diary, as he moved frequently during the years of his writing. In Jerusalem, he changed his domicile several times for financial and social reasons. When he found himself living alone in Jerusalem after his brother moved out, Sāmī moved to a smaller and presumably less expensive place. When he found a particular dwelling uncomfortable, he again relocated, even if it took him far away from his job and made his commute more onerous. From Jerusalem he moved to Ramla when he changed jobs to work in welding (Map 1). Throughout all of these moves, Sāmī reflects in his diary on his ties to his birthplace, Hebron. Sāmī describes Hebron with longing and its surrounding geographical vistas in romantic detail. Sāmī writes about temporary movement as he traveled back and forth between Jerusalem, Ramla, and Hebron, just as he creates something of a travelogue when he traversed the country visiting family.

The visitor to the West Bank today would not see Palestinians moving easily between the cities in which Sāmī moved from 1941 through 1945 or any other Palestinian cities that he mentions in the diary. The conflict that would

129. Eisenman, *Islamic Law in Palestine and Israel.* Al-Ashhab notes in his *Mudhakkirāt* (45), for example, that when he and his fellow organizers sought to have a workers association in Jerusalem, they followed procedures according to the Ottoman Law for Associations (*qānūn al-jamʿīyāt al-ʿuthmāniyya*).

come to engulf Palestine, dispossess hundreds of thousands of its indigenous Arab inhabitants, and eventually leave Palestinian land occupied now poses an obstacle to the kind of free movement that Sāmī enjoyed during that period.

Not a political treatise, Sāmī's diary captures elements of politics, economics, and social life, as he struggled through his late teens simultaneously with the World War II years in Palestine. Although those war years were relatively quiet in Palestine, Sāmī mentions war episodes in various passages, particularly early on in his diary. One might wonder why events in Japan (diary entry dated 8 December 1941) and India (entry dated 30 March 1942) raised his ire enough to write about them in his diary while local events of violence and uprising such as the 1936–1939 Arab Revolt did not. One might conclude that Britain's military posturing and its camps, soldiers, and police in Palestine were simply a fact of life.[130] By contrast, Sāmī's age might explain his failure to mention the revolt, as he was only twelve to fifteen years old at the time. By the time he set out to write his diary in 1941 at age seventeen, the challenges he encountered likely overshadowed the events of his younger years, when he might have had less understanding of politics, resistance, and revolt.[131]

Saʿdī's Experiences

The young diarist wrote frequently about his brother Saʿdī, whom he first mentions in the fifth entry of his diary, 19 November 1941, regarding Saʿdī's decision to join the British army. Sāmī's entries on his brother Saʿdī's experience give details of Saʿdī's situation and how Sāmī dealt with it. Without Saʿdī's own words, we cannot fully understand the decision he made that so upset his younger brother. Sāmī had his way of dealing with the mandatory authority, and Saʿdī, it seems, had his. Even a casual reading of Palestinian history during the mandate period affirms that some Palestinians opposed the British in Palestine and others collaborated with the British, believing that

130. See Kolinsky, *Britain's War in the Middle East,* and Jackson, *The British Empire and the Second World War.* Some former regular soldiers serving as police in Palestine wanted to return to their fighting units when World War II began. In Britain, a law came into existence that allowed this in a controlled fashion, and the same law was later adopted by the British Mandate government in Palestine but not enforced. The former soldiers, now policemen, who wanted to return to fighting could only do so by breaking a law and serving jail time. Once they did, they could return to military service. Horne says some Palestine policemen did so to get out of the police force; *A Job Well Done,* 265n3.

131. ʿAwdat al-Ashhab, approximately two years older than Sāmī, participated in the revolt along with his brother and wrote about it in his memoirs.

would help end Zionist colonization of their country.[132] This latter reasoning may or may not have been part of Saʿdī's decision to enlist. Possibly Saʿdī was more involved in politics than Sāmī, who was about three years younger, knew or understood. As more diaries come to light, future researchers can pursue the question of Palestinian Arab participation in the British war effort during World War II.

As Saʿdī took none of Sāmī's advice not to join the army, Sāmī wondered about his brother's emotional state that would lead him to enlist. The diarist writes, "I have not mentioned my poor brother before this whom I never got angry with even once, but for whom I have great sympathy. I lament him because I have learned that his mind until now is not stable or perhaps he needs many other experiences to make him realize the good from the wicked."[133] Sāmī continues, shocked not only over his brother's actions but also at what it meant for his brother (and perhaps all young Palestinian Arab men) to put on the British army uniform: "It is inestimable how much less freedom comes with the donning of that uniform, which now resembles the shackles of the captive and prisoner, the bonds of servitude, and submission to regulations." We have no way to understand what Saʿdī thought about the army, but conversations with Sāmī's widow suggest that Saʿdī joined whimsically, thinking that serving in the army was some kind of joke.[134] The younger brother, Sāmī, much more serious than the middle brother, Saʿdī, saw great repercussions in this decision.

Although Sāmī remarks on the loss of freedom that came with wearing the uniform, one later reads that it was the removal of that very uniform that led to Saʿdī's incarceration in a British prison. Based on Sāmī's diary entry of 15 November 1942, a year after Saʿdī enlisted, Sāmī raised the specter of his brother's troubles in the military. Within two months, in Sāmī's 1 January 1943 entry, Saʿdī had been sentenced to six months in prison for going AWOL. Sāmī learned within a year of Saʿdī joining the army that Saʿdī had been imprisoned, something that Sāmī describes as having caused his "belief in justice to waver."[135] He omitted in his writing the charges against Saʿdī, but Sāmī was certain that his brother did not commit the crime. Sāmī adds in his

132. See Khalaf, *Politics in Palestine*. Undoubtedly, as in all countries, there were people also who collaborated for more nefarious purposes.

133. Entry dated 19 November 1941.

134. Interview with Suhayla, 15 January 2006.

135. Entry dated 15 November 1942.

first entry on the subject in January 1943 that the charge against his brother stemmed from a plot by others while Saʿdī was in Syria. If indeed the mandate was intended to guide the local population toward self-government and how to live by the rule of law, this incident quickly led Sāmī to disenchantment with the British legal system in place in Palestine.[136]

It seems unlikely that Sāmī did not know at the time, as Suhayla said Sāmī told her about Saʿdī's incarceration soon after they married in 1945. She said she believed he knew the charge behind the incarceration although he did not mention it in his diary.[137] Perhaps the idea of putting the charge on paper was more than Sāmī wanted to face. Those who keep diaries often return to them to read what they have written; in this case, by later reading what he had written, Sāmī would have had to acknowledge again something that he seems to have preferred to keep tucked away. Furthermore, if the diarist intends for his or her diary to be published, one could expect certain omissions, such as the one about Saʿdī's conviction. Perhaps most importantly, if people write diaries to work through grief, Sāmī's omission of the reason for Saʿdī's imprisonment allowed Sāmī to create or control a situation in a historical period in which Palestinians had little control over the political direction of their lives and their country.

Suhayla stated very plainly that Saʿdī went to prison for going AWOL, a detail Sāmī told her, and she insisted that he knew at the time the reason for his brother's imprisonment. She added that when Saʿdī was taken to Egypt to serve in the British war effort, he treated it like a game and decided to escape. According to Suhayla, the story continued when Saʿdī took off his military uniform, left it on the banks of the Nile River, and bought and dressed in the clothes of an Egyptian peasant.[138] He then made his way back to Palestine, where the British caught him, and, as Sāmī relates, put him in jail, tried him, and found him guilty. Although he received a six-month jail sentence, it seems he served only four months before being moved to an army camp in Jerusalem and then back to a fighting unit in Egypt, something Saʿdī came to fear, according to Sāmī's diary entry of 12 May 1943.

In an entry dated 15 November 1942, in the style of a letter to his brother that Saʿdī may or may not have read, Sāmī expresses the depth of his love for

136. Sāmī must have thought previously that there was justice within the British system because he writes that his belief in the system wavered.

137. Interview with Suhayla, 15 January 2006.

138. Ibid.

his brother, who, he was certain, would come back to him, and they would have a blissful family reunion.[139] Despite all of the sadness Sāmī conveys and the uncertainty he notes at the end of the letter/entry as to what actually happened to Saʿdī, Sāmī encourages him to be courageous and to overcome the injustices that had been done to him. Sāmī's relationship with this brother with whom he had shared an apartment appears to have been complex. He clearly loved his brother a great deal and tried to help him in any way possible. Yet in an entry dated 6 April 1942, five months after Saʿdī joined the British army, Sāmī writes of the emotional distance between them:

> I am alone because no one gives me advice or sits next to me and takes an interest in me to ask any questions that I can answer or to whom I can ask questions and he can answer. Yes, I have a brother whom I live with . . . and we work together . . . but we are living in two completely different worlds, in spirit and in being.

Sāmī seems to have been quite pained by that, as he was looking for guidance and Saʿdī offered no counsel or companionship. He adds at the end of that entry, "I have to bear this awful loneliness and learn something from these circumstances." As for his eldest brother, Asʿad, Sāmī's widow said that he offered Sāmī almost nothing as an older figure in his life.[140] She recalled that it was Sāmī, the youngest of the boys in the family, who took care of family business. He took especially good care of his mother as she got older and needed more and more help, and she eventually came to live with Sāmī and Suhayla.

The imprisonment of his brother continued to affect Sāmī deeply for months after Saʿdī's release, and he reflects on the period in his diary several months later. On 12 May 1943, Sāmī writes about his weekly visits to the prison in the neighborhood of Jerusalem known as aṭ-Ṭālbīyya and comments on it again on 18 September 1943. Not only did the visits shake Sāmī, but he describes how painfully his mother took the visit to her son in the British jail. Sāmī's widow described her brother-in-law Saʿdī as continually having made things very difficult for his mother.[141] Sāmī writes that their mother cried and held Saʿdī tightly during these visits.[142] He adds that she appeared to want to take

139. No one in the family has any letters that Sāmī might have written. It is possible that Sāmī wrote the letter only in his diary.

140. Interview with Suhayla, 15 January 2006.

141. Ibid.

142. Entry dated 12 May 1943.

him home with her to Hebron, the city that factors so prominently in the life of the ʿAmr family and appears in the diary as a point of contrast for other parts of Palestine and as a reminder of the continuity of home life for the family.

Tradition and Change

At home in Hebron for the birth of his youngest sister's first child, Sāmī writes a diary entry dated 18 September 1942 in the form of a letter addressed to his brother-in-law, whom he calls "My Dear Friend," that illustrates the struggle he had with change and tradition in Palestine.[143] The newborn child, a boy, marked a significant stage in the life of that family, really of any family, as a son signifies the future of the family. Arab parents are renamed after the eldest son; in this case, Sāmī's sister became Umm Sulṭān, the mother of Sulṭān, and his brother-in-law Abū Sulṭān, the father of Sulṭān, leaving a constant reference both of the child's relationship to his parents and the parents' relationship to their eldest son.

For Sāmī, the birth of this child, the new generation, and the future made him reflect on what a name meant for one's identity and whether the child and his name truly mark the coming of something modern and new or the persistence of something traditional and old. A name, Sāmī writes, is "nothing but a special sound that a family gives to a child, releasing that sound or syllable especially given to that newborn to distinguish that child from others." He adds that "previous generations did not pay much attention to the naming of a child or to being creative with the naming of children, and thus they named their children Muḥammad, peace be upon him, after the Prophet of Islam, or after other ancient prophets" from the Qurʾān.

But, Sāmī notes, times had changed, and "names have become in the view of upper-class families in particular and middle-class families more generally an essential thing in a person's life." Not content to speak only of new generations, social classes, and the future when talking about the naming of children, Sāmī also writes about this in terms of progress: "The world is in accelerated progress with the passing of time, and the West is getting closer to the East." Sāmī recognized the progress the world was experiencing, which he says "will wipe out the old corrupt traditions, and what will remain from it

143. Sāmī's use of "My Dear Friend" here for his brother-in-law was not the same as his frequently addressing the diary itself as "my friend."

. . . is the triumphant city." The naming of Sāmī's nephew raised the issue in his mind of tradition versus progress.

One can best understand this matter if one first recognizes that Sāmī's brother-in-law ʿIzzat (Abū Sulṭān) came from a big Bedouin tribe from the Naqab (Negev) Desert. The stories Sāmī's sister Ruqayya (Umm Sulṭān) conveyed to me in a 2005 interview suggest that ʿIzzat had wanted to marry into the ʿAmr family and came to Hebron to do so.[144] Apparently ʿIzzat had studied in Jerusalem, and undoubtedly he saw aspects of modernity in the urban environment of Hebron as well, much as Sāmī expressed. He agreed as part of the marriage conditions to remain with his bride in Hebron once they married.[145] Abū Sulṭān occasionally worked in other parts of Palestine that led him to live periodically outside of Hebron, including at the time of his first child's birth. At age seventy-nine at the time of our interview,[146] Ruqayya laughed effusively when reminded of the story of the naming of her first son, Sulṭān. She immediately recalled how much Sāmī disliked the child's name, Sulṭān, and how offended her husband was when Sāmī gave him the letter, a version of which made its way into Sāmī's diary.[147]

In Sāmī's mind, this matter affected society at large. One must consider the way forward, he thought, and not rely on traditions of the past, traditions no longer relevant to the new world in which he lived. Beyond this clash of values, maintaining tradition or embracing modernity, for Sāmī a clash also arose between the city and the desert, city dwellers and Bedouin, that ʿIzzat moved past by marrying and relocating to the city. In the same entry, 18 September 1942, Sāmī disparages ʿIzzat's Bedouin origins:

> [C]ivilization will rise from the uninhabited places of the city itself and the Bedouin will emerge from their dwellings in goat hair tents and become civilized and live in palaces; then they will gradually move towards upward development and participate in the running of factories and administration buildings and office

144. Interview 20 December 2005. Ruqayya said her husband at first wanted to marry Suhayla, whom Sāmī would eventually marry.

145. See note 17 in the diary.

146. Interview 20 December 2005.

147. In single instances, it seems that parts of the diary were written on separate pieces of paper and later copied into the diary. It is not clear whether this letter was composed in the diary first, or if Sāmī reproduced it in the diary after ʿIzzat tore up the actual letter so that Sāmī could maintain his words in some fashion.

> work and leave this vast desert in which their forefathers lived for generations, suffering from the difficulties of living, hunger and thirst, not thinking that there is a better life, more comfortable, in the cities, or at least in the villages.

Not only did ʿIzzat move to the city, but he also took up work as a surveyor for the British government, thus answering Sāmī's call, arguably, for progress and change among the Bedouin. ʿIzzat did not remind Sāmī of this, most likely, but did become irate at his comments. For all of his philosophizing on such deep issues as tradition and modernity or progress, in the letter Sāmī calls on ʿIzzat not to take seriously his comments, his "chatter and nonsense" (*ath-tharthara*), but asks that he save the words (originally composed in a letter and given to ʿIzzat) for the little boy, "for whom I am now his uncle." Sāmī hoped—perhaps not seeing that he had made any headway with the father—that the young boy would read this when he was older, and it would be for his own good; this would never happen, as ʿIzzat promptly tore up the letter after reading it.

Sāmī's ideas of modernity, written when he was a young man, coincide with what ʿAlqām heard from his interviewees on the subject of intermarriage between social groups. Having lived through the British Mandate period, they described essentially three distinct groups within the Palestinian population—city folks, peasants, and Bedouin—that had a kind of rivalry for the most appropriate lifestyle. ʿAlqām explains that the Bedouin held their value of honor very tightly and considered that quality as lacking among the other two groups, while each of the other groups claimed to have the best values. Ruqayya, too, found that the city folk of Hebron viewed themselves as being a superior social group. She recalled that they were strongly opposed to the idea of her, a city girl, marrying a Bedouin.[148] In comparing Sāmī's family's story of the "mixed marriage" of a Bedouin with a city girl with the stories ʿAlqām heard during his interviews,[149] they all highlight a sense of social difference among Palestine's Arabs and illustrate differences in the ways people understood social distinctions in their own society during this period.

The theme of tradition and change appears again in an undated entry in which Sāmī discusses an Arab village in southern Palestine. The entry, titled "If I Were an Arab Leader," highlights Sāmī's desire for modernization in Pales-

148. See note 17 in the diary.

149. ʿAlqām, *al-Intidāb al-bariṭānī,* 42ff.

tine.[150] He says his "hopes will be fulfilled" if through his writings he could envision himself as a leader in one of the Arab villages in the south of Palestine, and he compares himself "to the Arab prophet, Muḥammad . . . [who] raise[d] his people [*yanhaḍu bi-qawmīhī*] religiously and politically." He asks: "Doesn't the secular reformer deserve credit as much as the religious reformer?" Sāmī grew up in the city of Hebron, and although his family maintained ties to their natal village of Dūra, he makes no other mention of wanting to be a village leader in the diary or even to living in a village. He does express his views on how life in the village should be. In imagining himself the leader of this nameless village, Sāmī saw himself "standing among the throng of villagers encouraging them toward modernity [*taqaddum*] and leaving the tribalism that tears apart their very being." To bring about modernization, Sāmī imagined

> extending the roads in the village, building healthy homes, including toilets, while demolishing the old dwellings infested with diseases; burning the long, loose-fitting robes in favor of something simpler and more tasteful; and putting shoes on those bare feet, which suffer from treading on the small white pebbles on the ground, of everyone in the village.

Sāmī saw value not only in changing the habits and living environments of villagers but also in making improvements to the way they worked. He wanted to "collect donations and bring tractors to work the pure land, dig wells, and assemble water pumps" for villagers to be able to work their lands better. He foresaw beautifying the land as well, "plant[ing] trees in an orderly fashion along the sides of the street and on the peaks of hilltops that lay barren." What would really turn the village into something modern or something of the future was the "establish[ment of] an office for trade of the products grown by the villagers," the opening of factories, and the creation of vocations such as sewing and hair cutting in which girls could work.

In talking about her childhood, Sāmī's youngest sister, Ruqayya, spoke of sewing classes in Hebron, and it is perhaps from seeing such experiences along with living under the British Mandate in Palestine that Sāmī conceived of ways to make village life more prosperous, healthy, and productive.[151] The discourse Sāmī used for this discussion of village life might seem that of a

150. The entry seems to have been written between 22 and 26 October 1943.
151. Interview with Ruqayya, 24 December 2005.

colonial administrator or urban planner, but Palestinians during the period recognized the differences in lifestyle between the urban areas and the rural ones. Progress and change would come by colonialist tactics, but Palestinians undoubtedly saw colonists (both Zionists and others) in Palestine employing mechanized farming, something not all Palestinian villages used prior to 1948. Mechanization of agriculture was limited mainly to the villages nearest the cities, as they tended to be wealthier villages that could afford to buy tractors.[152]

Palestinian Identification with the Land

Palestinians saw great change coming to their country not only from direct British rule but also from the Zionists who colonized Palestine, established agricultural settlements, and already in the early 1920s created one fully new city, Tel Aviv. So as not to lose their homeland, a goal that Sāmī states most definitively, Palestine's Arab population would have to change.[153]

Sāmī recognized the impact that the Zionists had made in Palestine in agriculture, the economy, and social life, but, he realized, the real challenge lay in the realm of politics. He acknowledged progress and development but would not countenance giving up the land to Zionists. In an entry dated 15 March 1943, Sāmī explains what he saw in the conflict around him between Jews and Arabs in Palestine with almost prescient accuracy:

> Palestine is a piece of land on which live two people [an Arab and a Jew], each of whom claims that he owns it. They fight each other until their fight becomes a conflict in which one grows stronger and the other weaker. The weaker one will lose his life and the stronger one will come to live on the remains of the weaker one.[154]

152. In his village memorial book, *Min dhākirat al-jihād al-filasṭīnī,* Abū Sabayh says about his village of al-Abbāsīyya, next to the German settlement of Wilhelma (established in 1902), that "the most important thing gained from the Germans was the use of agricultural plows for planting. They increased the yield manifold, not only in our village but in all of the villages generally" (64–65). On Palestinian village memorial books see Rochelle Davis, "Mapping the Past," 53–75, and "al-Kutub at-tidhkarīyya." For more on the modernization of agriculture during this period see Miller, *Government and Society.*

153. While undoubtedly others believed that change in Palestinian society was necessary, there was no single path to implementing such change. ʿAwdat al-Ashhab, for example, saw change best implemented by working on behalf of the proletariat and creating branches across the country of the Palestine Arab Workers Society.

154. In Arabic Sāmī employs *rajulayn,* meaning two men. The word *rajulayn* is better rendered in idiomatic English as "two people."

As World War II intensified the circumstances created by the Balfour Declaration and the British Mandate for Palestine, Sāmī understood very well that the Zionist Jews in Palestine had great ambitions to take over the country and bring their Jewish brethren from Europe to take the place of the Arab population of Palestine. He writes in that entry of 15 March 1943 that "if the Jews take over in Palestine they will close the sole and most significant gate from which the people of the Middle East import their goods for their livelihood and subsistence."

Sāmī saw the potential of the Zionists in Palestine, adding that "they will look at the surrounding and adjacent Arab countries and make them into a market for their manufactured goods and their trade and with it kill Arab trade, for they [the Arabs] will not be able to sell." All of the difficulties that the Arabs of Palestine would face with a Zionist takeover, Sāmī writes, would lead the Jews to expect that the "Arabs will get frustrated in Palestine and look to emigration (God forbid)." On the subject of Arab emigration from Palestine, Sāmī writes that "the Jews have measly excuses and unconvincing arguments about this, claiming that the Arabs have countries other than Palestine to which they can go." To this day Israeli and non-Israeli Zionist Jews and other supporters of Israel repeat this refrain to delegitimize the Palestinian connection to the land and strengthen the Jewish connection to it.[155]

Though focused more on self-expression, the diary may serve as an expression of resistance to the Zionist desires to take over and transform Palestine. This young defender of his country states that he and his countrymen "will not leave our country to satisfy [their] aspirations and facilitate their comfort in Palestine while bearing the pain of exile." For Sāmī, Palestine was his homeland, and Arabs "entered Palestine by the sword [probably through the Muslim conquests, or perhaps his own family's experiences] and would only leave it . . . by the sword and would take [their] last breath trying to save it."[156] While the diary has only this one nationalistic entry about politics and the rising conflict between Arabs and Jews, Sāmī also writes long, poetic descriptions in the diary of his country, from the *wadi* (valley) near his family's village of Dūra, outside of Hebron, to the area near the al-ʿAwja River where he visited with his cousins.[157] He writes passionately about his travels north

155. See George's "'Making the Desert Bloom.'"

156. All quotations in this paragraph are found in an entry dated 15 March 1943.

157. Sāmī erroneously identified this as the Jarīsha River. See note 70 in the diary. Israelis now refer to this as the Yarkon River.

to visit his sisters and his trips to Jaffa to visit his uncle and his uncle's family. Throughout such descriptions, one gains the sense that Sāmī felt that he and his fellow Palestinians were tied deeply to the land, every valley and stream, the riverbank, and the beach, as well as to the types of trees and flowers that grow there.

Sāmī's eloquent descriptions of all this in the early 1940s predate later kinds of literature that Palestinians would write to preserve their memories of their homeland. In her article "Mapping the Past, Re-Creating the Homeland: Memories of Village Places in Pre-1948 Palestine," Rochelle Davis describes the memorial books that Palestinians have been writing since 1985 as a means to document their identification with place in Palestine. In spite of at least forty years of exile, Palestinians writing memorial books have been able to recount the details of brooks and streams, hills and mountains, fields and trees and flowers in such minutiae that one would guess that they had inspected the land that day. In fact, in Sāmī's case, he often visited those places earlier during the day of his writing. But in the more recent efforts at resistance to the continuation of refugee status, Palestinians have relied on their memories to record the details and history of the country where they grew up, the country they knew, which has been subject to Zionist and Israeli colonial development plans for nearly a century.

Work and Relationships

Although Sāmī writes passionately about the growing conflict between Jews and Arabs in British mandatory Palestine, the conflict did not limit his career aspirations within the British mandatory government, nor does it seem to have affected his interactions with co-workers and supervisors. He writes about an angry complaint he planned to make to his supervisor at the NAAFI office, a Greek man whom Sāmī saw as preventing his promotion. Yet when he confronted Lorenziadis, the supervisor, Sāmī learned that he too would soon be ready for promotion. Sāmī did receive a promotion to clerk after some time in his first position as errand boy, but he never seemed particularly content at the NAAFI. When Sāmī sought opportunities outside the department where he worked for several years, the ongoing war likely gave him the opportunity he needed, as his British interviewers immediately accepted Sāmī into the training school for welders. He seems to have made solid relationships with some of the young men in his job and later in the welding school, but his relationships with women caused him great confusion, again related to the themes of tradition and change.

When reading the diary one recognizes a deep internal conflict about his acquaintances with girls. He expresses his shyness when talking to any girl, but in particular the barriers in Muslim society erected between young men and women led Sāmī to ask in his diary how he could in fact talk to a Muslim girl. Sāmī writes in an entry dated 6 April 1942 that regardless of what he might do to change the situation, he was sure that he would "not get anything, big or small, without talking to the girls." He was "not courageous enough to talk or say even one word to them because they are Muslim girls." On the impossibility of the situation, he notes that he was too "shy to open up to them what is inside me, full of infatuation, if that is in fact what is in my heart." Those with whom he could speak freely were members of his family; in the workplace he was able to speak with many non-Muslim girls, whether Greek, Jewish, or other.

In a few diary entries, Sāmī writes about several female co-workers, including one named Tsibūra (Tsipora in Hebrew), a Jewish girl whom he loved and by whom he felt scorned when he heard that she had married.[158] Prior to that, he had invited several girls to a picnic near his family village. Among them was Tsibūra, who accepted the invitation but did not show up. Sāmī's brother and cousins were there, as well as his uncle Jamāl. Though excited about his relatives' visit too, Sāmī writes intently about the young women who came to the outing. He asked why Tsibūra had not come, but the girls did not answer him. The outing took place in Wadi Nunqur, or Nunqur Valley, which Sāmī's relatives said is near Dūra.[159] The setting elicited from Sāmī a wonderful description of the area's geography, topography, and agriculture—of apple trees, apricots, plums, and almonds. Sāmī seemed momentarily to have forgotten Tsibūra, turning his attention to a girl named Lūbā. In writing about the beauty of the trees, Sāmī adds that he listened to Lūbā, "with her tenderness and charm," call the *wadi* a "small paradise." He found himself mesmerized by the

158. Sāmī mentions his feelings for Tsibūra in entries on 10 August 1942 and again on 7 September 1942, after learning that she had married.

159. Dabbāgh says in *Bilādunā filasṭīn* that Nunqur (here he is not referring to the *wadi* by the same name), was southwest of Hebron, as is Dūra. He notes that Nunqur is a *mazraʿa,* a farming community, and that in 1921 there were 102 people living there, all Muslim (156). Nunqur took on the status of a village after 1948 when the population increased (14).

opportunity, and he and Lūbā walked around by themselves for a while in the *wadi.* Sāmī helped her up and down the walls, without speaking. Reflecting on the day and comparing it to how he watched the Muslim girls and they him from the window of the house, with all of his shyness and the circumstances usually preventing any kind of relaxed, comfortable sentiment, he and the others asked each other, "Didn't we have a nice time?!" and responded, "Yes, very much so."[160]

Conclusion: To Write or Not to Write

Sāmī faced many challenges during the period in which he wrote his diary: the move to Jerusalem, his brother's enlistment and imprisonment, the sale of family property, his employment situation, and his awkwardness around girls, among others. He saw his life as a struggle and wrote about it as such. Yet whenever he could effect change, Sāmī dealt with the challenges thoughtfully. Within the pages of his diary the reader finds poems that Sāmī penned, letters to family and love interests (though it is not always clear that he sent them), and striking descriptive prose about his observations of the countryside, the human landscape, and the political situation looming around him. Without his written words and indeed those of others who share their written thoughts or memories, our understanding of the everyday lives of individuals in general and in Palestine during this particular period would be impoverished.

In fact, Sāmī himself limits our understanding of his life, as he stopped writing his diary with a single word pertaining to a single event: "marriage." If, as Philippe Lejeune suggests, writing a diary comes with some kind of trouble or suffering, it is unclear why Sāmī stopped writing his after sticking with it for nearly four years. One also wonders if the end of the war in North Africa in 1943 and in Europe in May 1945 that had most consumed the British, somehow influenced Sāmī's decision to quit the diary.[161] Perhaps, quite simply, in spite of the challenges he faced after he married—and of course there were many, such as the loss of Palestine in 1948 and 1967, dispersion of the family, relocation outside of historic Palestine, the birth and upbringing of his children, taking care of his mother as she grew older—Sāmī felt that the "struggle" was over, and thus he stopped writing.

160. Picnic quotes are found in an entry dated 10 August 1942.

161. The Pacific theater of war continued until September 1945, some six months after Sāmī stopped writing.

One might also say that the struggles increased and thus left him little time for self-reflection and writing. By then, however, Sāmī could rely on Suhayla and may have turned to her rather than the diary to work through his troubles. At the start of his engagement to Suhayla, Sāmī asks in the diary when facing difficulty: "To whom shall I talk now, you, my friend [the diary], to whom I always poured out my complaints, or to you, Suhayla, you who have now become my main goal in this life and my companion when I am lonely?"[162] In 2006 Sāmī's widow said she had encouraged him to write in those early years after they married and that he replied with "it is written down in my heart," meaning that he would remember everything. She said because he worked so much after they married he no longer had time to write.[163] One thing is quite certain about the diary: Sāmī processed situations, relationships, and obstacles in his life by writing them down. Through his diary we can better understand the social and political history of Palestine under the British Mandate from the perspective of a young Palestinian man. With conventional sources leaving the historical record somewhat wanting, the diary serves to fill that gap, as it leaves us with an affirmation of Sāmī's life more than sixty years later.

The particular circumstances of the British colonial mandate over Palestine bear the hallmarks of those in other colonized regions, from Algeria to India, albeit each inflected with local specificities and those imposed by the colonial power on each country. Questions of identity have been the fodder of innumerable studies on the former colonized world, and one might link Sāmī's struggles with the search for identity. Who was he, he might have asked himself, in a country ruled by the British, colonized by Zionist Jews, and experiencing World War II at somewhat of a distance? In the wake of the Palestinian Nakba (Catastrophe) that resulted from war between Jews and Arabs in 1948, Sāmī's diary becomes even more pertinent to gaining an understanding of the individual, of what he might represent, and of the remarkable—and unwanted—change that loomed for Palestinians in their country just a few years after Sāmī ended his diary, as understanding history requires understanding this kind of change over time.

Although this introduction to Sāmī's diary provides some historical and family background, one can easily make the short leap to realize that Sāmī's

162. Entry dated 10 July 1944.
163. Interview with Suhayla, 16 January 2006.

diary has created a space for his particular voice in the writing of the history of Palestine in the pre-1948 period, much as it allows us to see the universal struggle of youth looking toward an uncertain future. This introduction is offered to contextualize the diary within the history of Palestine during the British Mandate period from varied perspectives, including the historical and historiographical context, family history, and thematic content. Sāmī's writings are both rich and sparse in detail, depending on the subject or the day; they are passionate and dispassionate; they reflect his feelings of happiness and sadness, youthful optimism and experienced pessimism. Sāmī's entries invite the reader to learn about a variety of individuals, many of whom he names, but not all of whom are known by relation or family surname.[164] Above all, Sāmī's writings welcome the reader into the plurality that was Jerusalem during the mandate period, what Issam Nassar has described as "open, intermixed with different languages from different national, political, and denominational groups, which co-existed in the city."[165] Sāmī easily crossed what later would become sharply drawn boundaries among those groups and within the territory, while reflecting in his diary on his own sense of identity as a Palestinian and a Muslim.

164. Appendix 2 presents a list of all persons mentioned in the diary and their relation to Sāmī.

165. In Nassar's conclusion to Nassar and Tamari, *al-Quds al-intidābīyya,* 647.

PART 2

TRANSLATION OF THE DIARY OF SĀMĪ ʿAMR

MY MEMOIRS IN THIS LIFE | by Sāmī ʿAmr

[Presentation and introduction explaining your circumstances before beginning the writing of memoirs in simple and sincere language.][1]

[The presentation of the book is as memoirs, not as a story.][2]

THE BATTLE OF LIFE

A literary social story written from a compilation of memoirs put down in writing by a young man seventeen years of age.[3]

1. I have generally translated the term *mudhakkirāt* ("memoirs" in this title) as "diary" because Sāmī wrote regularly as events happened to him rather than as reflections on an earlier period in his life.

The introductory sentence here appears in the original Arabic text presumably as a later add-on in the top margin. For two reasons it appears that someone else might have written this sentence: first, paleographically, it does not look like the same handwriting that appears throughout the diary. However, if Sāmī did write the margin note after twenty years, his handwriting would likely have changed. Second, since the Arabic text reads *ẓurūfaka* "*your* circumstances" (emphasis added), it reads as if an external writer approached Sāmī as his addressee with the prospects of publishing the diary and adding an introduction. Sāmī seemed to have desired the publication of his diary, according to his eldest son, Samīr ʿAmr (henceforth Samīr). In correspondence of 1 February 2005, Samīr writes that his father told him on several occasions "that he wanted to publish the memoirs in the form of a story entitled 'My Struggle in This Life' and update it with events which took place later on in his life. He [Sāmī] never did that, and I [Samīr] am not aware of any additional or follow-up memoirs."

The photograph at the beginning of Part 2 is from Sāmī ʿAmr's passport, issued in 1943 when he was nineteen years old. The passport has only one visa in it, from the consulate of Lebanon in Jerusalem. Sāmī used this passport only once, for a trip to Lebanon in 1945 when he went to visit his brother Saʿdī at Dār al-Bāshiq Sanatorium. The sanatorium specialized in treatment of tuberculosis, which Saʿdī had contracted.

2. This bracketed sentence also appears in marginalia, on the right side of the first entry in the original manuscript. Like the bracketed sentence above, this appears to be a later addition, when Sāmī may have thought better of the idea to turn his diary into a story and clarified that the presentation of his words appear *not* in the form of a story.

3. Sāmī was born on 25 July 1924.

April[4]
30 April 1941
The Struggle Began:

My real life began during the second week of leaving school![5] That is because at that time I began to think. Yes, I began to think and look toward the future with a trembling heart and with a ray of hope that enlivens the heart. My sole hope is to complete my education at the technical school in Haifa, but it is out of the question. Can anyone answer my hope, while Haifa is currently under air attacks and lethal bombs?[6] I gave all of my effort to convincing my family to agree to my going [to Haifa], but it was to no avail.

With that, the glimmer that lit up my heart and kept it alive with hope ex-

4. In many places throughout the diary, double headings indicate the date. The first is often just the name of the month, and the second is the actual date, including the month. I have retained the headings as Sāmī wrote them. A second date sometimes clarifies when Sāmī made a mistake in his dating.

5. Completion of fourth or fifth grade was a standard education for the time period and in particular for those living outside of Jerusalem, which had most of the schools offering the sixth and seventh grades. One studied either a four-year or a five-year curriculum at the elementary level followed by a noncompulsory "higher elementary cycle." Sāmī took the five-year curriculum, which included English. It becomes clear toward the end of the diary that his knowledge of English would help Sāmī with a job interview. He also completed the higher elementary, or intermediate cycle, of two years, thus finishing seventh grade, probably at the age of sixteen. Life circumstances in Palestine led to pupils attending school when time permitted, making their ages and grade levels inconsistent. This could explain Sāmī's age at the time he completed seventh grade. In correspondence of 2 February 2007, Samīr suggests that his father probably stayed in Hebron for close to a year after completing school to help take care of his mother before heading to Jerusalem to earn money and make his way in the world. Sāmī was almost seventeen when he made his first entry in the diary. By 1945, there were only seventeen intermediate schools in Palestine of the kind that Sāmī completed, according to *A Survey of Palestine,* prepared in December 1945 and January 1946 for the Anglo-American Committee of Inquiry, volume 2, 650–651. See also Lindenberg, "Cultural Life of Palestinian Arabs," 233. One of the main sources on education in Palestine is Tibawi's *Arab Education in Mandatory Palestine*; see especially the subject of age and grade level, 45. In my introduction to this diary also see the section on Sāmī's education.

6. Italy was bombing the Palestinian coastline at Tel Aviv and Haifa at this time. The school that Sāmī wished to attend was likely the Haifa Trade School, which opened in 1936 and offered a two-year program in "fitting and machinery, carpentry and joining, and blacksmithing and welding, and car repair and maintenance"; Tibawi, *Arab Education in Mandatory Palestine,* 52.

tinguished. The world cast a darkened shadow over my face; I stayed at home, not leaving the house, thinking of my situation. We await the next set of tragic events and how they will change the path ahead of me.

I had given up hope of going to school but have also renounced my seclusion at home. There was only one door left in front of me: work! Yes! By being occupied with anything I can, I will be able to forget my pain and my memories of the sweet days that I spent in school, yes! There is nothing left for me except that door. I waited a short period and after that began working in a simple job at the NAAFI Department.[7] I was very angry for all of the period that I worked there. During that period, my calm, composed spirit died and was replaced by a spirit full of bitterness.[8]

May
6 May 1941
The Defeat:

I am returning to my writing, we have moved from aṭ-Ṭūr,[9] that dreary, deserted place in which catastrophes and accidents befell us; there is no need to mention them because they will remain inscribed in my memory for my entire life!!

I have now sat down at my table, after having left it for a month, lacking the means to facilitate my thinking and writing, so long . . . ![10]

7. The Navy, Army, and Air Force Institute (NAAFI) is a canteen service of the British military that provides members of British armed forces and their families overseas with recreational services and familiar retail goods in Palestine and throughout the world. Sāmī began to work at the NAAFI when he was seventeen years old. According to the NAAFI website, at http://www.naafi.co.uk/history.php?menu_list=111, the NAAFI was established in Palestine in 1938. For more on the NAAFI see *Naafi Up!: The Official History of NAAFI Commemorating 75 years of Serving the Services.*

8. This is the only indication that Sāmī may have written at a different period only to later pen it in his diary, suggestive of a memoir.

9. It is not clear to whom Sāmī refers when he writes "we" and "us," but the reader will discover that Sāmī lived at times with his brother Saʿdī in Jerusalem. He may well have been referring to his brother here. aṭ-Ṭūr is a suburb just east of the Old City of Jerusalem (Map 3). This may have been the first place in Jerusalem that Sāmī lived after moving from Hebron, when he began to work for the NAAFI.

10. Sāmī exaggerates the time since his last writing; the elapse of time was approximately one week, not one month.

September
13 August 1941[11]
Disturbances:

As I write these lines the situation is becoming worse for the ʿAmr family, wearing themselves out, losing their minds, although I am not referring to all of them. For example, Yūsuf ʿAbd al-Ḥamīd wants to take by force fifty pounds from ʿAbd ad-Dīk, actually, the woman whom he [ʿAbd ad-Dīk] had married.[12] If she refuses then he [says he] will take her to court; she refused, of course, and it was decided that the court date would be next Tuesday, 16 September 1941. Muḥammad Salīm and Saʿdī came that night to the house and consulted on this case, asking how Yūsuf ʿAbd al-Ḥamīd could take their cousin to court, and they threatened and scolded him and then they went to bed!![13]

11. Sāmī's writing "August" for the date is undoubtedly incorrect. September, as he lists the heading, is most likely correct. If one looks at a calendar for September 1941, one notes that "next Tuesday," as Sāmī writes about the scheduled court date, was in fact Tuesday, September 16, 1941, and so he presumably was writing on 13 September, not in August.

12. ʿAbd ad-Dīk is a nickname for a man whose real name is unknown who married a woman from the larger ʿAmr family, making her a relative or cousin of Yūsuf ʿAbd al-Ḥamīd. It was from her that Yūsuf ʿAbd al-Ḥamīd sought the money through her husband, ʿAbd ad-Dīk; correspondence from Samīr, 27 December 2007. Yūsuf ʿAbd al-Ḥamīd, according to Sāmī's wife, Suhayla ʿAmr (henceforth Suhayla), became the *mukhtār* of Dūra. He was a second or third cousin of Sāmī. Suhayla said Yūsuf's wife was from the as-Suwaytī family; interview with Suhayla, 16 January 2005. Little is known about the incident Sāmī mentions here, but Sāmī's youngest sister, Ruqayya ʿAmr (henceforth Ruqayya), said it probably had something to do with land sales, noting that fifty pounds was quite a lot of money at the time; interview with Ruqayya, 23 December 2005. The currency in Palestine during this period was the Palestine pound, which was tied to the British pound sterling; see Berlin's *The Coins and Banknotes of Palestine.*

13. Muḥammad Salīm was a relative of Ḥusayn ʿAmr but was not well identified by Sāmī's family in interviews and correspondence. Saʿdī was clearly Sāmī's older brother about whom he writes a great deal throughout this diary. ʿAwdat al-Ashhab mentions Muḥammad Salīm ʿAmr in his memoirs as "the perfect friend," by which he means trustworthy and reliable. Muḥammad Salīm tried to find ʿAwda work in the British military camps, which "absorbed large numbers of workers in a variety of jobs in the service of officers and soldiers in the canteens among others" (*Mudhakkirāt,* 41–42). As ʿAwda speaks of family and friends from Hebron, it is most likely that this is the same Muḥammad Salīm ʿAmr whom Sāmī mentions as a relative.

Tammūz[14]—October
18 October 1941
A Rare Occurrence:

On this day we celebrated the wedding of our beloved sister, may God find favor with her.[15] Her betrothed husband, the respectable al-Sayyid ʿIzzat Effendi al-ʿAṭāwna, loved her.[16] May God grant her sons and please them with His affections and His good fortune, and may God nourish us and our brother [ʿIzzat], Amen.[17] A splendid party was held and many distinguished members of the city attended, as did a not so small number of English ladies, who sat with our folks and ate with their hands—I mean without spoons or forks.[18] I think that they found special pleasure by eating the food this way.

14. Sāmī wrote *Tammūz,* an Arabic month, next to "October," but Tammūz corresponds to July, not October. It is unclear why the months appear this way. In some cases, Sāmī wrote only the transliterated English month name, for example, Abrīl or April, or only the Arabic month name, Nīsān; in other cases he uses both the English transliteration and the Arabic month name, as he does here. I have retained Sāmī's original usage throughout, as the mixed usage suggests questions of identification with language and change.

15. Here Sāmī is referring to his youngest sister, Ruqayya. This was the actual date of the wedding. Ruqayya was fourteen years old when she married; interview with Ruqayya, 20 December 2005.

16. The title "Effendi" was inherited from the era of the Ottoman Turkish rule, generally denoting a respected government officer. ʿIzzat worked as a surveyor for the government. It could also be an honorific title for a well-respected man. The transcription of the Arabic is indeed *Afandī*; however, the word "Effendi" has been standardized in English.

17. Ruqayya married ʿIzzat Effendi al-ʿAṭāwna, a man from a large Bedouin tribe of the Naqab (Negev) Desert. Ruqayya said he was one of very few from Bʾir as-Sabʿ [Beersheba] who were educated in Jerusalem. ʿIzzat had wanted to marry Suhayla, the daughter of the wealthy Abdullah Bashīr who would become Sāmī's wife. But Abdullah Bashīr continuously put off ʿIzzat, who gave up on Suhayla. Mukhliṣ ʿAmr interceded at this point and suggested that ʿIzzat marry his cousin Ruqayya, a beautiful young girl whose father had died. Ruqayya, who related this story, said she resisted as much as possible, including rejecting his gifts, as she felt too young to marry. She added that the people of Hebron complained about a city girl being given in marriage to a Bedouin. Mukhliṣ ʿAmr prevailed, but the condition for the marriage was that they would stay in Hebron. ʿIzzat built Ruqayya the house in Hebron where I interviewed her on 23 December 2005.

18. Ruqayya said these English women who attended her wedding were possibly from Sāmī's work, although she did not see any English ladies at her wedding; interview with Ruqayya, 23 December 2005.

November
19 November 1941
Sorrows:

I returned to my writing from which I think I have been separated for a month. My heart has preoccupied me and errands have taken me away from my writing. And now, we are like the nomadic Bedouin, not settling in one house before moving to another. Today we moved to a different house from the one we were in, which caused us great danger because it was not [built] strong or stable and we have enemies . . . !?[19] I have not mentioned my poor brother before this whom I never got angry with even once, but for whom I have great sympathy.[20] I lament him because I have learned that his mind until now is not stable or perhaps he needs many other experiences to make him realize the good from the wicked.[21] Yes, I did not mention that he joined the Army Corps without anyone asking him to. I do not know what his frame of mind was when he did that, when he entered the officer's office and said that he is twenty years old and that he would like to be a soldier.[22] He put on the soldier's uniform with his eyes closed. It is inestimable how much less freedom comes with the donning of that uniform, which now resembles the shackles of the captive and prisoner, the bonds of servitude, and submission to regulations. I often advised him and tried to deter him, but he closed his ears and ran away like a fugitive when he heard my advice. May God reform him and put him on the straight path.

19. It is not clear to whom Sāmī is referring when he mentions "enemies."

20. Here Sāmī is undoubtedly referring to his brother Saʿdī.

21. Ruqayya repeatedly referred to her brother Saʿdī as having suffered a great deal in his life. Regarding many of the incidents about which Sāmī writes referring to Saʿdī, Ruqayya either did not know or did not remember; interviews with Ruqayya, 30 December 2005 and 7 January 2006.

22. At the time of this diary entry, Saʿdī would have been twenty or twenty-one years old. Family members recall his birth year as either 1921 or 1922. It seems from the diary entries that Saʿdī worked with Sāmī at the NAAFI office and then decided to join the British army, an enlistment that would prove quite difficult for him, as is apparent in later diary entries. Hurewitz notes that despite British pleas for young Arab men of Palestine to enlist in the military, limited numbers did; Hurewitz, *Struggle for Palestine,* 119. There is little scholarly literature about Palestinian Arabs serving in the British military during this period.

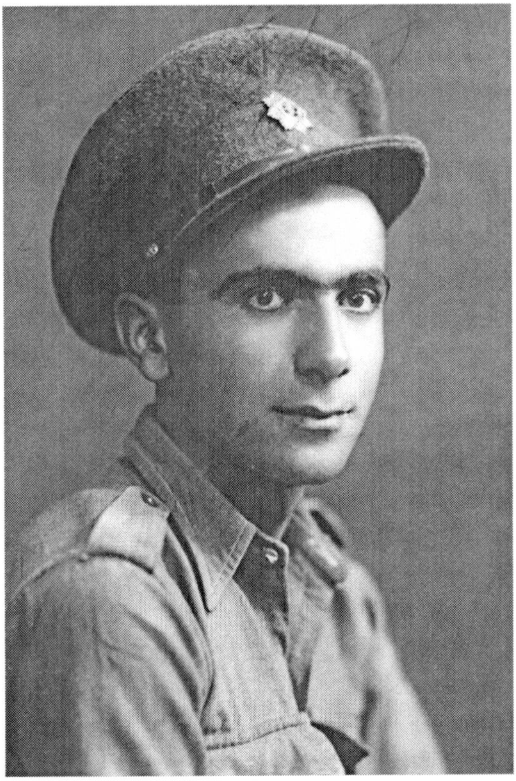

Figure 2. Saʿdī in British military uniform, circa 1942. Courtesy of Samīr ʿAmr.

30 November 1941
Hope:

I have not mentioned my older brother Asʿad because he is always calm, concentrating on how to live without burdens or troubles. He took his wife with him to the village where he works, and he bought a radio and he only comes to Hebron on rare occasions, once every three or four months.[23] He sends

23. Asʿad lived in Dawayma, a village close to Dūra. He was a schoolteacher, assigned to teach there by the government. He also moved from one town or village to another, as determined by the director of the Department of Education. Asʿad was not a "villager" but rather was a teacher assigned to the schools of particular villages; correspondence from Samīr, 5 February 2005.

ʿUthmān, his cousin, to the bank to collect his salary. May God strengthen his fortitude in this difficult life and on this rugged path and grant him wealth and children.

December
2 December 1941
A Wave of Compassion:

The war is at its peak along with the rise in prices. The pound does not equal a quarter of its actual value, and the government is exerting its greatest effort to compel the population to volunteer [for the military], not by force, but by starving them out and hindering [opportunities for] work. The government spreads only dejection, as it waits to break their spirit on the one hand and starve them on the other.

There were no signs in Palestine of war, by that I mean killing, but I think that it is just being postponed to a later date.[24]

December
8 December 1941
Aspirations:

I am waiting, and I am full of hope that I will become a clerk of some worth in the NAAFI Department, so that I can finish with this exhausting job that I am now starting to do.[25] But my hope freezes when I think of that wicked Greek man, Lorenziadis, who puts me off from one day to the next. Every time he needs a new clerk, he brings a Jewish girl or a Greek girl. When I had lost hope in convincing him [through words] to choose me as the next clerk, I gave him a gift of a turkey that I had bought for one pound.[26] And now I

24. Sāmī mentions that there were bombs falling in Haifa in the first entry of his diary. In this December entry, he seems to mean that there is no ground warfare in Palestine.

25. Sāmī began his work at the NAAFI as a *murāsil,* an errand boy.

26. One pound for the turkey would have been a generous gift, as Samīr said his father's salary was probably five to six pounds a month; correspondence from Samīr, 20 January 2008.

see that he has forgotten it and increased his deception and his cunning and his debauchery. Yes, I am waiting, and in the meantime Japan declared war on America and England yesterday.[27] That is a piece of information that will make the world stand up and take notice, no doubt, as they were waiting for Japan to do that.

December
16 December 1941
Jealousy Does Not Harm, but It Is Useful!

Every day I see new girls coming into the office and entering Lorenziadis' office, leaving immediately as clerks. Jealousy has eaten up my heart. I have talked to myself about writing a letter to Lorenziadis to remind him of the promise that he had made to me months ago. So I did this. I quickly wrote him a letter and went into his office to put it on his desk when, at the same moment, he came into the room and asked what I wanted. I gave him the letter and he read it and laughed, saying: "Yes! I have not forgotten you, Sāmī, and you will receive a position as quickly as possible and I will make every effort for your sake, Sāmī." I thanked him and left his office happy, my heart throbbing joyfully, filling with hope! . . . I will return to writing [in the diary] when I become a clerk in the NAAFI Department. God knows what is destined and He is capable of everything.

December
17 December 1941
Surprise!!

Poor me!! I feel so sick my chest is nearly bursting and the cough is shaking my being. I feel myself broken, I feel such pain in my chest and my throat, and

27. In fact, Japan attacked British, Dutch, and American territories, the latter being the well-known bombing of the American naval fleet in Pearl Harbor, Hawaii, just before Sāmī's entry on 8 December 1941. That same day, the U.S. Congress declared war on Japan and three days later on Germany and Italy. Japan's "declaration" of war against America and Great Britain, as Sāmī mentions, came by way of attack rather than declaration.

I do not know whether this sickness will go after my youth and exterminate a young man?!! . . .[28] He [God] is capable of everything.

[No Date][29]

Groaning

I have nothing but moans and groans
  Of my present and the darkness of my future
I have nothing but tears
  For they are relief for the misfortunate and the sad
Patience, O my heart, patience
  Perhaps luck has left on the straight path
How lost I have been
  How many years have passed
Have mercy, O God, on your obedient servant
  For sorrows have troubled his heart
A self-denying traveler in the world
  His family, freed from this life
Tears of a loved one were shed
  That will extinguish the flame of his feverish heart

Hope

O sad heart
  Pour tears on the grave of happiness

28. Samīr said Sāmī was concerned about contracting tuberculosis, which was common in Palestine during that period; correspondence from Samīr, 19 January 2008.

29. This entry of a poem was not dated in the diary. As it ties to no historical events, I cannot verify its date completely, but after careful examination of the diary and the entry dates, I find it most likely that this entry belongs here. I have taken the liberty to make an educated guess as to where it belongs, based on my understanding of how Sāmī made entries at the beginning of the diary. The groaning here may have been tied to the illness he mentions in the previous entry, when Sāmī would have been at home with time to write. It is possible that this entry belongs elsewhere.

In it sadness scatters
And disappears between the folds of space
And after patience and loyalty
Sadness is buried and happiness is sent from the grave

---

20 January 1942
Description of My Residence

Damn cave, destiny put it in a grave[30]
A human at the beginning of his life
Ick, if you see it you would consider it a shelter
It was prepared for times of danger[31]
It has three walls with the highest a barrier[32]
Against the sounds of the cold of winter and the flood of rain
There is no light except for a small glimmer
It began to freeze the darkness like the grave
I can see from it but cannot be seen, but
What does the [inside] viewer see [outside]
Used baggy pants, others new
Skin-colored stockings of the best trademarks
Small shoes and big shoes
New ones and very worn ones
Soft, white legs
Others, you can see aging.

30. This poem, according to Samīr, is based on the configuration of Sāmī's domicile, partially below the street level, with a window that revealed the street level. When looking out the window, Sāmī saw the lower part of people's bodies as they walked past. When he refers to women's legs and shoes of small children, he means those of the pedestrians passing by; correspondence from Samīr, 14 January 2006.

31. Sāmī probably means a bomb shelter, as the context for this is World War II.

32. He seems to have counted three walls inside the room and the wall facing the street as a barrier.

10 March 1942
Famine Threatens Us from One Day to the Next!!

We have breakfast at the club where we buy a bit of a sandwich and we drink a cup of tea.[33] As for lunch, we try our best to get some bread from Ayyūb, the owner of the restaurant, who sells nothing other than hummus. In the evening no one among the food sellers admits to having any bread left. Will we go to bed without having dinner? I try most of the time to find bread at lunchtime, and if I have been able to, I usually am not able to buy more than one loaf. Yes, we have money, but no one wants to sell. Take rice for example: Someone who requests rice from a seller, it is as if he has requested something forbidden (like hashish) and he [the seller] repeats the words and says "rice, there's none," and he [the buyer] leaves him and moves to another until you pass by all of the shops and hear the same answer. Isn't there anyone who wants to draw out his lie and say "I wish [I had rice to sell]." And also bread found in the shop—you request bread from the seller, and he looks directly at you and he says "there's none, sold out." O what wolves they are, the greed will kill them and lead them to death; that is their unalterable fate.[34]

I am awaiting a full, general revolt ignited only by the poor to humiliate the rich people who are sucking their blood and starving their children. They grasp onto materialism and close their ears to the calls of humanity—to hell with them. It is necessary to ignite this revolt, using hunger as the common basis for its uprising. The poor will use their torn rags as high-flying flags; its frontlines will be the naked children, who have mouths gaping from hunger, and girls with tousled hair and flimsy robes resulting from poverty and hardship. I am awaiting this day in which they lay siege to the rich in their homes; we will not cause them harm except to embarrass them for their cruelty and for their offspring.[35]

33. Based on the entry dated 30 March 1942, the club was located below the NAAFI office and may have been part of the NAAFI.

34. In his *al-Mufaṣṣal,* al-ʿArif lists the difference in prices between 1939 (just before the war) and 1947. For example, in 1939 a *raṭl* (2.884 kilograms) of rice cost six Palestinian *qurūsh,* while in 1947 the price had quadrupled, and the same amount cost twenty-four *qurūsh.* A list of prices for staples in Palestine in this comparison is in *al-Mufaṣṣal,* 466.

35. Sāmī displays a high sensitivity to the plight of the poor in society, yet he also seems to have some resentment for how they lived their lives. See the undated entry titled "If I Were an Arab Leader," which follows the 22 October 1943 entry.

Where do they put them, those hanging sheep in the slaughterhouse,[36] which the poor see, sighing not for themselves, but for their children who have not tasted meat for such a long time because it is too expensive? The poor man overflows with grief when he sees the rich with a porter filling their basket from whatever is in the market—fruit, vegetables, and meat—while his own wife, who recently delivered her baby, writhes with hunger, in pain.[37] In front of her there is nothing but the bread that she could not get without great effort, and the poor man remembers his children who are fighting over crumbs of bread.

Where are you, O Government, save the people, those for whom you see yourself as the protector!!

March
18 March 1942
Victory![38]

I promised earlier in my diary that I would return to writing when I became a clerk in the NAAFI Department, and it did happen, two months ago. I am praising and thanking God for what has been granted to me by this promotion. This has, in effect, changed the direction of my life in small, or possibly big, ways. I am changing everything completely from what I was two months ago, since during those two months there has been this development in my daily life. In fact, Sāmī the errand boy, always dissatisfied and full of complaints toward himself and toward God, has disappeared. Filling his place is Sāmī, the clerk, full of laughter, cleverness, and jokes, Sāmī who is seen by all the girls in the office with an eye of wonder and appreciation; they all like him a little, but especially adoringly in the eyes of Marīkā, when she turns to

36. Here Sāmī is referring to the hanging animals in the butcher shops.

37. Wāṣif Jawhariyya says in his memoirs that there were no shortages in Palestine during the war; see Nassar and Tamari, *al-Quds al-intidābiyya*. Sāmī's widow, Suhayla, suggested that there were shortages during the war but clarified by saying that staples such as rice and sugar were available, although very expensive and sometimes difficult to find; interview with Suhayla, 15 January 2006.

38. It is interesting that Sāmī uses the word "victory" (*intiṣār*) rather than "success" (*najāḥ*). Perhaps this fits in with his view of his life as a struggle, a battle to be won, not merely successes to achieve.

look at me, and in the tender voice of Lūbā, when she speaks to me.[39] I now have a position that is not bad among everyone [in the office], and my salary is not too bad either.

March
19 March 1942
Praise to God:

After always being alone and lonely, I now have plenty of friends in the office. The most respected among them is as-Sayyid Abū Sawwān, who is polite, has high morals, and helps me out in all that I ask him at work. We engage in deep conversation during our free time. I have not seen a young man in Jerusalem who has a combination of knowledge, hard work, and high moral values other than this young man. At first impression, I might have taken him for a young woman, as he is very shy and polite. I would sincerely like it if all young people or at least some of them were like this young man. Also among my friends who advise me are as-Sayyid Ilyās Habbash and as-Sayyid Hannā Yaghnam.[40] These are two guys who study Arabic, [and] the first one also studies journalism, at the Egyptian Correspondence School.[41] I would love to study poetry and Arabic poetry in strophic form at this school because I am especially inclined toward poetry and its rules and structure. I do not know if I can manage to study or not. It is not likely, as I remind myself of what is going on now—these days are days of war. It is rare to be able to help a person use his mind and exercise his imagination to write poetry.

39. These girls were probably Jewish, Samīr said, of Eastern European origin, based on their names, which are not Arabic; correspondence from Samīr, 19 January 2008. The British Mandate, with its reliance on the Balfour Declaration, opened the door to Jewish immigration to Palestine, and many came from Eastern Europe.

40. Both of these young men were Christian Palestinians.

41. Sāmī also studied through this correspondence school. See note 162 below.

March
30 March 1942
My Life Without Secrets:

Maybe, my friend,[42] you would like to know something about my home life. It differs from my work life completely. I live in a house in al-Baqʿa near the office,[43] and I begin work each morning at 8:00 and I leave at 1:00 in the afternoon. I have my breakfast in the club just below the office, and I have my lunch in a restaurant nearby. After that I go home and stay there until the time comes for me to return to work on those days during the week that we work from 3:00 until 6:00 in the afternoon. If I don't have to work then I go to the cinema if there is a good film showing,[44] or I stay home and read some of the novels I have or I write in my diary or I talk to one of the (female) neighbors, like Umm Aldū, who is affectionate toward me like my mother and takes an interest in my personal life and always asks how I am doing.[45] She spends a lot of time with me in the evening, and I talk to her about the political situation and about the war and its progression in India. Will Japan march on Calcutta or not?[46] Is the situation still the same in Libya?[47] Will the Russians in Russia

42. The friend to whom Sāmī refers here is the diary. He repeats this several times throughout the entries.

43. This is a neighborhood in Jerusalem where Sāmī lived for a period and where the NAAFI Office was located (Map 3).

44. al-ʿArif notes that there were eight cinema houses in Jerusalem in addition to the occasional screening at the YMCA; *al-Mufaṣṣal,* 443. Films screened were British, American, or Egyptian; Lindenberg, "Cultural Life of Palestinian Arabs," 233.

45. Umm Aldū was an Italian woman from whom Sāmī rented a room. It seems a bit of a curiosity that while Germans in Palestine during the war period were sent to detention or exiled by the British, an Italian woman lived freely, leasing rooms to locals and even, in this case, trying to seduce one of them. In her diary of life at the American Colony in Jerusalem, Bertha Spafford Vester notes that her German husband, long affiliated with the colony, was arrested under order of British Mandate authorities as part of a policy to arrest Germans in British Mandate Palestine as the war heated up. In this particular case, Mr. Vester was released almost immediately due both to his service in the country through the American Colony and to his connections. Undoubtedly not all Germans in Palestine at the time received the same consideration. See Spafford Vester's *Our Jerusalem,* especially 321ff.

46. On 23 March 1942, Japan invaded the Andaman Islands in the Bay of Bengal, to the east of the Indian subcontinent. Sāmī might have taken a strong interest in this, as the presence of Japan so close to India pushed the hand of the British in India to offer autonomy to the Indians; this also firmed the resolve of Indian nationalists who now sought full independence.

47. It would not be until November 1942 that the British would push the Germans and the

move forward and drive out the Germans? Will the Germans push forward in the spring, which has already begun now? These are the questions that we repeat each day, and there has not been a definitive answer until now. Then Umm Aldū decided to teach me Italian, and she gave me my first lesson yesterday. I noticed during her lesson a meaningful glitter in her eyes toward me, and I do not know what it meant. She was giggling a lot during the lesson, and she asked permission to leave despite her not wanting to. She left, promising to return today. I waited for her tonight but she did not come. I grabbed the opportunity to write in the diary after a long time [away from the diary], but I did not write a thing.[48] See you later, my friend. I feel sleepy and my eyelids are heavy, urging me to sleep . . .

Nīsān, April[49]
2 April 1942
Caution and Hope:

Such is fate to prepare me for its trap—Umm Aldū has fallen in love with me, yet it is not clear up until now whether it is in fact infatuation or maternal love. She tires herself out making me content, and she finds happiness being near me, without my doing anything. She frequently visits me and asks me to come to her house. Will she turn my life upside down, or will she throw me to the ground, as happens to young men who follow their loves and follow their passions? Your mercy, O God, free me from this frightening nightmare that sits on my chest whenever I imagine myself in such a situation of moral depravity that weaves through my pure [virginal] mind, which has never before imagined such vices. Every time I intended to move from that house, these incidents increased, holding me back and doubling the circumstances of my subjugation. I am just a man who wants to live. I want to live among people and compete with them. I want to become famous and gain prominence. Whenever I engage in spiritual reflection, the paths of success multiply in front of

---

Italians, who controlled Libya as of 1911, back to French-controlled Tunisia, where they were met by British and American forces.

48. It is unclear what he means when he says "I did not write a thing." Perhaps he had hoped for something more philosophical, spiritual, or otherwise, but instead came up with a recounting of such mundane things as the days' events and the war abroad.

49. *Nīsān* is the Arabic word for April.

my imagination, and my heart soars with joy when I imagine everyone echoing my name. I have tried all jobs, but in my imagination, I have succeeded and failed, gained and lost, from my delusions and hopes. Will these hopes be realized, and will these fantasies materialize and become true? Yes, I want to live and I do not want to get tied up now with silly talk of deceptive love and animalistic desire. I have many years ahead of me to satisfy myself. This is the right thing for me to do. As for now, I am still in my formative period! I am in the period in which I am laying the foundation, which must be strong and firm for my future life. I have great hope and it is not far off in the future that I will be a respectable person. What will raise me to the level of elites is not my physical work or my financial situation but my hard work and fear of God and control over myself.[50]

As-Sayyida Umm Aldū asked me to dine at her house today and I accepted her invitation, fearing that she would get upset if I did not. She filled me a big plate of macaroni cooked with peas and veal. It really was delicious food, and as-Sayyida sat down next to me. I put food on her plate and she began to eat. She was looking at me from one moment to the next. She stared at me with her piercing glances, but they became routine for me because I am not interested in her. Then, she offered me some fruit and a cup of coffee, and I stayed with her for not too short of a period, pretending complete ignorance for this banquet of hers and the reception. The most amazing thing about this woman is that at the beginning she threatens and acts in a menacing, aggressive manner towards anyone who dares to play romantic games with her or try to get close to her! Following that she starts talking about her romantic adventures and starts laughing, mouth wide open, as if she did not describe herself a moment ago as the lethal courageous woman she claimed herself to be. Do not bother with her, my friend, because I do not care about her anyway. See you later on, on a day of self-reflection, as I feel myself quite tired and I am desirous of sleep. . . . I wish you a good night. . . .

50. Sāmī ultimately did well for himself in his life. After working in government service for a number of years, he opened a real estate office and made quite a bit of money. He was able to give his children a solid university education, something he was never able to have. Throughout my interviews with his sister Ruqayya, she wondered why Sāmī did not continue to write, considering how well he did in his endeavors later in his life.

April

6 April 1942

Blaming the Soul and Cautioning the Mind:

Frequently, what happens to me is I find myself in some situations having to deal with sexual relations. Usually I am tranquil, remaining at a standstill, but on that day you will see me frantically coming and going, trying to pay attention to that which does not concern me but rather issues that concern women and girls. With my shyness, I comb my hair many times, but there is no need for that; I look in the mirror a number of times to find the place of weakness in my handsome face. We have Muslim [female] neighbors who appear sitting in the window, and when these feelings come over me, or illusions, call it whatever, I run to the bathroom that faces opposite their window. I pretend that I have only come to the bathroom where I stay for a minute, then leave, pretending to button my pants. Then I return to where I was, pretending that I do not know anything. O God, I steal a few glances toward the window and I find the girls stealing back a look at me. Then when I look, they pretend, in turn, to look at something else other than me. All this is to no avail because I know with certainty that no matter what I do, I will not get anything, big or small, without talking to the girls, just as I know that I am not courageous enough to talk or say even one word to them because they are Muslim girls. If I were to talk to them, it would be impossible, as I am so shy to open up to them what is inside me, full of infatuation, if that is in fact what is in my heart . . . Caution, Sāmī, before making mistakes like these that you always seem to face.[51] Be careful and take every caution to refrain from those orders to

51. Sāmī seems to have faced such situations more than he relates in his diary. Samīr relays the following about life in cosmopolitan Jerusalem during the period as told to him by his father: "Even married Muslim women would get involved in relationships with young men, especially if they were married to older men. Sāmī told me more than once about a Muslim landlady who leased him a room, and who one night knocked on his door telling him that there is a pretty young woman who has 'many gold bracelets on both hands' (meaning rich), who was married to a rich old man incapable of doing 'any good', and she wanted to get pregnant to keep her 'status' with him by giving him a son. With no DNA analysis or blood group testing available to the public in those days, this woman (and others) went looking for a 'bull' to inseminate her—perhaps she would also become his [Sāmī's] mistress—with promises of gold and money. Concerned with his purity [apparent throughout the diary], Sāmī bolted the door, barricaded [himself] in his room, and the next day he fled in the early morning

do bad things, as you are still at an age in which you should not allow this to yourself and your subconscious, and in which you should, before everything else, remember God, before doing any act, great or small. For whoever has God in his heart and in his mind and continues to remember his God, does not make mistakes while living life in this world . . . !

April
6 April 1942[52]
Quiet Pain:

I am alone because no one gives me advice or sits next to me and takes an interest in me to ask any questions that I can answer or to whom I can ask questions and he can answer. Yes, I have a brother whom I live with under the same roof, and we work together at the same job, but we are living in two completely different worlds, in spirit and in being, and whenever there is a meeting of spirit and being, with the material, he asks for the material, crushing the place of spirit and being from existence. I have to bear this awful loneliness and learn something from these circumstances.

---

10 April 1942
[Untitled]

Farewell to the one whom my heart loved at first sight, farewell as I failed tremendously in love, which I thought was a game:[53]

with his few belongings"; correspondence from Samīr, 24 February 2008. Sāmī expresses his concern with his purity most clearly in the entry dated 11 November 1943.

52. 6 April 1942 has two entries. It is not clear if indeed Sāmī wrote twice on this date, as he does not mention that he was writing a second time that day. This is the only date for which there seems to be a double entry. As this is the date that appears in the diary for this entry, I have left it as is.

53. This is a salutation to an unnamed girl. From the context it seems that this was directed to a girl at work; Sāmī writes as if this is happening in front of him and she does not know that he is writing about the scene simultaneously. It is either one of a few letters that Sāmī copied into his diary from actual letters he wrote or the only version of the letter in which he wanted to tell the girl how he felt but was too shy to do it in any other form than in a letter in his diary. In either case, it is probably safe to assume that the unnamed girl never read how Sāmī felt about her.

In fact, your love affected me and made me a different man, as if I now know life in its entirety having tried all kinds of things. Farewell, O dear one, you who have buried your love in my heart, as I refused to ruin my honor.

Yes, I have placed love on one side of the scale and honor on the other side, and honor weighed more than the memory of love; now eternal craziness has won and is what remains after I have pasted your image in my mind and accustomed my hearing to your sweet, beautiful voice. Farewell, after my heart is broken apart with jealousy over you from those dastardly people who have gone to extremes in their harassment of you and making advances toward you, yes, I hate all of those men. Now it is 12:45 Monday, and you are telling me that the flowers that (——) gave you have filled the room with their scent;[54] I responded by nodding my head, as sorrow was about to kill me. You were waiting for me to laugh, but I am very far away from doing that.

Sāmī

April
21 April 1942
Speech:

Dear Gentlemen, a good evening to you,

We have tried frequently to get over our sadness, for if we continued to think about it we would hate life. However, a human being, in his essence, is stubborn and strong-willed to get past the black days. He can make great effort to turn those dark days to happy days that can make him feel better and let him enjoy life. Yes, it is necessary to cheer someone up, using a variety of ways to get rid of his sadness and pain. Imagine, O friends, how many men at this very moment are waiting for death, in their bunkers underneath the cold of the wind and perhaps the drizzle of rain, yes! Imagine those men and imagine people who are deprived of food and sleep, with the path to fortune closed off in front of their face. Think about a bleak future—I hope that is not what is waiting for you—this future that awaits the masses. That day that will show the face of the war, in all its force and its might! The war and its

54. It seems clear that Sāmī knew who gave the flowers to this unnamed girl, but he writes a dash in place of the name.

starvation! The war and its hideousness! Yes! Think to that day and compare it to a day like this when I see you quarreling and arguing as to which song you will start with! Think about your brothers and sisters who are waiting for help from you regardless of how little it is, and your mothers who are now at this moment sitting, sleepless, worrying, waiting for you . . .

You are excused . . . now that I hear your songs and listen to your voices. I find them all expressing the suffering and the sadness of the pressures in the heart. You try to escape from your pain through singing. I am wrong when I said a few seconds ago that you are filled with delight; it is only now that I have learned that you are sad and wistful . . . I see your eyes and your facial expressions and I do not find any trace of happiness in your faces.

And, finally, I recommend that you forget about the alcohol. It is useless although you think that it makes you happy, but in fact it is to no avail. It is out of the question that it makes the sad person happy. In fact, sadness will overflow into the heart and will make the happy person sad. Even if you drink bitterness instead of alcohol, take it as a fact that alcohol will not make happy the one who is not already happy, just as it increases the sadness of one who is already sad.

Peace be upon you.
(I gave this terse rambling speech when Saʿdī convened a group of friends for a late-night gathering one evening at our place, including Mūsā al-ʿAṭāwna;[55] they brought the oud,[56] which pleased them that night.)

April
27 April 1942
Sorrows:

((Money . . . money . . . where can I get money? From where? From where? Yes! There is the settlement of the trees that were cut from our land, and per-

55. Mūsā al-ʿAṭāwna was the brother of ʿIzzat al-ʿAṭāwna, the husband of Sāmī and Saʿdī's sister Ruqayya.

56. An oud is a wooden, stringed instrument popular for public audiences and for private gatherings such as this one that Saʿdī held at his and Sāmī's flat. The memoirs of musician Wāṣif Jawhariyya (1904–1968) provide a deeper look at the oud and entertainment in Palestine during this period. Wāṣif left his memoirs, which were published in two volumes edited

haps the sum of that will be a substantial figure, yes I must go to the location where the settlement is taking place. It is in the Governor's Office, yes! I am going!!))[57]

This is what was going on in the mind of my oldest brother, Asʿad, when he arrived at the Governor's Office asking the permanently gloomy clerk: "Did the agreed upon settlement for the sale of the cut trees from our land arrive?" The clerk said dryly: "No settlement has arrived, get out, I am busy!" And my brother said: "Please look in the register in front of you, perhaps you will find the report." The clerk got angry and screamed in his face. My brother lost his patience and screamed in turn and he said "I will not get out until I show you [a thing or two]!" The clerk hurried to the Assistant Governor and told him that this man is scum and the Governor got angry and called for the police to arrest my brother. They arrested him and he spent the night in jail. If not for the Education Inspector, who told them that one night in jail was enough, the Assistant Governor would have given him seven days.[58] He got out the next day, sad and depressed, and wanted only to go to the village where he works, but he couldn't find a car until 6:00 in the evening. He went to his job, but this was after his name had become gossip on the tongues of everyone in Hebron. The name of that wretched clerk is Shafīq Musallam, Christian, peasant.

April
28 April 1942
Love or Exaggeration and Lies (Waterlou Bridge Film):[59]

She sat down to tell me the story [of the film] that she had seen in the cinema.[60] She was repeating that sentence with passion: "then he fell in love

---

by Nassar and Tamari, *al-Quds al-ʿuthmānīyya* and *al-Quds al-intidābīyya*. See also Tamari, "Jerusalem's Ottoman Modernity."

57. Sāmī seems to be quoting what he thought his brother Asʿad must have been thinking prior to arriving at the governor's office and thus put the first few lines in double parentheses, after which he explains that these are his brother's thoughts.

58. The education inspector probably knew Asʿad and vouched for him because he was a schoolteacher.

59. "Waterlou" is written in English but misspelled in the title of this entry.

60. This woman is probably Tsibūra, as his feelings toward her become clear later in this

with her and then she too fell in love with him." At that point you could see a glimmer shining out from her eyes that captivates hearts. Yes, she sat on the edge of the window, and from one moment to the next the breeze played with her short dress, revealing her pure white legs; it makes the mouth water. She was speaking in that voice that rings as if it is full of strong emotion and passion like that woman who fell in love [in the film] and she wishes that she could be her. She carried on talking until she finished, and I was listening to her pretending to understand, when in fact, all of me had turned to look at her beautiful, seductive qualities that make her so feminine and well developed.[61] She was talking to me and I wished that she knew what was pounding in my heart. Every few minutes, she would playfully stretch her beautiful neck toward the yard where the cars are parked, waiting to see when the bosses leave and clear out the club for us to play that game that we recently learned called billiards. We played for the first time on Thursday, 23 April 1942, and since that time we have been eager to play again. We played that day because we were working in the afternoon. We began the game at 2:15 in the afternoon, Tsibūra, Nikōlā, Marjarīt, and I,[62] and we seemed happy with the game and our faces overflowed with exuberance and joy with the blissful solitude we found in the billiard room. Tsibūra radiated like a gem under the light of the moon, and she had a smiling mouth and a resplendent face, always laughing and full of enthusiasm for the game, which you could tell by how sad she got if she did not win the game and how happy she got when she did. So, we promised that we would return to play on Thursday, the day after tomorrow, as we had become so enraptured by that game.

I don't know if we love it simply for the game or to enjoy that happy solitude. I feel that I lose control over my nerves when my gaze meets that of the magical Tsibūra, who emits an attractive and enticing light or when it falls on her thin waist and slender body. These are the first words that I say that are said with affection. I am not accustomed to love and passion, which are still

---

entry and are repeated in a few places in the diary. The Arabic transcription, Tsibūra, is used here, as that is how Sāmī refers to her in the diary; however, the name Tsipora is a Hebrew name.

61. An interesting note as one reads how much Sāmī was influenced by this woman's description of the film is that when he came to work in the Ministry of Interior in Jordan, part of his responsibilities included censoring films; interview with Suhayla, 19 January 2006.

62. The girls must have been Sāmī's co-workers. There is no further information available about them, other than the references Sāmī makes to them in the diary.

off in the future. [I said] This because I feel, truthfully, [the emotions] I have written!

Ayyār[63]
29 May 1942
Rare Amusement and a Short Trip:

The head of the office decided that my annual vacation would be 17–31 May 1942. On Saturday, the sixteenth of Ayyār, my mother and I headed to Hebron because as-Sayyid Sulaymān Budayrī and his mother were coming to our house.[64] We stayed there until Tuesday, when we traveled to Jerusalem and from there to Nablus, and from Nablus we took a car to ʿAnabtā, where we stayed as guests at the home of ʿIzzat Effendi al-ʿAṭāwna, the husband of my sister Ruqayya.[65] We stayed two nights at his place, and during the two days I looked around that small village, and I met some of the people from the village. On the whole, they have high morals and a peaceful character, as well as being educated. Then, on Thursday morning, we traveled to Nablus to visit our older sister Yusrā;[66] we stayed with her, and she was pleased at the outset with our coming. We stayed with her for one night and then left on Friday after walking around the Old City's streets and markets. My mother and I were on our way to Tulkarem but when we reached ʿAnabtā, my mother

63. *Ayyār* is the Arabic word for the month of May.

64. It seems that Sāmī's reference to Sulaymān Budayrī may be incorrect here; he also omitted the definite article *al-* in the last name. Sāmī's mother had a sister named Nuzha who married into the al-Khālidī family. Sāmī incorrectly identifies Nuzha's son here as Sulaymān al-Budayrī. He was Sulaymān al-Khālidī; interview with Suhayla, 16 January 2006. Ruqayya also clarified this, noting that Sulaymān's last name was al-Khālidī and that his mother was from the Budayrī family; interview with Ruqayya, 20 December 2005.

65. ʿIzzat worked as a surveyor for the British Mandate authorities, and this work sometimes led him to live outside of Hebron, where he had settled with Ruqayya after they were married.

66. Yusrā had a different mother than Sāmī and the rest of the siblings. Saʿīd, Sāmī's father, was married to Yusrā's mother, Nuzha ʿAbdīn, and they had a few children, but only Yusrā survived. Saʿīd then married Sāmī's mother, Zahīya ʿUthmān al-Budayrī, and the rest of Sāmī's siblings are the children of Saʿīd and Zahīya. Yusrā and her husband, ʿUthmān Amīn al-Ḥammūrī, lived in Nablus for quite some time while her husband worked there as an inspector for the Department of Forestry. They only returned to Hebron when her husband retired. See Appendix 1.

stopped there again while I continued on to Tulkarem, as I was on my way to Jaffa. I reached Tulkarem and stayed there an hour before continuing on to Jaffa. Once there (in Jaffa) I stopped at the main street, where I got out of the car and I saw the coachman and asked him if he knew the home of Jamāl al-Budayrī or not.[67] He said that he would try to find it. I took the carriage, the time was 7:30 and the sun was disappearing in the distance; the evening wind was gently blowing, satisfying with a slight coolness from the sea. The carriage took me along as the breeze disappeared. I imagined myself a French duke in times gone by . . . Finally, I reached my uncle's home, and I went up the stairs and knocked on the door. I entered the house and when my uncle looked at me, I told him "I am Sāmī," fearing that he might have forgotten me. He received me hospitably and his wife was delighted, as were [cousins] Muḥammad, Fakhrī, and ʿAlyya. I sat with them on the balcony and engaged in deep conversation until ʿAbd al-Karīm entered (he is my cousin) and looked at me first without knowing who I was. Finally, I told him who I was and he was very happy. We sat to have dinner and later went to the bedrooms to sleep. In the morning, after eating breakfast, I went with Fakhrī, who is six years old, to the beach, to bathe there. We reached the beach of Tel Aviv and it was Saturday, so there were plenty of people there to bathe, and they began to play different games in the water.[68] I left my clothes with the boy [Fakhrī] and snuck among them as if I were one of them.[69] The most wonderful thing that I saw in that scene was when a wave came and splashed all of the bathers; the strength of the wave pushed all the people together, unintentionally, into the arms of each other—the lucky one found a woman in his arms! One time it happened with such a wave, and I raised my head until I found an older woman and she grabbed onto my neck. I moved her away from me gently and she apologized while laughing. We returned to the house and ate lunch, then ʿAbd al-Karīm and I went to wander in the streets also looking at the cinema from the outside. Finally we reached the beach and we rented two chairs and

67. Jamāl was Sāmī's maternal uncle, from the al-Budayrī family. In some cases, Sāmī uses the definite article *al-* with names, and in others he does not. I have followed his usage directly, which accounts for the inconsistency.

68. Tel Aviv was a recently built Jewish city (1909) in British mandatory Palestine. Saturday is the Jewish Sabbath, so it is not unusual to think that there would be many bathers on the beach that day.

69. It is possible that Sāmī says this here because most of the people on the beach in Tel Aviv were Jews, and he may have felt an outsider in this environment.

we remained sitting in them until 7:00, when we went home and ate supper. After that we went to the cinema, which is called Cinema as-Sharq. It is a summer theater, with no roof to it, and it begins at 9:00 and ends at midnight. I saw *Awlād ash-shawār*[c] [Children of the Street] and *al-Majd al-Khālid* there, two wonderful films, the first an English film . . . After that, we went home and early on Sunday ʿAbd al-Karīm and I went to the sea and we did not stop swimming until 2:00 in the afternoon. We rode what is called *ḥasaka,* which is a small boat, but there is no place to sit in the middle, there is only sitting space on the edges of it, and it suits only three people. We stayed on it for two hours circling the calm, beautiful sea. From time to time a male or a female bather splashed us and we would stop near him—we would stare at him and he would stare at us, then he would rest a little from tiredness and place his arms on the *ḥasaka*. Finally, we returned to the house with our skin almost having burned from the heat of the sun that sank into our wet bodies. In the morning of the following day, we went to the sea, as usual, and swam until noon. We returned home to eat lunch, then we agreed to go to the Jarīsha River [Figure 3],[70] and ʿAbd al-Karīm, ʿAlyya, Muḥammad, Saʿīd, and I rode the bus until we reached the road that leads to the river, and we walked a not so short way until we finally arrived, and we saw the place immersed with people. There were some boats for rent. We rented one and bought some oranges. ʿAbd al-Karīm took control of the boat and the oars and took us between the trees that grow along the sides of the river. Many people rented boats like we did and among them was someone with a gramophone, and he and his friends enjoyed music while they were in the boat. There were small, beautiful waterfalls, whose water does not stop, flowing until it comes crashing down and becomes foam. We all enjoyed that beautiful, interesting trip. Finally, we returned after having ridden a carriage, which took us all the way home. The same program was repeated in the morning. We went to the sea and ate lunch at home, then ʿAbd al-Karīm and I went to Cinema al-Ḥamrāʾ,

70. The young man in the boat with Sāmī in Figure 3 is probably his cousin ʿAbd al-Karīm, son of Sāmī's maternal uncle Jamāl al-Budayrī. It seems that Sāmī is referring to the al-ʿAwja River here. He may have called it the Jarīsha River because the village of Jarīsha sat just on the south bank of the al-ʿAwja River before its destruction in 1948. Walid Khalidi suggests that the village of Jarīsha may have gotten its name from the Arabic verb *jarasha,* which means "to mill" or "to grind," and indeed there were grain mills along the river. A photo called "The Mill of Jarīsha on the al-ʿAwja River," dated 1917, is in Khalidi's edited volume, *All That Remains,* 246–247. ʿAwja, the name of the river, is a variation on the Arabic verb *ʿawwaja,* "to bend" or "to curve."

Figure 3. Sāmī and cousin on the al-ʿAwja River. Courtesy of Samīr ʿAmr.

which was showing *Sī ʿUmar* with Najīb ar-Rīḥānī.[71] I was delighted to see it. We went out from the beautiful cinema, the building with its expensive furnishing and furniture. I said goodbye to ʿAbd al-Karīm and I took the bus to Jerusalem arriving there at 8:00 in the evening. I spent that night in my house after the neighbors had told me that my brother traveled to Syria.[72] I woke up early the next morning to inquire from the clerks at the office about what happened and I was told that he had been requested to travel to Syria for work in the office in Beirut.[73] At that point, I went to Hebron and Asʿad informed

71. *Sī ʿUmar* (Master Omar) is a 1941 Egyptian comedic film by Niazi Muṣṭafā and starring Najīb ar-Rīḥānī, Mīmī Shakīb, and Mary Mūnīb. *Companion Encyclopedia of Middle Eastern and North African Film,* s.v. "Egyptian Cinema," 51, 121. A poster image of this film can be seen at http://photos1.blogger.com/blogger/3388/941/1600/Si%20Omar.jpg.

72. This is a reference to Saʿdī.

73. It is interesting that Sāmī still considered Beirut in Syria in 1942. By that time, Beirut had become the capital of French Mandate Lebanon, a country that was separated out from the larger Syria as a result of the post–World War I peace settlements devised mainly by Britain and France (Map 2). Lebanon would gain its independence one year later, in 1943, with Beirut as its capital.

me that Saʿdī had taken from the bank ten pounds and traveled to Beirut. Our mother still does not know that he went. And finally, I went back to my place of work on Sunday evening. I moved my things from the house that I was living in to another house, one I had lived in six months prior, which I did because I was now going to be alone in the house and there is no need for a big house, like that other house, for just me.

July
5 July 1942
[Untitled]

I stopped writing for a long while for which I am very sorry. The only reason for it was that I had moved to a different house, as I mentioned previously, not the one I had been in before. In this house, actually around it, there are many neighbors with whom I spend much of my time, which did not facilitate my writing a thing about my life during the whole month. I will make up for it, God willing, without anything disappearing from my memory.

---

10 August 1942
[Untitled]

It is now 10:00 in the evening. Marīttā and Rudaynā have left after having taken a lesson in English and after they gave me a lesson in French.[74] After they left, I ate and sat down to write what I neglected to write in the recent few months. To you, my friend, here is what happened to me during this period.

After my annual leave had ended, I returned to the office, suntanned, from time in the sun at the beach. The clerks in the office welcomed me with many questions about how I spent my vacation and whether or not I enjoyed it. My answer was: "Yes and I really wished that you had been with me," this answer coming spontaneously to the question of a girl. One day, as I was sitting at my desk, which is across from the desk of Lūbā, Lūbā said to me "are there

74. These girls may have been Sāmī's neighbors or co-workers. Marīttā was most definitely Christian, as hers is not a name Muslims used. Both Muslims and Christians used the name Rudaynā, but it is likely that this Rudaynā was also Christian.

cherries in Hebron?" I told her yes. She expressed her desire to go to Hebron and I told her to ask Tsibūra and see if the others wanted to come. Tsibūra agreed and expressed her desire to come. We planned a time to meet, set for Sunday at 8:00 [in the morning], when Lūbā, Mary, Lūbā's sister [Barbara], and Tsibūra would meet at the Jaffa Gate to come together.

Of complete surprise, my brother Asʿad had invited the son-in-law of my uncle Jamāl to his place in Hebron on the same day that the girls from work were coming. It was to my great pleasure that they [the girls] were going to the same place as my uncle's son-in-law. On Saturday evening, my uncle and his two daughters [Hind and Faṭṭūmah, or Fāṭima] and Hind's husband came to our house to spend the night. In the morning the girls waited a little [upon arriving in Hebron], and I came exactly at 9:00, but the one whom I love was not with them.[75] I wonder why she did not come with them?! I asked the girls the question a few times, but their answer to me was nothing other than a few darting glances until I shut up about this question. I convinced myself that it was in the hands of God. We went down to the house and everyone was sitting in the sitting room when the three girls, Lūbā, Mary, and Lūbā's sister came in. They were quite happy prior to the entry of Hind and Faṭṭūmah, when their happiness lessened and the extent to which they felt relaxed subsided.

Then we all agreed to go to Nunqur,[76] so we arranged a bus to take us there and we decided that we would eat Qidr,[77] which is made in the oven. And with this, we rode the bus together to Nunqur and Lūbā sat next to me and we began to talk the whole way about the weather and the agricultural products during which time my poor brother Asʿad stole my mind as he began to look in turn at all of the girls and decided that his choice would be Lūbā's sister, Barbara, and he began trying to get her attention. Ḥāfiẓ Kamāl [uncle Jamāl's son-in-law] sat next to his wife and my uncle and his wife and my mother and Naʿīma and Faṭṭūmah sat in various seats of the bus.[78] Finally the bus reached

75. Here Sāmī is referring to Tsibūra.

76. Sāmī is referring here to Wadi Nunqur, the Nunqur Valley, between Hebron and the ʿAmr family's village of Dūra, according to family members. Nunqur, southwest of Hebron, like Dūra, has been considered a village since 1967 because of the increase in its population; Dabbāgh, *Bilādunā filasṭīn,* 14.

77. *Qidr* is a well-known dish in Hebron made from rice and lamb. The name comes from the cooking pot in which the dish is made, which is called a *qidr.* In Palestinian colloquial dialect, the dish is pronounced *idrī.*

78. Naʿīma was Sāmī's oldest sister with the same mother.

our destination. We took the bags down and headed in the direction of the beautiful Wadi Nunqur [Nunqur Valley], which, if you stopped there, sounds of the babbling streams, mixing with the singing of the birds and the trees, would fill you with delight. The green that extended from the very beginning of the *wadi* to its end would delight your mood along with the water that encloses you wherever you go, with the beautiful blue brooks scattered here and there. From one stretch to the next there are tall walnut trees with their broad leaves and their penetrating, gripping scent. There are also apple, plum, and apricot trees, which, by their blooming, have taken over the *wadi* with their colors that spread and splash across its dress of green brocade, the most beautiful red and blue and violet.

We walked down in that *wadi* that Lūbā described as a "small paradise." The group picked out a high point in the *wadi* that looks over all the rest of it and faces a high rock on which the water breaks and flows to the bottom. It fills the numerous brooks quenching the thirst of the trees nearby and the herbs spread out among them. We scattered to all parts of the *wadi*: Asʿad went with Mary and Barbara and I went with Lūbā. Ḥāfiẓ went with Hind. Every time Lūbā would face a series of intertwined trees or a high wall, I would pick her up and carry her down without speaking, and like this we wandered around the *wadi,* finally returning when everyone was looking for us! Time came for food and we sat to eat it and it was delicious in its simplicity. The girls loved it and with the food there was a bottle of wine, and they drank from it and Asʿad drank with them in turn as well. The wine made the following question repeat on our tongues: "Didn't we have a nice time?! A very good time?" And the answer would be: "Yes, very much so, as there were no troubles."

Evening began to approach, and we walked like ghosts [tiptoeing to enjoy the atmosphere]. Our hearts were still connected, tied by that little paradise, as Lūbā had described it. We began the return, and in our eyes there was a lesson and in our hearts pain: as for the lesson, it was the tears of joy that filled our eyes when we were in that paradise. As for the pain, it was that we had to leave that paradise on earth that Lūbā gave new life to, and gave it a name with her tenderness and her charm. We returned without uttering a sound, utterly speechless and in reverence, as if silent with awe.[79] The family returned

79. Sāmī uses an expression that literally translates to "as if birds were on our heads" to describe just how gently they moved and how silent they were, as if in awe of the place, so as "not to scare off the birds from their heads." He uses this wonderful expression again in the entry dated 12 March 1945, indicated in note 186 below.

to the house [in Hebron] while we returned to Jerusalem. O, how I left this place, my heart overflowing. See you later, my friend.

---

13 August 1942

Mentalities, Spiritualities, and Materialities!?

It is 9:30 in the morning. I hope you do not get bored by my words, O my friend, for I find in them something of an excess and an exaggeration, nevertheless I am forced to write, so bear with me and this coldness in my writing, yes!!

Whatever kind of troubles or disappointments happen to me, you will find me not paying any attention to them or considering them harsh or out of the ordinary. This is because I am waiting for great and better things to turn me away from what is happening currently. I see things that I want and I see girls whom I like but rising from deep inside of me is a screaming voice telling me no! Don't do this and don't take that. The time will come when it will announce it: "Control yourself from everything you see and touch." I have become completely faithful to these emotions. In fact, they have prevented me from making many mistakes. This is due to the fact that I am very clear about the many things that I want and have come to realize in my mind. Just look at the periods in which these feelings have led me. Now, I am working at a normal job . . . I quickly threw the work papers aside and I took out this small piece of paper to write on it what is going on inside of me, ignoring the conversation of the clerks who share this room with me, and even the desk.

Today, at 1:30, I will go to pick up my suit from the tailor, which he kept for four weeks without doing anything; when he needed money, he moved his hand quickly to his work.

Saturday
15 August 1942
11:00
A Mother:

A mother is a treasure to her good, obedient son. My heart pounds when I remember that I have not seen my mother for two weeks.[80] The beauty of a mother cannot be compared to the beauty of a lover; the voice of a mother does not vie with that of the singing of the birds; the sympathy of a mother surpasses all others as does her happiness. Naturally, as the mother only finds her happiness after ensuring the happiness of her son, she would burn herself at the altar of her son's enjoyment and happiness.

For a son the mother must be the second whom he worships, following God the Almighty. Damn me! What is this lack of attention and neglect [for my mother]? I don't deserve motherly love because I don't take care of her and appreciate her as she deserves to be appreciated.

I am waiting for the end of the workday impatiently, so that I can go to my mother and find from her some peace of mind and comfort. I wonder what she is doing now and what she is thinking, whether she is happy or not. May God be gentle to her and lead her on the straight path.

As a young woman she exhausted herself raising us and staying up late for our comfort, and now she is in the throes of death and she has begun to take steps toward the end![81] Damn me! What am I saying, is she in truth coming close to the end, no! No!! You are the healing balsam for me in my life, O Mother, peace be upon you and kisses to you every time the sun rises and the moon breaks forth.

80. Sāmī had a very close relationship with his mother, and after he married, even though he was the youngest of the boys, it was he who brought his mother to live with him and Suhayla. Sāmī's mother lived with them for thirty years, until her death in 1975.

81. Sāmī's mother lived for more than thirty years after this entry.

24 August 1942
7:15
[Untitled]

Now I am sitting in my seat looking around me while listening to music, and I see in front of me the wealthy men, women, and young girls sitting in their boxes.[82] What are they other than old, middle-aged men, who have lost their hair—they are bald.

Among the Muslim women there is abundant beauty; all Muslim women resemble each other when they are made up. If only the Muslim woman had the desire to become civilized as she has the desire for entertainment and excess.

In fact, the *hijab* [veil] has begun to gradually disappear in Jerusalem;[83] ahh, the windows have closed and now the lights are beginning to go out, I cannot continue [writing], the movie has begun.

25 August 1942
Not a Bad Trip:

I cut off from writing for a while, for no reason other than little time, and it has been on my mind. As for this time, I will recall my trip south to Bʾir as-Sabʿ and from there to al-Jammāma where we attended the wedding of Mūsā al-ʿAṭāwna.[84]

82. Sāmī is writing this while at the movie theater.

83. al-ʿArif mentions this in his *al-Mufaṣṣal,* 486.

84. Ruqayya said the al-ʿAṭāwna family owned property in al-Jammāma; interview, 30 December 2005. According to Walid Khalidi, al-Jammāma, prior to its depopulation following an Israeli military assault on 22 May 1948, was located on the back of Wadi al-Madabbaʿ in the northern Negev. Khalidi states that "it was linked via a secondary road to the village of Burayr (Gaza District) . . . which was itself on a highway that led to Gaza and ran parallel to the coastal highway. Because a network of similar roads linked it to other villages as well as to the Beersheba-Gaza highway, to the southwest, al-Jammāma was considered a gateway to southern Palestine." Khalidi also refers to the al-ʿAṭāwna Bedouin tribe that lived in the village prior to its depopulation and gives details as to the village's socioeconomic structure; *All that Remains,* 73–74. See also Benny Morris, *The Birth of the Palestinian Refugee Problem Revisited.*

On Sunday morning, 23 August 1942, ʿIzzat, our brother-in-law, passed by my place and we went to the car station and rented three cars. Members of the an-Natsha family went in one of them.[85] As for the other two cars, members of the ʿAmr family went in them, including Ḥusayn ʿAmr, Maḥmūd Muḥammad ʿĪsa, and I, as well as Ṭalab ʿAbd al-Majīd and Yūsuf ʿAbd al-Ḥamīd and others.[86] We began to travel at 10:00 reaching Bʾir as-Sabʿ first. We waited there a short time until all the cars caught up. We then continued north heading toward Gaza. All along the way between Bʾir as-Sabʿ and Gaza there were large military camps full of cars and equipment, just as the way was crowded with cars full of foodstuffs for the horses and the soldiers heading toward Gaza. In the middle of the way between Bʾir as-Sabʿ and Gaza, we passed a wide airport that accumulated airplanes from all over and was well parked [organized].[87] Between one and the other [each airplane was] fifty meters at least. In the middle of the air base a number of air-raid shelters hexagonal in shape have been built; sand is then placed in front of it when it then becomes a small hill that is impossible for the enemy to notice. We also saw piles of petrol barrels in the middle of the sand all along the way.

Then the car went off the path into the plain, leaving the paved road, and it went wherever it wanted in these soft sand dunes. After a long while we tired of the up and down [movement] of the car on this ground that [seemed to have] no end to it. We reached our destination, which was the place where the wedding was to take place and we were received by a number of horsemen who guided us until we reached the Bedouin tent where seating had been prepared. We sat looking out from our place over a broad *wadi*;[88] the Arab youths began to show off, racing each other on horseback.[89] Then the food was brought in and we ate. We stayed there for a while until a gypsy woman came and began to sing some songs and dance recklessly, taking the hearts of

85. According to Sāmī's family members in 2005–2006, the an-Natsha family was related to the al-ʿAṭāwna family and lived in Hebron but had roots in Bʾir as-Sabʿ.

86. These were all distant, and older, cousins of Sāmī. Ṭalab ʿAbd al-Majīd ʿAmr and Yūsuf ʿAbd al-Ḥamīd ʿAmr were both from the ʿAmr clan in Dūra, where the ʿAmrs built their power base initially. The rest were from the ʿAmr clan in the city of Hebron, including Sāmī. It is not clear what, exactly, their relation was to Sāmī, but they were all family leaders (*mukhtārs*) or elders. Their children were of Sāmī's generation.

87. For Palestine's role in Britain's war effort see Kolinsky, *Britain's War in the Middle East*, and Jackson, *The British Empire and the Second World War.*

88. Sāmī is referring to Wadi al-Jammāma here.

89. By "Arab," Sāmī probably means Bedouin.

the Bedouin. They began to clap for her wanting more, but ʿIzzat complained saying he did not want to hear her or see her dance and sing.[90]

We took the car after we asked permission from ʿIzzat [to leave]; after we gave him a gift of one pound we [all] returned, heading toward Hebron. Actually, we took a different route from the one that we came on and we were completely absorbed the entire time until we reached the paved road. We then continued the way on the paved road until we reached Hebron at 6:00. I spent that night there and I woke up early and went to my job, in Jerusalem, and I arrived there at exactly 7:30.

September
1 September 1942
Illness:

There are only three things that break the soul of an individual: death, poverty, and illness. It is illness that sticks its nails into my weak body; I have no power and no strength. Illness is a hell in itself, and if God wanted someone harmed he would make him poor and make him sink low, or he would make a deadly disease take control over him, causing him a variety of disabilities without killing him. "To God we belong, and to Him is our return."[91] I say this as the illness flows through my veins just as the water flows away from the branches of a tree. Violent pain occurred throughout my body, nothing comes out of me except deep sighs. During this I imagine all kind of frailties which the disease will leave in my body. Your mercy O God, God save me.

If you only knew when I wrote this. I am now writing and the clerks are resting and going and coming and work is piling up in front of me to be entered into the registers, but I have no patience. I began this scrap of paper to write what is going on around me. Blessed are the healthy, for they are the rich.[92] Blessed is he who is not sick; as for the ill, the sickness troubles him all night long and keeps him away from his work.

90. Ruqayya recalled immediately that her husband, ʿIzzat, would not have liked to see this scene with the gypsy woman dancing and singing; interview with Ruqayya, 30 December 2005.

91. This expression is something that one would only say upon death, and Sāmī says this in an exaggerated expression of how he felt, so awful it seems that he thought he was dying. An example of this saying is found in the Qurʾān, 2:156.

92. Sāmī uses a word in Arabic that is particularly connected to Christian blessings.

4 September 1942
Friday night
Dream:

I saw what the sleeping person sees: I am with lots of people whom I know, standing in a carriage taking us straight to the top of a high mountain. We were all afraid that the carriage would tip over on the steep slope, but all of the passengers remained in the carriage. As for me, I got out, afraid of falling. I stopped on top of a rock that was unsteady under my feet because I felt that I had been in a situation in which if I had tried to ascend with the carriage I would have fallen into the deep ravine. But suddenly I saw a woman, with a Jewish face, in her 40s, lean over from above and extend me her hand. She pulled me up, which made me very happy. I was overjoyed and thanked her in English, but she responded to me in Arabic that there was no need for all of that gratitude. After that woman pulled me up, I saw a broad, plowed land full of trees, with a stream running through the middle of it shining with clear water. I saw another path in the other direction of the plain with people whom I know, walking, happy. Then I stopped at the base of a tree and stayed there a moment, content. After I opened my eyes, I saw the morning light sneaking into my room and I got up, washed and moisturized my body with a treatment good for the skin. I ate my breakfast and I went to the office to begin work.

7 September 1942
Reflections

He was right, the one who said the following:
The days will show you what you had been ignorant about.
And the news will be brought by someone whom you did not hire [or pay for the news].

How I admired Tsibūra's beauty and how the shine of her eyes did magic to me. Now, finally, after I have spent nights thinking about her, she has married, yes, married an ugly rich guy. I do not think that she loves him. Why did this happen? If only I had not reined in the bridle on myself at that moment, and if I had gone with the flow of my feelings. If that had happened, the only thing that would have harmed me was failure, [as] I would have fallen in front of everyone. Yes, God has granted me something and it is emotional coldness, which is the opposite of irritability and hotheadedness.

Now I remember my brother Saʿdī when I recall boiling blood for he is hot-blooded in character, with nerves of fire. Yes, I am thinking of him and sympathizing with him to a degree that I cannot describe. A sympathy of the pitying kind and lamenting, with sadness and happiness, when I feel his sadness and his happiness, those brotherly feelings that one brother feels towards a beloved brother of his.

Nobody feels this emotion but the one who is out of sight from his distant brother and longs for him and extols his praises and forgets his flaws.

---

18 September 1942
A Letter[93]

My Dear Friend,[94]
How happy and joyous I was at your steadfastness of opinion and for your adherence to your principles when we argued about the naming of the protected one, by the grace of God, Most Esteemed. May God make him among the helpful, may He make your eyes pleased and overjoyed by him.

93. Sāmī actually uses the word *taḥrīr* here, which usually means "editing" or "liberation," even "recording" or "writing." In this case, Samīr notes, the word is used to mean a letter, which was the end product of an editing process; correspondence from Samīr, 28 January 2008. The notion that a letter comes after a process of editing is suggestive for the various letters that Sāmī included throughout the diary, such as this one given to Sāmī's brother-in-law ʿIzzat at the birth of his and Ruqayya's first child, Sulṭān. The context for the letter is not clear, as Ruqayya said ʿIzzat was outside of Hebron working in ʿAnabtā at the time of his son's birth and that it was Sāmī who brought her, along with their mother, to the Hajjār Hospital in Jerusalem. Perhaps ʿIzzat read the letter once he returned after the birth of Sulṭān; interviews with Ruqayya, 23 and 30 December 2005. The Hajjār Hospital does not appear among the list of hospitals in al-ʿArif's *al-Mufaṣṣal*. In his article "Tawfiq Canaan: His Life and Works," Khaled Nashef mentions that one of Canaan's friends was Dr. Yūsuf Hajjār, a physician and general surgeon of Lebanese origin at the Government Hospital in Jerusalem. Ruqayya mentioned that the doctor who delivered her baby was named Hajjār, and it is likely that Dr. Yūsuf Hajjār delivered Sulṭān in the Government Hospital, not in a hospital named after him. The Government Hospital was opened by the British in 1917 initially for government employees but later opened to the general public; *al-Mufaṣṣal,* 458.

94. This is directed not to the diary as in so many of Sāmī's other entries but rather to Sāmī's brother-in-law ʿIzzat, as confirmed by the content of the entry and comments by Ruqayya.

1. What is a name?[95] A name is nothing but a special sound that a family gives to a child, releasing that sound or syllable especially given to that newborn to distinguish that child from others, giving a name so as to call that name from the other names of his siblings, making it easier to call him and get his attention.

2. Creativity in Names. Previous generations did not pay much attention to the naming of a child or to being creative with the naming of children and thus they named their children Muḥammad, Peace Be Upon Him, after the Prophet of Islam, or after other ancient prophets, Peace Upon Them. As for today, names have become in the view of upper-class families in particular and middle-class families more generally an essential thing in a person's life. A beautiful name has its privilege, as a beautiful face has its privilege.

3. The world is in accelerated progress with the passing of time, and the West is getting closer to the East and with that the masks that hide, held onto by Easterners, will disappear and they will think that they have the right to do this. Then there will be nothing unusual resulting from this "removing of the masks." Yes! The world is progressing and will wipe out the old corrupt traditions, and what will remain from it, what is appropriate from it, is the triumphant city; civilization will rise from the uninhabited places of the city itself and the Bedouin will emerge from their dwellings in goat hair tents and become civilized and live in palaces; then they will gradually move towards upward development and participate in the running of factories and administration buildings and office work and leave this vast desert in which their forefathers lived for generations, suffering from the difficulties of living, hunger and thirst, not thinking that there is a better life, more comfortable, in the cities, or at least in the villages. And here, the uneducated Bedouin and tired peasants feel their way to the city that will receive them with welcoming arms on one condition and that is to forget the worn-out traditions that bring them closer to the Jahilīyya than to the prosperous modern times.[96]

4. I have gone on too long in my speech and I hope that you do not take my words seriously that are nothing more than chatter and nonsense. But, I hope that you will save this in a record or a book and give it to the little one for

95. Sāmī's discussion here is about the name of his nephew.

96. The term *Jahilīyya* here is a reference to the period before Islam, the Age of Ignorance, when people were ignorant of the existence of God.

whom I am now his uncle. He will read this when he grows up and I hope that he will be an upstanding young man. Why not?!? He is the son of ʿAṭīyya,[97] and his maternal uncles are from the ʿAmr family, who have a respectable lineage and ancestors. ʿIzzat, kiss the little one for me, and, my sister, you kiss him for me too; that will equal two kisses that I ask of you to give him from me, and I will give him the third when I see him, when he begins to speak nicely and he says to me: "Uncle!" Send my regards to Mother when you see her, for I am missing her a lot.

You call your son Sulṭān
  I do not see any need for this title[98]
The days were as oppressive as death
  And they [the days] threw them [the people] into the pits of graveyards
Why did you not name him Ḥāfiẓ, the defender of the homeland,
  Or Zuhayr, the one who has eternal glory
Or Karīm, who reveres his morals
  Expressing them in generosity or in love
Or Sharīf, steadfast in his land
  Keeping the promise as a promise of responsibility[99]

Peace
Note: This letter did not please as-Sayyid ʿIzzat, and he tore it up and threw it on the ground.[100]

97. This is a reference to the al-ʿAṭāwna tribe of ʿIzzat's origins that took its name from ʿAṭīyya.

98. ʿIzzat named his son Sulṭān, which carries the connotation of a ruler. Indeed, the Ottoman Empire, which ruled for four hundred years in Palestine, was led by *sulṭāns*. To Sāmī, ʿIzzat's choice for his son's name was more like a royal title than a true name; correspondence from Samīr, 28 January 2008.

99. Sāmī constructed this poem in a way that the Arabic names he uses are defined by what follows the name.

100. Ruqayya confirmed that her husband tore this up; interview with Ruqayya, 30 December 2005.

2 October 1942
[Untitled]

When a man gets sick, he finds his family around him easing what ails him and helping him to bear the pain. When people get sick they find their house clean, their bathroom and kitchen, and other comfortable things, which help speed up their recovery. As for me, I have a small house, lacking any of these conveniences, lacking water, lacking a bathroom, lacking the necessary food to help the blood of an individual to overcome the illness and bear it. In addition to all of that, I work from dawn to dusk, I prepare the food, I wash the dishes, and, if I have to, I sweep the house and clean it. I open and close [come and go from] my house, alone except for the shadows I visualize and talk to, while my soul is far away. These shadows were my neighbors and I do not interfere in their affairs, and they do not find from me anything other than reliance on privacy. I close the door and lie down on the mattress and I stay there until it is time for work or a meal. I go to work or I prepare food—that is my mere life. I receive a meager salary every Friday and I spend it with caution until the next Friday comes, which by then, I have nothing left of my previous week's salary except for a few *mils* and *qurūsh*.[101] I have a passion for studying, which, whenever I try to begin, many reasons get in the way; the biggest reason is the lack of the necessary money.

6 October 1942
[Untitled]

The act is done, I have moved from a room in Umm Mikhāʾīl's [rooming house] to another, much better than the first by far, in the house of ʿAwdat al-Māliḥī.

My life has begun to change a little, corresponding with the environment in which I have begun to live. In the house next door live a woman and her daughter and young son. As for the house, it is new and strong and clean, but,

101. The *mil* was the smallest unit of currency in Palestine, equal to 1/1000 of a Palestinian pound. *Qurūsh* are standard piasters, 1/100 of an English pound; see Berlin, *The Coins and Banknotes of Palestine*.

I am sorry, far from my place of work and it requires that I wake earlier in the morning to prevent arriving late.

Now I do not feel like I am a stranger in my country because I have people surrounding me who are like me and share my religion. Before, I used to feel deathly alone when I lived at Umm Mikhāʾīl's, where in their view I was an infidel, since I did not share their religion.[102] All of their actions were wrapped up in hatred and disdain.

I discovered this great social difference only when I moved away from the Christian neighborhood to a Muslim neighborhood.

Thank God for the Islamic faith.

Jerusalem
10 October 1942

My Dear Fāʾida:

I awoke from my sleep to the sound of your melodious voice in my ears. I wanted to see you at that very moment but I remember many things: First, I am dressed in pajamas that make me look as if I am naked, and second, it is the greatest fear in my heart that your lady chaperone would be with you. After you walked away, my pain began and I could not sleep completely. I stayed sitting on the bed until the kerosene ran out from the lamp, as the hour closed in on 3:00 in the morning.

102. Umm Mikhāʾīl was Christian. Sāmī's wife and sister both showed great surprise that he would express such a sentiment, as they knew and were friendly with Jews and Christians during this period; interview with Ruqayya, 30 December 2005; interviews with Suhayla, 15 and 19 January 2006. Samīr added that whatever unpleasantness Sāmī experienced in this Christian neighborhood in Jerusalem, it did not have any kind of lasting effect on his father. Samīr recalled that when he was young in the 1950s, Sāmī would invite American Christian missionaries in Hebron into their house for meals, even though he knew they were looking to convert Muslims and was not interested in their message. Sāmī simply thought they were doing humanitarian work for the needy and the sick and thus admired and respected them for their work. Further, Sāmī's closest business partner in his real estate business was a Palestinian Christian; correspondence from Samīr, 29 January 2008. This entry seems like an exception to Sāmī's outlook toward non-Muslims and probably was just Sāmī venting to his "friend," the diary, about his troubles.

I lay down like a log, motionless. I sank into a deep sleep with dreams pervading it. Yes, I could see visions that I cannot remember. I remained sleeping until 7:20, which then left me only 10 minutes to wash my face and dress, which I did very quickly. I did not spend more than that to eat breakfast and I hurried to the bus. No sooner had I arrived but my body was flooded with sweat. I reached work at 7:40 and the supervisor advised me not to be late again.

My Dear:
I have gone on a long time about myself and the time has come to speak to you on the page of this little notebook, as we have been prevented from speaking freely. Today is Saturday and I have to go see my mother and spend a day or two with her. I find a sense of security and comfort when I am with her, but I wish that I could go back on this trip and stay here by your side.

The beating of my heart accelerates when I think of you or when I see you or when I hear your voice. You changed my life, my beloved, and you made me forget everything tied to the past. One of these days I will read to you from my diary and I will let you know what kind of adventures I have come across.[103]

Don't travel in my absence for if you do that you will hear what I have done with myself and you will learn that I have loved [you]. My love differs from all other loves and if I am sad, also, my sadness is like no other sadness. I hope you will not be bored by me or reproach my words in your response to them. Don't leave, for I will suffer.

(Throw your letters from the window, it will make me extremely happy when I get them.)[104]

The Lover,
S.A. [Sāmī ʿAmr]

103. Ultimately, when Sāmī did marry, he read the contents of his diary to his bride, Suhayla; interview with Suhayla, 15 January 2006.

104. Suhayla said it was Fāʾida who wanted to marry Sāmī, but his family would never have accepted this Lebanese girl. There is no further information as to who Fāʾida was; interview with Suhayla, 15 January 2006.

30 October 1942
[Untitled]

From now on I will not trust anyone unless I am certain of his words and I will not think of anything until I am sure of its success. I will not hold on to hope or imagination, both of which, since my heart has flown away, control my feelings to the point that I forget myself and all material things and I fly to faraway places impossible to reach except through suffering and rigorous exertion.

Yes, I had believed in everything and everyone and I would imagine myself in situations greater than reality. I would trust in people when it was necessary to scorn them. I must not take advice from anyone because every person offering me advice does so aiming for his own benefit. I must not respect anyone because people, regardless of whether I respect them, turn out to be lower than you think or imagine. Of course they have flaws, and perhaps I even imitate them thinking that they are good customs.

I must not open my heart to a woman until God strengthens my financial situation and brings upon me His grace. There is no way for the destitute to go; he can't sleep easily for sleeplessness dries his tired eyes thinking how much he will be spending tomorrow. When something comes to him, he realizes that he does not own a thing to please the woman he loves and whom he promises to provide with all the reasons for comfort and happiness.

Jerusalem on 15 November 1942

Dear Brother,[105]

I sent you a family photo once and I wrote to you another time. While I am getting ready to send what I wrote, news has reached me that has shaken my being and definitely caused my belief in justice to waver, just as it has torn my heart and signaled a tear to my eye and a wound to my heart.[106]

105. Here Sāmī is writing to his brother Saʿdī.

106. Sāmī is talking about Saʿdī going to prison. Although Sāmī states that his belief in justice wavered because of this incident, Suhayla stated very plainly that Saʿdī went to prison for going AWOL, absent without leave. She related that when Saʿdī was taken to Egypt to serve the British in the war, he treated it like a game and decided to escape. Apparently Saʿdī

Yes, the driver told me the news and I received his words pretending I did not care. Afterwards, that news left sadness deep inside of me. I could not free myself from it, and inside of me there was a vileness caused by guilt of my not being able to defend [you] and clear [your name]. While I was in distress and feeling grief, the messenger came. I wanted to give him a letter for you, but he looked at me saying how can I give him a letter when he is in the dungeon of the prison? I became silent from the torment and I let him go and returned to my desk, shocked and going out of my mind. Every time I grab a pen to try to work, my spirit rejects it and I throw it to the side. Finally, I picked it up and looked at it apologetically and I began to write these words to convey on this small piece of paper my feelings of pain and my sadness.[107]

How I have dreamed of happiness that can only happen when we meet again. I remained taking care of myself, trying to fill this happiness, but fate did not happen to us as expected. It stopped and tossed us aside by its disaster, whose [unfortunate] circumstances are endless and have no mercy.

It must not find a path of despair in our hearts, O brother; we must believe in fate and destiny after our faith in God, exalted and fortified. Perhaps this little dilemma that you have fallen into is the key to the situation that you are in. As a result of a moment of not thinking, it placed you in a situation for which you did not consider its consequences every night. O brother, I meet you and my heart gladdens when I dream about you near me, and how my sadness appears when I awaken and the bitter truth shines through to my eye. But, I am optimistic of your arrival, O brother, which will happen only when I see you in my sleep. You know that I am a *darwīsh* and believe in the power of such good omens.[108] Have courage, O brother, may God strengthen your fortitude against the one who eats and does not want to give sustenance and the

---

took off his military uniform, left it on the banks of the Nile River, and dressed in the clothes of an Egyptian peasant. He made his way back to Palestine, where the British caught him; interview with Suhayla, 15 January 2006. As Sāmī relates in the diary, Saʿdī was put in jail, tried, and found guilty.

107. Sāmī may have written down his thoughts when he had the time and then copied them into the notebook that became the actual diary. His mention here of a small piece of paper on which he wrote his thoughts is an example of this.

108. Samīr explained that in Palestinian colloquial Arabic, *darwīsh,* the word Sāmī uses here, means a simple or ascetic individual, like the mystic who receives good omens through dreams. Thus, when Sāmī says he dreamed about Saʿdī, he accepts that as a good omen, as if he would see him soon in reality, not just in his dreams; correspondence from Samīr, 29 January 2008.

one who has oppressed and pretends to feel justice. As I write I do not know what happened in your case, but I have great hope in fate and God's mercy. Whenever Mother asks me about you and about the letters that you send her each week, I tell her that I forgot them in Jerusalem and that you are fine and in good health.

Your sincere brother,
Sāmī Saʿīd ʿAmr

Kānūn ath-thānī (January) 1943
1 January 1943
[Untitled]

On this day my brother Saʿdī was sentenced to prison for six months for a crime that he did not commit,[109] a plot hatched by someone else while he was in Syria. I am here with a heart full of sorrow and pain, which is due to my inability to do anything to help my poor brother; how can I do that when he is under Army regulations. All I could do is to write a letter to Major Tate asking him about my brother, reminding him of his innocence and our collective anxiety about him. I will make efforts to get him out of the trouble he has fallen into.

---

17 January 1943
[Untitled]

I went today to the bank with my brother-in-law ʿIzzat. He guaranteed a loan in the amount of fifteen pounds, which I borrowed to pay someone who pledged to find me a job in the court. I still have the money, and if I do not get the job that he promised me, I will return the money to the bank again. My

109. Sāmī does not mention the crime with which Saʿdī was convicted; see note 106 above on Saʿdī's crime of going AWOL from the army. Hurewitz notes that "the number of Arab deserters from the British armed forces was known to be considerable in the spring of 1941 and even more numerous in the summer of 1942"; *The Struggle for Palestine,* 119. Saʿdī joined the British army in November 1941 and deserted about a year later.

salary in my current job is very small, and I do not know how I will live if I continue to work there.

---

19 January 1943
[Untitled]

This morning I received a letter from my brother informing me of the disaster that has happened to him.[110] Since that time I am absent-minded and my nerves are weak, as if I had received a blow to the head; I have no ability to work. O God, free the shackles of my brother and comfort him and comfort us, and make this difficult world in front of us easier so that we can be like regular people.

---

15 March 1943
[Untitled]

Every time I think of that issue it increases my fear and my heart beats for the blood of the innocent, which is shed in vain from both sides, the Jews and the Arabs.[111] Palestine is a piece of land on which live two people [an Arab and a Jew], each of whom claims that he owns it. They fight each other until their fight becomes a conflict in which one grows stronger and the other weaker. The weaker one will lose his life and the stronger one will come to live on the remains of the weaker one. It is a lofty issue, and it is incumbent on the Arabs to prepare for the day in which the Jews find themselves overly confident and try to hurt the Arabs and expel them from Palestine. The Arabs must not overlook this issue because the Jews' greedy aspirations in Palestine have no boundaries and do not stop at any limit. They want to bring all of

110. This seems to be a repetition of information Sāmī already knew. Perhaps this was the first time that he heard directly from Saʿdī about his incarceration, so he mentions that he received a letter about the matter.

111. This is the only diary entry in which Sāmī directly expresses his understanding of and opinions about the growing conflict between Arabs and Jews in Palestine during the mandate period. Much of this entry is almost prophetic in its expression of what would come within five years between Arabs and Jews in Palestine.

their brethren from the European countries to settle in the "Promised Land," as they maintain.

If the Jews take over in Palestine they will close the sole and most significant gate from which the people of the Middle East import their goods for their livelihood and subsistence. If the Jews take over in Palestine, they will look at the surrounding and adjacent Arab countries and make them into a market for their manufactured goods and their trade and with it kill Arab trade, for they [the Arabs] will not be able to sell. Their livelihood will be squeezed and instead of the Arabs, the Jews will gain their income, trading easily. From there the Arabs will get frustrated in Palestine and look to emigration (God forbid). The Jews have measly excuses and unconvincing arguments about this, claiming that the Arabs have countries other than Palestine to which they can go. But these insane people [the Jews] have forgotten that we will not leave our country to satisfy [their] aspirations and facilitate their comfort in Palestine while bearing the pain of exile and dispersion. In fact, we entered Palestine by the sword and would only leave it, God forbid, by the sword and would take our last breath trying to save it.

---

25 March 1943
Questions That Have No Answers!!

I wonder who she is!
　The one I will live with forever
The one whom I am going to please
　Always my love for her is strong
O People, what is her name?
　O People, what does she look like?
What does she do? Where does she go?
　I see her in my imagination, her and the children
I see myself in their midst
　I will raise them and walk proudly
I will call one of them Samīr
　The second Zuhayr, and the third Amāl[112]

112. Figure 4 shows Sāmī and his wife on 26 June 1952 with their first two children, four-year-old son Samīr and two-year-old daughter Amāl, whom he names here in the poem. The

Figure 4. Early family photo. Courtesy of Samīr ʿAmr.

They all love me and call me Daddy
  I spoil them and their mother
For she goes with the family
  To the cinema or to a picnic spot

God knows!!

---

12 May 1943
Pains:

Now it is 2:00 in the afternoon. After having eaten lunch in the office restaurant, I sat to record what happened to me in my diary during the last few months. During the past three months, I was constantly thinking of my brother Saʿdī, anxiously worrying about him. I would go to visit him every Sunday at 2:00 in the afternoon. I would be in Hebron at 10:00 and I would have to hurry to find a car to take me to the prison at the appointed time. When I would arrive at the prison, I would stop at the gate with the others standing there, waiting until the sergeant called us in. We would stand for an hour or half an hour under the glare of the sun, waiting impatiently until they would finally let us enter, threatening that anyone who brings in cigarettes or food will be prevented from seeing his prisoner again. At that point, they would lead us to a place nearby where they cleared a space for benches and the visitors [would] sit with the prisoners who cannot decide whether they should turn right or left, fearing that the sergeant would see him or hear him. We begin to talk, pretending as if we are not talking, and the prisoner tells about the harsh treatment that they face and the grueling work activities that they undertake. He then persists in asking questions about his friends on the outside and begs us to send them to visit him next week. After a quarter of an hour or more, the sergeant screams out that visiting hours have ended and we say goodbye to them and leave them so that they can continue on with their work.

That is how I spent every Sunday of every week for these three months.

I used to take my mother along to visit Saʿdī and she would suffer consider-

---

couple would indeed name their next son Zuhayr, who was born after their second daughter, Samīra.

ably from the exhaustion of waiting under the blazing sun and the cold winter until she would enter and find him in a state of weakness, pale and in dirty clothes and her eyes would tear and she would bring him close to her chest, as if she wanted to take him with her . . .

As of now, he has been released from jail, in peace, but he has stayed in the Army camp in Jerusalem, not knowing what happened with his case. He is uncertain and afraid that they will transfer him to another of the Army's fighting units. I do not think that will happen because none of the NAAFI employees has been transferred. He is, in fact, completely free, O God, except for the fact that he sleeps in the camp, which depresses him, but God is with those who are patient.[113]

I have informed you, my friend, that during these last three months I have wrapped my thoughts around my brother and wrote a letter to the NAAFI director hoping he would set him free, while seeking the opinion of various people on this subject.[114]

Now, my brother is free. I have woken up, I have returned to my old self, finding that I had been asleep for a long time permeated by troubling dreams.

These three months have passed without my thinking about the fact that I have a debt, whose repayment date is approaching. Yes, the repayment date is quickly arriving in a frightening way and I have wracked my brains trying to think of ways to repay the sum. I have seven pounds, but I still owe eight more. What am I going to do?

I shared my situation with some friends in the office, and they suggested that I write a letter to the director requesting a loan from the office funds. I clung to that hope like a drowning person clings to a twig trying to save himself. After some give and take with myself and my wishes, and my sensitive compassion, I decided to confront the head of the office to deal with this. I knocked on his door and entered. I found him engrossed in crunching the

113. Saʿdī was sentenced to six months in jail but seems to have served only four, as mentioned in the diary, before being moved to an army camp in Jerusalem and then, according to Sāmī, back to Egypt. What is unclear is Sāmī's reference on 1 January 1943 to Syria, where Sāmī says Saʿdī had been "when the plot was hatched." This did not come up at all in any of the conversations I had with either Sāmī's wife or his sister. Based on Sāmī's comment here, it seems Saʿdī was not the only NAAFI employee who became a soldier in the British army.

114. The NAAFI director whose help Sāmī says he would seek may have been Major Tate, whom Sāmī mentions on 1 January 1943.

numbers. I stood in front of him without moving. He looked at me while he was still crunching the numbers and he said: "Yes, tell me what you want, Sāmī!" I answered him in a breaking voice: "I want to ask you if it is possible for me to take a loan [from the office] in the amount of eight pounds. As repayment you will take a specified amount from my salary each week. I am really in dire need of this money and I have no one else who can help me but you." At that point my heart palpitated quickly and I looked at his wrinkled face, aged by the years. He raised his head and said, "No! It is not possible; someone else came and asked for two pounds and we refused him as well. Do not waste your time on this point." He continued his work as if my issue did not bother him in the least bit. I left his office unsuccessful and dejected. I came up to the office I work in, but I am unable to do anything.

I am drowning in a sea of horrifying thoughts. Yes, I was very afraid. I did not expect that when one borrows money from the bank he puts himself in such a nightmare and he experiences such a fright. How easy it is to extend your hand and take ten or fifteen pounds, but how difficult and troublesome it is when the repayment day comes and you do not have the money to pay. Will the bank sell the furniture in the house to recover its money?!

The entire week I remained unable to settle down. I did not enjoy my sleep and I am still battling the waves of the sea and the storm. The twig still floats by me and sinks [leaving him with no way to keep afloat]. Finally, I insisted on trying my luck with it. Yes, I had one remaining hope and that was to inform Captain Pudrell of the matter, either orally or in written form.[115] I wrote him a letter to explain the situation and I insisted that he had to help me. I apologized to him for bothering him every once in a while and I promised that I would not bother him with my personal trouble again.

The internal office phone rang and the [female] operator told me that I was to go down to the office of the Head Clerk. I went down quickly and I entered his office where he was sitting at his desk with the letter that I had sent to Captain Pudrell in front of him. He said: "You are an annoying boy. Do you want the Captain to give you this sum from his pocket?" I replied: "If I do not obtain this sum I will be arrested and put in prison. Do you want that?" He said: "Sorry, I understand . . . listen, you are going to receive [a raise of] five pounds on the twenty-seventh of this month and you will collect this raise

115. It is unknown what position of authority Captain Pudrell had in the office where Sāmī worked at that time.

for a month or two." But I told him: "The repayment date is scheduled for the seventeenth of the month." He assured me, however, that the bank can wait ten days and if it will not wait then he will personally telephone [the bank]. I thanked him and told him that that was all that I wanted and if that is the truth then I did not need a loan from the office.

My dear friend, if you become broke, so much so that you do not have even one *qirsh,* do not approach the bank. I felt during this period that all I could think about was that I did not have the resources to repay my loan. Yes, I felt that I was crazy and I was thinking of suicide! Yes, by God I am telling you the truth. In fact, I seriously considered that while I was sitting up in my bed, and the middle of the night came with its darkness intensifying. At that point these thoughts came to me and made me crazy.

But now, my heart rests easier because my brother advised me to go to the bank and tell them that I will pay back the money at the end of the month. In fact, it is certain that we will get the raise that the boss told me about.

A Prayer and a Remembrance:[116]

Dear Mother,

I send my greetings to you and kisses to your hand as a sign of my loyalty and obedience, as I ask for your blessing. Now to the following: If it was not for you, I would not know where I am; my thinking about you and my fear of disobeying you prevented me from wandering aimlessly in this wide world. Rather, I have gained your spiritual strength for myself which has prepared me for any path that I choose. Without you, I would have become a soldier in the Army and requested to be transferred to India or to the furthest point on earth.[117] Your strength, which has no superior except for the strength of the

116. This may or may not be the continuation of these last several pages. The subject changes, as it did throughout the previous long entry, but by this point in the diary Sāmī appears to have written chronologically, listing a date per entry. This may or may not be an exception to that, as a new title appears here but no new date. As in other entries in which Sāmī appears to be writing a letter, it is not clear if this was a letter he might actually have sent to his mother. Suhayla said Sāmī's mother was literate, so it is not out of the question that he sent her a letter like this; interview with Suhayla, 19 January 2006.

117. Based on this and on Sāmī's impressions of Saʿdī's experience in the army, it seems that the army for him was a punishment or an option of last resort for a young man traveling the journey of life.

Creator, powerful and mighty, imprisons my soul in a cage of obedience and [I have a] lack of courage to come and to do any job without your consultation and listening to your blessing.

O Mother, with what can I repay you? When I am sad, you are sadder, when I am happy, you are happier. Is a mother anything other than a second spirit that complements the spirit of a human, supporting him when he is touched by weakness and confusion? Isn't it a mother who seeks to absorb all the harm that faces her child's spirit, acting to break the fall when her child is the victim of a bad situation? Isn't the mother the one who takes all that is bad away from you? Why not, for you are a part of your mother when you are in her womb day after day. You were nourished by her blood, then, after birth, by her milk. What a favor and a blessing she has done for you. When you screamed with hunger or freezing cold, she would nourish you and wrap you up, enveloping you in warmth. When you grew up, she sent you to school and she made every possible effort to satisfy you and make you like your schoolmates. Can one do for someone else something of this great magnitude without, in this case, the child being forced to respond, to repay? Imagine when you feel this debt upon you.

---

18 September 1943
Eight Nerve-Wracking Months:

O, such carelessness . . .
Eight months have passed and I have not penned a letter in this book, while these eight months were full of events that must be mentioned.[118] But, I do not know where to begin . . . Let me think a little, my friend, and gather up what has become lost in my thoughts. Everyone knows what has happened to us during these past eight months with regard to the great rise in the cost of living. It has become so bad that the pound does not equal twenty *qurūsh*. The price of gold has increased and now one gold pound equals six paper pounds. Many necessities can no longer be found such as rice, flour, and eggs. Yes, they have disappeared from the regular market and have emerged in the black market, as it is called. The price of a cheap suit has gone from six pounds to twenty-three

118. The dating is off here. Four months, not eight, had passed at this point since Sāmī's previous entry. Based on what Sāmī writes here, he was simply reflecting on the first eight months of the year. Some of the stories are repetitive.

pounds, as have shirts and all clothes. This is daily life in general and that is what everyone is complaining about, whether young or old, rich or poor.

As for my own personal life, during this period I was living in a house far from the rest of the world, far from people and the city. I spent most of my time reading books and magazines, so much so that it weakened my vision. Friends advised me to ease up on the reading. I was not influenced much by them and not one night has passed without my reading a book.[119]

I had neighbors whom I did not talk to unless it was absolutely necessary and I spent that time as if in exile, lost in the desert of thought and illusions until I almost went crazy. However, I contacted the Arab Workers Society and I began to start helping them, extending my hand [as a volunteer], and I became a member of the Society.[120] I spent most of my time there except for the period of winter rains and cold when I did not go. I met a girl who lived there and being that I am a young man, I began to be kind to her, finding in her tenderness and sweetness. But my heart did not feel for her even a little bit, in spite of the fact that I used to accompany her to the cinema and pretend to like her while with her. God did not lengthen her stay and she traveled from Jerusalem before I had known her for two months.

My brother Saʿdī was locked up in the prison in aṭ-Ṭālbīyya, notorious for its horridness, and I used to go visit him every week on Sunday when my heart would break with sadness for him.[121] He rained many questions on me about life in Jerusalem and Hebron and I would try to assuage his concerns. He left

119. In his *Reading Palestine,* Ayalon offers an interesting discussion of Arabic word usage for reading. The two words for "reading" that Sāmī uses here, *utāliʿ* and *aqraʾ* (the former in the first two appearances in this paragraph and the latter in the third), reflect two practices of reading: *utāliʿ* connotes individual, silent reading, while *aqraʾ* historically means reading aloud, as the root itself is tied to the meaning "recitation." This latter meaning has ties to the Qurʾān, itself a word that shares the root *q-r-a* and can mean "recite" or "read." This discussion is particularly interesting in the historical period addressed by Ayalon, the one in which Sāmī lived and obtained his education and wrote his diary, as the etymological analysis allows the reader to grasp the monumental changes that occurred during that period as mass literacy emerged. See Ayalon's discussion of individual reading in *Reading Palestine,* 111–124.

120. The *jamʿiyyat al-ʿummāl al-ʿarabiyya* of which Sāmī writes is most likely the Palestinian Arab Workers Society. For more on workers in Palestine during the British Mandate period see Lockman, *Comrades and Enemies.* In his *Mudhakkirāt,* 44ff, ʿAwdat al-Ashhab describes his involvement in the Arab Workers Society, including its establishment in Jerusalem as a branch of the main organization in Haifa.

121. Interestingly, the main prisons in mandate Palestine were the Russian compound in

prison after serving four months and he was transferred to an Army camp in Jerusalem and from there to Egypt. There things happened to him which I will mention later on . . .

As for my internal life, I mean private life, my days all seemed similar and passed slowly, heavily. I went from work to home and from home to work. I would eat, sleep, and read, all of which would repeat itself every day of every week of every month. By God, these days were boring . . .

I contacted a middle-aged man during that period of time who gave me hope with the most appealing of promises—that he would find me a job in the Ministry of Justice.[122] He was bleeding me dry of my meager few *qurūsh,* until I moved to another house and got rid of the evil shadow of that man forever. Nevertheless, sometimes I remember his promises, which give me the urge to go and meet him and discuss that matter with him, but I halt [word missing, probably "because"] the call to common sense makes me wary of him.

I now live in a house that I share with a guy who has high morals and is highly esteemed. My life in it is empty; there is no pleasure; I feel incomplete, as if one of my organs had been amputated. There is a deep abyss in my chest filled with a scary emptiness. Such, you will find me always quiet and withdrawn around myself. I do not wish to talk to anyone ever, but I am looking around for that severed part to join it to my body and complete my "being" with it.[123] My work has improved at the office, but my rights are oppressed and my salary money is stolen from me.[124] I have no choice but to leave the office totally and find a different job that considers my work and my rights.

Jerusalem and the main prison in Acre. ʿAwdat al-Ashhab does, however, mention that at the time of his imprisonment by the British he was taken to the prison near Bethlehem, on the way to Hebron. That prison was probably the one in aṭ-Ṭālbīyya, as that Jerusalem neighborhood is on the way to Bethlehem; see his *Mudhakkirāt,* 26.

122. This seems to be related to the story of Sāmī borrowing money to give to a man who promised to help him get a job in the court.

123. He is undoubtedly talking about finding his soulmate. One may read this comment philosophically—the idea of another person making one "complete," which is how Sāmī describes how he will feel when he finds that "severed part" and joins it to his body, has a long history in the Mediterranean region. It brings to mind Aristophanes' speech on humans and genders and the separation of humans, who are now constantly looking for their other half to reattach to their bodies. It is doubtful that Sāmī read the works of Plato, but adaptations from classical Greek works have made their way into Arabic writings and Arabic traditions from the early Abbasid period; see Plato, *Symposium* 189E–194E. It is completely a matter of speculation, however, as to what Sāmī might have been thinking when he wrote these lines.

124. Sāmī's reference to his rights here may be a direct result of his membership in the Pal-

My brother Saʿdī returned from Egypt looking despicable, gaunt, and pale. He does not have a single *fil* in his pocket and as such, my oldest brother, Asʿad, was forced to pawn off some of our olive trees in Hebron, for which he received 100 pounds, to spend on this wretched brother of ours. The matter did not end with the pawning of the olive trees; rather it brought out my oldest brother Asʿad's candidness and daring—he insisted on selling the only store in Hebron.[125] After dealing and negotiations, the buyer agreed to pay 950 pounds as payment for the store. He put 300 pounds up front, until the transaction was completed. At this point I began to feel that I had some wealth, even if only a small amount, so much so that if I were to leave my job, I would be able to live and work with it.[126] Yes, I will gain 300 pounds from this sum, at least. Often what appears to me in my sweet dreams quickly disappears when it becomes certain that the war is without end and that these banknotes do not equal anything. My destiny is failure, if I wish to work with this money.

I do not know what fate is hiding for my poor brother Saʿdī, for every moment we expect the police to come. As a result, he is now far away from the house, fearing that someone will surprise him [and take him away].[127]

Four months ago I bought a flock of chickens and some rabbits; some of the chickens have died, leaving only five now, along with two rabbits. The amount that I had paid for them up until now is seven pounds, but I have also spent in excess of five pounds on them for food and seeds. Finally, some of the chickens have begun to lay eggs.

---

estinian Arab Workers Society discussed above. He may mean here that he was very poorly paid, or he may be referring to the money he spent to try to find another job.

125. The brothers owned three shops; it is not clear why Sāmī says there was "only" one, unless they had sold the other two; correspondence from Samīr, 14 January 2006. Ruqayya said the reason their family managed better than others, although they had had no salary income, was because they could sell olives and wheat from their land and sold the shops too. She also mentioned selling the land; interview with Ruqayya, 23 December 2005.

126. It sounds like Sāmī wanted to run a business with his money.

127. This is likely tied to the story of Saʿdī's escape from the army, although this entry was written after he was released from prison.

6 October 1943
[Untitled]

Is hope ever realized? Can it become actual truth? Today I wrote a letter to the Inspector of Education requesting work as a clerk in the Ministry of Education.[128] I gave the letter to as-Sayyid ʿĪsa, who teaches Muḥammad, my roommate. He assured me that I will not fail, and I do not have to worry, for his part, because he will convince the Chief Clerk. He asked me to go to the ministry office next Sunday at 10:00. Perhaps God, You have eased the path, enlightened the heart, and had mercy on Your servant; You are the exalted one of this world and the next.

22 October 1943[129]
[Untitled]

Is hope ever realized? Can words become deeds? Does vision shine true? That is not far off for God for He is the exalted one of this world and the next. We met last night in our first meeting to arrange our company, the three of us, and to agree on the necessary conditions.[130] I am bursting with hope for our success. We will borrow twenty-five pounds either from the bank or from one of our friends. Perhaps God will fulfill this aspiration.

128. Here Sāmī refers to the Dāʾirat al-Maʿārif (Department of Information), the predecessor of the Ministry of Education.

129. This entry is a good example of the inaccurate chronology that the original diary manuscript occasionally bears, as it carries a date in the original of 22 October 1942 but falls between entries dated 25 February 1943 and 6 October 1943. It is neatly placed in its location, thus making it unlikely that Sāmī's usage of 1942 is accurate. Still, it is problematic that an earlier date appears after this entry, even when corrected for the year. Based on thorough study of the diary and with attention to contextual accuracy, this entry is best placed here with the altered date that it now bears.

130. There are no details as to who met with Sāmī or what kind of business they wished to run, but it may very well be tied to the money Sāmī was going to get from the sale of the shop.

[No Date][131]
If I Were an Arab Leader:

Perhaps my hopes would be fulfilled if I end my writing with the following: I imagine myself the leader among leaders in the Arab villages in the south [of Palestine].[132] I see myself like the Arab Prophet, Muḥammad, who raises his people, religiously and politically. Doesn't the secular reformer deserve credit as much as the religious reformer?

I imagine myself standing among the throng of villagers encouraging them toward modernity and leaving the tribalism that tears apart their very being. I also imagine myself with the villagers, extending the roads in the village, building healthy homes, including toilets, while demolishing the old dwellings infested with diseases; burning the long, loose-fitting robes in favor of something simpler and more tasteful; and putting shoes on those bare feet, which suffer from treading on the small white pebbles on the ground, of everyone in the village. I would collect donations and bring tractors to work the pure land, dig wells, and assemble water pumps. I would plant trees in an orderly fashion along the sides of the street and on the peaks of hilltops that lay barren. I would establish an office for trade of the products grown by the villagers, which would save them the hardship of traveling. I would build a Dār an-Nadwa [assembly hall],[133] where the notables [*shuyūkh*] of the municipality would meet in order to discuss their affairs and other matters of interest.[134] I would bring seamstresses to teach the girls of the village and barbers

131. It is not clear at all when this entry was written, but it seems likely that it came sometime in late October 1943 or after.

132. Although some of the entries in the original diary were out of chronological order and this one has no date, there is no reason to believe that this was the last entry. This is an example of Sāmī philosophizing on a subject about which he thought and cared.

133. The Dār an-Nadwa to which Sāmī refers has both pre-Islamic and early Islamic connotations. Muslims recognize Qusayy, understood as an ancestor of the family of the Prophet Muḥammad and believed to be the founder of the Kaʿba in Mecca, as the builder of the Dār an-Nadwa assembly hall in Mecca. In the Dār an-Nadwa, all-important matters, including war council and marriage, took place. The Dār an-Nadwa remained at the rise of Islam, fell into disrepair, received renovations during the ninth century, and was annexed to the Masjid al-Ḥaram (Mosque of the al-Ḥaram) in Mecca; *Encyclopedia of Islam,* s.v. "Dār an-Nadwa."

134. *Shuyūkh,* in this context, are the village elders, the leaders. *Shaykh* is also a title for a religious leader or scholar, head of a tribe, or a patriarch, among other meanings.

to cut hair. I would establish a factory to preserve milk and dairy products in cans. I would bring a variety of new trees for planting in the most appropriate places.

---

26 October 1943
[Untitled]

I am in a state of hesitancy. I am currently working as a clerk in the NAAFI Department, but the [Arab Workers] Society has facilitated my entrance into the technical school. I would only get a salary from that job of about half of what my salary is now. Despite that small amount I will leave my job and work in this vocation, by the will of God the Great.

Tomorrow morning I will go with a group of guys to the Office of Workers' Affairs to take an oral exam [in English], which I do not think is difficult.

I spent the evening at the cinema, where I saw the movie *Awlād al-fuqarāʾ* [Children of the Poor], which affected me a great deal.[135] I was saddened to see this interesting drama for it is truly a film with a meaning and a message.

I am making great progress at work, but I do not care, because I am certain that is temporary. I will not be sorry to leave the office, regardless of the conditions.

---

29 October 1943
[Untitled]

Facilitated by the offices of the Society, I went on Wednesday to the Office of Workers' Affairs. In the room [where he was to take the exam] there were five English men who began to pose questions about my age, the school where I studied, and then asked why I wanted to leave my job at the NAAFI Department. I told them I had decided that I like mechanical work and that I prefer

135. The film *Awlād al-fuqarāʾ* was made in Egypt in 1942 and was directed by Yūsuf Wahbī. Wahbī also starred in it with Amīna Rizq, Maḥmūd al-Malijī, and Ruḥīyya Khālid. He is notable for producing the first "talkie" film in the Egypt/Arab world. *Awlād al-fuqarāʾ* was originally written as a play and performed by Wahbī's theatrical company in Egypt; Armbrust, *Mass Culture and Modernism in Egypt,* 252n32.

it to clerical work. Finally, they told me that I would become a metal worker [welder]. I accepted and left them, heading back to the office.

---

4 November 1943
[Untitled]

God's will has allowed me to be free from the NAAFI Department, and God has granted me great help to facilitate my way out. On the day that I submitted my resignation, I received a letter from the Post,[136] telling me that I had been accepted to the technical school in Jerusalem and requesting me to take up my work there on 15 November 1943. I waited for a response from the office director agreeing to my resignation letter of 29 October 1943. I received an answer on 2 November 1943 with the director accepting my resignation. Today, I am very happy, [and] nothing can bother me except the period of waiting that I now have remaining in the office, until 12 November 1943.

I asked many people about the trade that I am going to study in the school. Some of them said that it is good, while some of them told false stories about those who lost their vision from their work in oxygen welding.[137] However, this does not frighten me because I am certain that there are special glasses [one wears] during work.

On Monday, 1 November 1943, we received 570 pounds from the man who bought the shop. He has until the end of the transaction and its registration to pay the remaining 400 pounds.[138] We divided the sum [of the sale] with each of us taking 175 pounds, without expenses, which cost each of us five pounds.[139] We gave our mother 13 pounds now, and we will give her 28 pounds upon completion of the transaction, when we collect the rest of the money.

I took the initiative to put the money that I received in the Arab Bank, in

136. The Post (al-Bōsṭa) used here is not a post office; rather it is the name of a vocational school for young men that had a factory attached to it to allow students to gain practical experience in fields such as welding; correspondence from Samīr, 21 January 2006.

137. There is no welding process that relies solely on oxygen.

138. This does not add up to the amount Sāmī mentions for the sale of the shop in the entry dated 18 September 1943.

139. Here Sāmī is referring to himself and his two brothers, Asʿad and Saʿdī, who received the profits of the sale of the shop.

a checking account, which means that I will not earn any interest on it.[140] I bought a checkbook so that I can withdraw money when I am in need of something.[141] Do not think, my friend, that I am not thinking about investing my small sum, for I am striving diligently to find ways to make money out of it.

---

5 November 1943
[Untitled]

The Minister of Workers' Affairs in Greece came to the Society yesterday accompanying Mr. Shadley, Director of Labor Affairs in Jerusalem, at 4:30 in the afternoon.[142] We sat around them as they posed questions to us about the Society and about the progress that it has achieved. As-Sayyid Ḥasan Abū ʿAysha spoke in Arabic,[143] and as-Sayyid Jiryis Yūsuf translated his speech into

140. Founded by ʿAbd al-Ḥamīd Shōmān, the Arab Bank was licensed in Palestine in May 1930; its capital at establishment was 550,000 pounds; al-ʿArif, *al-Mufaṣṣal,* 476.

141. Samīr said his father probably paid a fee to get the checkbook. He recalled having seen some old Palestine mandate checks bearing revenue stamps, a sort of government tax, and thus assumed that those who opened a checking account in a bank in Palestine at that time had to pay a fee to get the checkbooks; correspondence from Samīr, 2 February 2007.

142. For Arabic names, Sāmī introduces them by using *al-Sayyid*; for the Englishman's name, Sāmī uses both the Arabic definite article *al-* plus a transcription of "Mr.," calling him "al-Mister Shadley," a kind of hypercorrection in usage. ʿAwdat al-Ashhab says the British established the Department of Labor Affairs (he calls it the Department of Labor) in 1941, two years before Sāmī mentions it. Al-Ashhab mentions both Shadley and Jiryis, to whom Sāmī refers in this entry, and that the latter was an assistant to the former; *Mudhakkirāt ʿAwdat al-Ashhab,* 47. It is entirely possible that Sāmī and ʿAwda knew each other. Sāmī does not mention ʿAwda in the diary, but ʿAwda mentions Sāmī's relatives Muḥammad Salīm ʿAmr (41) and Mukhliṣ ʿAmr (49). Muḥammad Salīm ʿAmr is discussed above in note 13. Mukhliṣ, ʿAwda states, was the editor-in-chief of *Majallat al-Ghad* and an author. Samīr conveyed that Mukhliṣ was Sāmī's first cousin (their fathers were brothers) and that he "was one of the pillars of the Palestinian Communist Party in the 1940s, which included Arabs and Jews. He was educated, articulate, and politically a leftist. He used to write a column in the newspapers in Jerusalem during the period of Jordanian rule"; correspondence from Samīr, 8 August 2007. Based on ʿAwda's memoirs, Mukhliṣ had apparently begun writing even earlier. Historian Muṣṭafā Dabbāgh notes that Mukhliṣ was best known as a nationalist; Dabbāgh offers very little on his communist activities, focusing instead on his role as a teacher and later as an education inspector as well as a prominent writer for several newspapers, including *al-Ghad* and *ad-Difaʿ* of Palestine in addition to Lebanese and Iraqi newspapers; Dabbāgh, *Bilādunā filasṭīn,* 151–152.

143. It seems that Sāmī may have known this fellow from his hometown of Hebron, and an

English. He said that the movement for workers' organization in Palestine was not new but that it arose decades ago. Several organizations had emerged that lasted a year, but they eventually collapsed, either over competition among their leaders or political inclinations. As for this Society, we hope from God that it will survive and dedicate itself to organize Arab workers and unify their voice. After that, they [the Greek minister and Mr. Shadley] posed a number of questions to those present and excused themselves and left.

---

9 November 1943

Reflections of One Who Has Resigned:[144]

How happy one feels when he works in one of the government offices, yet he finds the world too small to contain his happiness and his success. The days leading up to the departure of that individual from his job following the submission and acceptance of his resignation are long. I, for example, am counting the days and hours and minutes, waiting until the twelfth of the month comes when I leave the office never to return. I cannot describe my feelings now! I am working now [and it feels] as if I am going to remain forever. I answer the questions of the clerks about work, as if it is a natural thing, and as if I am not leaving them all of my registers and record books, my desk, my ink well, and my pens.

I am now like the dreamer. I look at everything in the office; I look more reflectively at everything. I look at the shelves of registers and at the bookcase, and at the faces of the beautiful girls. They work seriously and energetically and do not feel what is going on in my heart, feelings of sadness and regret over leaving their smiling faces. I look at my writings that I have done throughout my tenure in the office; I look at the letters that I sent, flipping through them one by one then hiding them in their files. I put them back

association with the family continued after the British Mandate period. When Sāmī worked at the governor's office in the Jordanian era, he had a colleague named Hāshim Abū ʿAysha, a young man with whom he also worked in Ramla; correspondence from Samīr, 14 January 2006.

144. The title of this entry and the first two sentences are written in the third person, probably to generalize how everyone must feel when finding a path forward from a job that is unsatisfying. By the third sentence in this entry, Sāmī brings this sentiment back to himself.

in their place on the shelf saying farewell to them, imagining the clerk who will work in my place and find them useful while also criticizing them. I am completely confident that I will not care what he says because I will be at my new job. I do not think that I will think about the office at all because I have something else to keep me occupied.

But what?! Is it the will of God that is changing my life's path, or my will? Am I free to do this or is there a higher power compelling me to do what I have done? I tendered my resignation and received an answer as if I was writing a letter to one of my friends. Do not ask my feelings when I received the director's letter accepting my resignation and the Post director's letter accepting me in the factory on Sunday. That day was my happiest day in comparison to these days now.

I feel that I am a stranger to this office despite having spent three years in it. There is also an incentive pushing me away from my fellow clerks. I talk to them as if I had not seen them before and as if I do not want to see them anymore. The day has nearly ended and I will wait until tomorrow comes to register what I will feel then.

---

10 November 1943
[Untitled]

My health today is not well and I feel that my head is nearly pounding. I have gotten a bad cold and I do not know if I can come [to work] today but I am at the end of my time at the NAAFI.

I still feel as if I am a stranger in the office, but nevertheless, and unfortunately, I am working and working seriously, as if I had sworn that I would not stop working until the very last moment.

My hope for the trade I am going to learn is great; yes, welding by oxygen and electricity is a good profession, few know it in its modern, technical way.[145]

145. The first half of the twentieth century brought great change in the field of welding. The one Sāmī mentions, using oxygen and electricity, seems to have been on the cutting edge of welding, as the patent for this technology, known as heliarc welding and requiring gas and electrodes, was only finalized in 1942 in the United States. Developments continued, and the process seems to have become widely known as the tungsten inert gas (TIG) process, which the British adopted into their Ministry of Aircraft Production and put into selective use in

I am waiting for Monday, the fifteenth of this month, impatiently. I have two days left in this office and they are the heaviest two days that I have faced, as I am [also] sick now. I have a toothache and my head is spinning like a wheel. I do not know what caused this—is it from the cold or something else?!

11 November 1943
[Untitled]

No!! I am fine, my health has improved today and I do not feel the pain I had felt yesterday. I am also energetic, working without stopping. They brought a young Muslim man for training and examination. I think that he is the one who will replace me. He was able to answer whatever they requested from him with regard to bookkeeping questions.

We got together last night with some people. We talked about the restaurant that the Arab Workers Society will establish and in which I shall have shares. Yesterday, I wrote a letter to Mr. Jones Nather, Supervisor of Provisions, requesting that he give the Society a permit to establish this restaurant for the Arab workers.

I stayed out late last night with Muḥammad Salīm ʿAmr. I saw that he is in extreme distress and I understood that he is in need of fifty pounds or less and I promised to help him.

Until this date and until this very moment, girls have not occupied my thoughts.[146]

No obstacles have come in my path caused by problems related to girls. Thank God I have reached nearly twenty years of age without tainting myself with one of those,[147] and I did this because I have great hope that I will get

---

1943. It seems that Palestine may have been one of the places selected for its use and that this is what Sāmī studied and practiced in his welding job. See *Inert-Gas Arc Welding,* especially 151ff, and Simonson, *The History of Welding,* 1.

146. Other than his poem about his unknown future wife on 25 March 1943, Sāmī's last mention of love or infatuation with a particular girl was more than a year prior to this entry, on 10 October 1942. Although he did not write every day and we cannot know that he did not think about them, the expressions of his emotions throughout the diary, particularly with regard to love, women, and relationships, suggest that he probably would have written had there been something to say.

147. Sāmī might have meant "loose" girls or even possibly prostitutes.

married to a girl who will compensate [me] for all that I have refused [thus far] of forbidden pleasures.

---

24 December 1943
[Untitled]

Here I am, I have left my office job in the NAAFI and entered into the technical field. I am now at the Post School to study oxygen welding. I feel that my health is improving from one day to the next because at this job I wake up energetic, which comes from the demands of the body. I wear armor, blue in color, and covered in grease and oil on many parts of it. I have a big appetite for food now; I eat five times a day and in the morning I feel very hungry. As for my stomach, it is in excellent shape.

I have found new friends in this place, not like my old friends, who are proud and show off. These are workers like me, and they have the same way of thinking as I do and they are, of course, Arab. We are impatiently waiting for the appointment of our departure to the place of work in Ramla or its environs, hoping very much that we will be happy there. We also hope to rent a house together, for we will have a lot of troubles if we do not end up living together.

My siblings raised the prospect of my getting engaged to the daughter of my Uncle Abdullah, but I refused the offer. I am too young and I do not want to marry yet. I do not regret that [decision].

---

8 February 1944

Ah, Dear Friend:
I have turned my life upside down. I am now living in between different workers' shifts. I go to work at 10:00 at night and finish at 7:00 in the morning.

I am working in a factory that manufactures gallon drums. I have been working there since Sunday. I sleep at 9:00 in the morning and I wake up at 2:00 in the afternoon. My current life is very harsh. I am preoccupied with returning to Hebron, but embarrassment prevents me from [doing] that.

From the ten students who studied [at the Post], only three of them are working: Hāshim, Bishāra, and myself.[148] I think that I will live with them because I cannot remain in the monastery.[149]

I am feeling a loss of strength and dizziness in my head and I think that is because of the change in my activities: staying up late and working all night.

---

9 February 1944

Ah, Dear Friend:
I am biting with regret over what I have lost.[150] I am stupid and I do not know what I will do. I do not see anything pushing me to stay in this city now.

148. Samīr said his father remained friends with these two colleagues for years afterward. Hāshim Abū ʿAysha, also from Hebron, later worked with Sāmī as a clerk at the government office in Hebron. The two maintained a long-lasting friendship; Hāshim died several years before Sāmī. Bishāra Saḥḥār was a Palestinian Christian from the Bethlehem area. Sāmī maintained his friendship with Bishāra until the late 1950s, the years when Sāmī remained in Hebron after getting married. Bishāra sent letters to Sāmī, apparently in an exchange of letters between the two men. Samīr said he read Bishāra's letters, which were filled with utopian thoughts and idealism, and suggested that he had a socialist, possibly communist, political ideology; correspondence from Samīr, 8 February 2008.

149. Suhayla said Sāmī had been allowed to live in a monastery because they thought he was Christian, as his name was a name Christians gave to their children. Suhayla related that he ate well at the monastery, including oranges from the orchard outside the monastery. She said no one knew Sāmī was Muslim, and one of the men who lived at the monastery and possibly worked with Sāmī said he had a daughter whom he wanted Sāmī to marry. Sāmī's reaction to this was to take his belongings in the middle of the night and flee from the monastery. When Sāmī reached the door, it was locked so no one could come or go at night, and Iskandar, the doorman, told him that he could not unlock the door. Sāmī, apparently frightened at the prospect of this marriage proposition, paid Iskandar a few *qurūsh* to bribe him into opening the door. Sāmī left and did not return to the monastery. Suhayla laughed when recalling this story; interview with Suhayla, 15 January 2006. Samīr noted that this monastery belonged to the Coptic Church in Jerusalem and might in fact be the Dayr as-Sulṭān Monastery. Sāmī apparently told Samīr that Iskandar, the gatekeeper, a one-eyed Egyptian guard, allowed him to lodge there; correspondence from Samīr, 20 January 2008.

150. Perhaps he is talking about his office job. Sāmī seems to regret his decision to work in welding. His work had become very difficult, and he writes in the entry of 8 February 1944 of longing for his hometown of Hebron.

27 February 1944
[Untitled]

Today I am fine. I have come to love the job that I had previously found difficult.[151] I am now living in Ramla, renting a house with two others. I bought shares in the canteen of the Arab Workers Society, paying 50 pounds, and my brother Saʿdī paid the same sum. I hope that the project succeeds.

My sister Naʿīma married after staying a widow for five years. Yes, she married Rashad al-Bakri. I went to [visit] her yesterday and I found her happy, but she thinks about her children a lot.[152]

My brother Asʿad is sick and his situation is not good. I wish him a speedy recovery. I saw Suhayla yesterday. Her figure and her beauty pleased me and I hope that she will be my wife in the future.

21 May 1944
[Untitled]

This life is amazing and full of surprises. God has allowed me to finish at the factory of Bayt Nabala.[153] I was accepted in the Airplane Camp after passing

151. By July 1944, Sāmī would again be looking to change jobs.

152. Naʿīma's children went to live with the mother of her deceased husband. Suhayla said Naʿīma would see her children from her first husband at her and Sāmī's home. Naʿīma went on to have children with Rashad al-Bakri, which was his reason for marrying her in the first place, as he only had a daughter from a previous marriage, according to Ruqayya, and wanted sons. Naʿīma's first husband's name was Amīn Abū Khālid. They married in 1936; he was killed while passing through a British curfew by a British soldier who shot him. Apparently the British mandatory government gave her a kind of compensation for the death that amounted to three *dinars* (probably monthly), which would not buy much to support the children. For that reason, Naʿīma had to marry again; interviews with Ruqayya, 20 and 24 December 2005. According to Suhayla, Rashad al-Bakri's first wife could not have children at all. Naʿīma had not wanted to marry so she could be with her children, but her mother convinced her by reminding her that she would not be able to take care of them after her husband was killed; interview with Suhayla, 19 January 2006.

153. Bayt Nabala was a village ten kilometers outside of Ramla. The population at the time was 2,310, according to Walid Khalidi. Khalidi notes that the British had set up a military camp in the vicinity of the village, which coincides nicely with Sāmī's description of his work in welding in this area. The village was a good location for the military camp, as it was near a secondary railroad track connected to the Rafah-Haifa main line, thus linking the village

the exam. The style of my life will change completely from that of a few weeks ago. I will never work nights again. There is the canteen, which I am keeping a close eye on, keeping the books, collecting its earnings, and eating in it as well. The work there is fair and you could even say light.

My brother Asʿad talked to me last week about Suhayla and that he was asking for her for me. I told him that I do not want marriage at this time, but he scolded me and attributed that to my lack of understanding and appreciating this opportunity. My sister Yusrā was at our house, and they agreed that she and Ruqayya would go to arrange the engagement to Suhayla, so we went, but I left [Hebron] without knowing the results of their conversation with Abdullah Effendi Bashīr![154]

---

17 June 1944

[Untitled]

I went to Hebron this week and I learned that my Uncle Abdullah has agreed to accept me as fiancé for as-Sayyida Suhayla.[155] I revealed my happiness to my mother and my siblings, but I was apprehensive of this, as if there was something out of the ordinary in the situation. My nerves shook violently and I could not sleep that night. I went back to Jerusalem early.

---

25 June 1944

[Untitled]

I came to Hebron today and my mother suggested to me that I go to my Uncle Abdullah's house. I went, hesitatingly, but finally I entered the house and I found my uncle at the door. He led me into the reception room, and I sat down

---

to Palestine's larger urban centers. Later, Israeli soldiers attacked Bayt Nabala after their capture of Lydda and Ramla. The village itself was destroyed, and some village lands were used to build Israeli settlements such as Kfar Truman (named for U.S. President Harry S. Truman) and Beit Nechemya; Khalidi, *All That Remains,* 365–366.

154. Ruqayya said their mother went with them to discuss the engagement for Sāmī and Suhayla; interview with Ruqayya, 23 December 2005.

155. Sāmī's usage of *as-Sayyida* is incorrect here, as an unmarried woman would be called *al-Ānisa.*

after he had left me and gone out. I was waiting for whom I would see, when my uncle's wife, Ratība, entered. I greeted her and she sat down. She seems like a youthful woman, with a beautiful face, but the illness has betrayed her and has wasted her figure, which is still fighting the illness.[156] When she spoke, she did so gracefully. She was lovely company, modest, with a lovely disposition.

She began to offer me a variety of sweets and fruit, which I ate happily. At midnight, I left her and went to our home. Once there, I was showered with different questions, which I answered, embellishing some, while withholding information on others.

Of course, the next day, as usual, I traveled back to Ramla.

The conversation, the sweets, and the respect, all of it does not compare to a gaze upon Suhayla or having a word with her.

---

10 July 1944

[Untitled]

This week I went to my uncle's house, and I found that my uncle's lovely wife had made me a sumptuous dinner of lamb's ribs. It was a long time since I had been here, and the waiting was very difficult. I ate and was very content. But, to whom shall I talk now, you, my friend, to whom I always poured out my complaints, or to you, Suhayla, you who have now become my main goal in this life and my companion when I am lonely? Yes, shall I complain to you about the customs of our people, shall I complain to you about what I have suffered when I would come to your house and see everybody, but I was forbidden from seeing you? Is that justice or the correct opinion of those who see the situation and think that they understand? How will I win your emotions and your love and how will I be for you that love in your heart when you are far away from me?

156. Ratība had rheumatic heart disease.

31 July 1944
[Untitled]

I went yesterday, with my mother, sisters, and brother Asʿad, to Jerusalem and we bought what is called *mlak* [bridal gift] for as-Sayyida Suhayla.[157] I took it last night and went to my uncle's house. My uncle's wife was pleased or so I thought, and I sat and talked to her. My mother and sister Ruqayya are coming here to sit and talk with them.

Finally, after some give and take, they decided to let Suhayla in to see me, but she refused to enter, so I went to another room and took her hand, and my heart was racing and the blood was rushing to my head. She came with me to the room that I had been sitting in and we sat, without talking, and I put the engagement ring on her, as she put it on me as well. From there, I spoke in a shaky voice and said to her: "This is the moment for which I have been waiting for such a long time and it is the happiest moment in my life." She was silent, breathing quickly with her chest moving up and down rapidly, and her nerves were frozen still; she did not release a reply and did not speak except for a little bit. I wonder, is she always like this or did she want to show me all of that shyness? She did not stay long with me, for she became very shy, as Ḥamdī and Nayyif were sitting across from us.[158] I got angry and called my mother to leave and we said our goodbyes. I kissed Suhayla's hand before leaving, hoping for myself that I would see her the following week.

I could not sleep that night because my thoughts were scattered between two things: the first was Suhayla, and the second was that I was meeting the Deputy District Governor the following day. My torment did not last long as morning came, the sun rose, and the birds sang. I got out of bed and dressed

157. Layla al-Ḥammūrī, Suhayla's niece, explained that the *mlak* was part of the agreed-upon gifts that Sāmī would provide for his bride-to-be, including nightgowns, undergarments, and material to make clothing; interview with Layla, 24 December 2005. That could also be the explanation for *jahāz,* but as Sāmī explains in the entry dated 22 August 1944, the *mlak* was originally intended as a monetary gift until Suhayla's mother wanted the amount in actual purchases. Samīr distinguished between the two: the *mlak,* he said, was a monetary gift, intended for the bride to buy gold and dresses, while the *jahāz* was a gift of more practical items, cloth for nightgowns and undergarments, blankets, towels, and such; correspondence from Samīr, 2 February 2007. The concept of *mlak* and *jahāz* may both be thought of as a trousseau.

158. Nayyif was Suhayla's brother, and Ḥamdī was her cousin.

and asked my mother for her blessing. I went to the division in the department of the Deputy Governor, and I waited more than two hours. Finally, my turn came and I entered the office of the Deputy Governor. He asked what I wanted and I told him that "I had sent him a letter on 12 July 1944 and I had received a reply to come to meet him."[159]

He told me to sit down and he looked at the dossier in front of him. He asked me if I wanted to work as a tax collector.[160] I replied that it would be better if I worked as a clerk in this department, but if there was no other job, I would accept that. He informed me about the salary I would receive. He was pleased with my English skills and told me to follow him to the office of the Governor of Hebron, whom I greeted. Finally, the Deputy Governor told him about me and that he found me better than any other person who had applied for the job in the District Office. He also told him that I am the nephew of Abdullah Effendi Bashīr as well as his son-in-law, and the Governor of Hebron said to me: "Wait a little in Saʿdī Effendi's office until I call you."[161] I did that and he called me and wrote some information down about me and told me that I might get the job in a month's time or after two years. I left him, with distraught thoughts and an anxious spirit, fearful that I had failed this time. But I must be patient. I will return to my difficult job in Ramla; God is with those who are patient.[162]

159. Suhayla remembered that her father wanted Sāmī to work in the Office of the Deputy District Governor in Hebron and that he helped Sāmī get the job to which Sāmī alludes in this entry; interview with Suhayla, 15 January 2006.

160. Sāmī's father had been a tax collector under the Ottomans.

161. Saʿdī Effendi was Saʿdī Abdullah Tahbūb, who was working at the Hebron governor's office before Sāmī began working there. The Tahbūb family is a well-known Hebronite family, and many of its members were educated, even in the 1930s and 1940s, and worked in government positions or in the Shariʿa court as judges (*qāḍis*), like Saʿdī Effendi's father, Sheikh Abdullah Tahbūb, did. Sāmī became Mr. Tahbūb's colleague, and they worked together for many years during the Jordanian period in the West Bank. Like Sāmī, he moved to Amman in the early 1960s and worked at the Ministry of Interior. Samīr added that he died several years ago; correspondence from Samīr, 8 February 2008.

162. Sāmī does not mention it in the diary, but Suhayla said he got this job in the district office and that the British official in charge, by the name of Somerville, liked Sāmī quite a lot. He worked there as a clerk, not as a tax-collector. Suhayla said the office benefited from his skills in English, which he improved through a correspondence course. Sāmī continued in this office, which became part of the Jordanian Ministry of Interior after 1948. He remained with the Ministry of Interior, and in 1961 he was transferred to Amman, where he initially lived by himself for six months before bringing Suhayla and his family to Amman, where they continued to live. Suhayla was quite upset about the move, but she managed it along

15 August 1944
[Untitled]

I decided not to go to Hebron this week; [however,] my longing to see you [Suhayla] propelled my coming at the last minute. Yes, I had no patience with my separation from you. The car snatched me away to Jerusalem and from there to Hebron. I did not arrive until nighttime, and I went down to our house where my mother welcomed me after having given up hope of my coming. She prepared the bed for me to sleep on, but I asked for her permission to go to my uncle's house. She granted it to me and I rushed to your home hoping to see you and enjoy conversation with you, O Suhayla. I had not arrived at your house without my heart nearly breaking over my desire to see you. Do you remember when I found you outside of the door, sitting with your mother, how I greeted you and how your mother stood in between us? From there I entered the [reception] room and waited for your arrival, as your sister brought me coffee and sweets without you. I asked [as to your whereabouts] and no one answered me so I repeated the question. Your good mother laughed and said that my uncle got angry because I saw you and that I would not see you again until our wedding. The news hit me like a lightning bolt. You had made me delicious sweets but I was unable to eat them except for a very little bit, due to my great sadness and my failure [to see you]. But why did they not know that I had come this distance for one thing and that was to see you and for my hearing and vision to be fulfilled by your words and the sight of you. Yes, it was a crushing blow, O Suhayla, but I handled it and asked for permission to leave. I left your house with a broken heart, blaming myself and feeling weak. I complained about the matter to my mother but she reassured me and said that these are the customs of our people and one must not go beyond the limits allowed. I lay in my bed feeling full of troubles. I finally submitted to sleep during which I had disturbing dreams.

---

with the children. As part of the job in this ministry, Sāmī finally got the opportunity to continue his studies. He was sent to the American University of Beirut for a yearlong study of general administration and received a certificate of course completion at a graduation ceremony attended by Suhayla and their eldest son, Samīr, who was approximately fifteen years old at the time. Suhayla said Sāmī also studied in the Egyptian correspondence school mentioned in earlier entries, from which he also received a certificate; interviews with Suhayla, 15 and 16 January 2006.

22 August 1944
[Untitled]

The sacred month of Ramaḍān descended upon us a few days ago, but I have been unable to fast more than one day. Indeed, I went to Jaffa on Sunday and headed out to the section of the beach allocated for men. I began to swim in the sea until noontime, then I got dressed and left in the direction of Jaffa. I thought to return to Ramla but I wanted to go to my Uncle Jamāl's house. I went to their house and found him there and we sat and talked and he was happy. But, he began to count for me the mistakes my mother had made and the damage that my mother had caused him. He was gone when I sent the *mlak* to my fiancée, but my mother had not informed him about this. He insisted that I tell him how much I spent on this. He said that Asʿad told him that we had first taken seventy pounds but my uncle's wife would not accept this and asked me to make purchases [in this amount]. Hind began to express some kind of anger about the money that my mother and my brother Asʿad had spoken about, but I denied all of that and reassured them. I did not see the reason for all of that anger and I think that they in fact regret what they did.[163] Were they going back on the decision to end the engagement?[164] God knows!?

I did not stay there more than one hour. I went at 3:00 to Cinema al-Ḥamrāʾ to see the film *Barlantī*.[165] It is a remarkable masterpiece and an impressive lesson in social values. Finally, I went back to Ramla to begin my difficult job.

O dearest love, I am waiting impatiently for a response to my application in the District Governor's office. My heart is pounding to go to Hebron so that

163. Family members recount that Jamāl was upset because Sāmī's mother did not tell him about the purchases that they had made for the *mlak* for Suhayla; interview with Suhayla, 15 January 2006.

164. Behind all of this is Jamāl's rejection of Saʿdī, Sāmī's brother, as a husband for Hind because he did not bring her the proper gifts for the *mlak*. Perhaps when they saw what Sāmī did for Suhayla, they came to regret that decision, so it seemed that Jamāl might have been trying to cause a rift over the matter; interview with Suhayla, 15 January 2006.

165. *Barlantī* is an Egyptian film released in 1944 starring Yūsuf Wahbī, Nūr al-Hūda, and Bishāra Wakīm. It was directed by Yūsuf Wahbī and produced by Aḥmad Darwīsh. Barlantī (often written as Berlanti when anglicized) was the name of the heroine, played in the movie by Nūr al-Hūda.

I can be near you. However, circumstances do not always help the individual; sometimes the wind blows against the sails of the ship.[166]

---

29 August 1944
[Untitled]

I have performed the ablutions awaiting the Maghrib prayer and I am not fasting!![167]

It occurred to me while I was sitting in my dreary room to write what I am thinking about. I went an hour ago to see Muḥammad ash-Sharabati to ask him if I had received a letter and he told me that I had not received a thing. I am impatiently awaiting a reply from the office of the Deputy Governor. I have become frustrated by my life in Ramla and I have resigned from my very difficult job.[168] I am always thinking of Suhayla and my mother and my life in the future when I will be in Hebron.

I am still continuing my studies at the correspondence school.[169] I study

166. Here Sāmī employs part of a poem by the well-known tenth-century Arab poet Abū aṭ-Ṭayyib al-Mutanabbī titled *Mā kullu mā yatamannā al-marʾu yudrikuhu*. The full verse, the twelfth of twenty-five, is: "Not everything one desires one obtains; sometimes the wind blows against the sails of the ship." Al-Mutanabbi wrote it upon hearing that rivals claimed that he had died and had an obituary read about him at the court of Sayf ad-Dawla al-Hamadāni in Aleppo. This poetic response told his rivals who wished he were dead that not all of their wishes would be fulfilled, using ships and wind as a metaphor. Al-Mutanabbi's poem can be found in *Dīwān al-Mutanabbī*. Sāmī uses the poem to make an analogy to his life, meaning here that although he is desperate to see Suhayla, circumstances are preventing it, and he did not get everything he wanted. Samīr recalled, "In those days the curriculum in Arabic language was very strong, and students had to memorize Arabic poetry and read prose. That is why he [Sāmī] used al-Mutanabbī's poem in this entry"; correspondence from Samīr, 14 May 2007 and 7 February 2008.

167. This period corresponds with Ramaḍān, the month of fasting on the Islamic calendar. It is not clear why Sāmī was not fasting during Ramaḍān, but it may have been due to the difficult nature of his work in welding. Suhayla said that after they were married, Sāmī always fasted during Ramaḍān, as did she, although he did not want her to, fearing it would be difficult for her delicate body; interview with Suhayla, 19 January 2006.

168. This is unclear, as Sāmī mentions in an entry dated 21 May 1944 that he had ended his harsh work in the factory after he passed the exam to work in the Airplane Camp. It seems that he either returned to or had not fully left the welding job, as he continues to refer to it in later entries.

169. Suhayla said Sāmī took several courses in journalism and received a certificate in journalism from this school; interview with Suhayla, 15 January 2006.

every evening. I ate two figs and I feel pain in my stomach and my head is spinning. I will never have the taste of figs again in my life.

9 September 1944

Dearest love,
I am now sitting in the canteen in the Airplane Camp in Ramla, yes, sitting, as the evening begins to lower its veils and the stars to shine in the center of the sky. The music plays loudly nearby. I sat by myself to contemplate my issues in this life and what the future holds for me with regard to happiness and sadness, failure and success. At every minute or period of quietness, I find you standing in front of me as a torch, illuminating the path in front of me, filling my heart with hope and taking any sadness away from me. I hope I will see you on the *ʿid* [feast] to complete my happiness and solidify our love and share with each other our hopes and our pains.[170] I am afraid that custom and tradition will stand as an obstacle in our path, but I will not be sad because perhaps we will marry in six months. I am still holding onto the hope that I will get work in the Deputy District Governor's office, and I am still waiting from day to day to be informed that I have gotten the job.

10 October 1944
[Untitled]

The days are gloomy and treating me with contempt. I do not know why I feel this way. Is what is going to happen to me that which I do not like? Will I find days crueler than I have already faced? I am pessimistic . . . May God keep troubles away from me. I am full of sadness for no reason and in my heart there is a deep and profound emptiness; in my soul there is a feeling of boredom so much so that I have tried to please it like a small child.

My body is nearly shattered. My bones emit a muffled sound, and my eyes

170. This entry date on the Gregorian calendar corresponds to 21 Ramaḍān 1363 on the Muslim calendar. The *ʿid,* or feast, Sāmī spoke of then was *ʿId al-fiṭr,* which marks the end of Ramaḍān and the period of fasting. This exchange between the Gregorian calendar and the Muslim calendar was calculated at http://www.calendarhome.com/converter/.

are so sore, as if there is sand in both of them. My spirit is broken, my pride is wounded, and my soul is shattered.

When, O God, will I be finished with this harsh life filled with fear and instability? When will I gain work that does not destroy me, sap my blood, and take away my vision?[171] When, O God, will my heart be reassured by the presence of my beloved wife, and when will my chest fill with delight over the sight of my children playing around me? When, O God, will I be able to have a calm life in my hometown, the place where I was born, near my mother and my wife?

---

19 October 1944
[Untitled]

To return to you, my friend, you who have listened to all of my words without protesting, you who have brought tears to your eyes when I have told you about the sorrows in my heart and what kind of sadness we are passing through; your face has radiated with delight when you learned of my success.[172]

My heart is wounded, and every time the wounds heal, blood flows from it as the wounds reopen; my soul is imprisoned and my spirit is tortured. I do not know why there is all this torment and why there are all of these wounds.

Listen, O my patient friend, to my speech and do not get bored from me, for I see life as a continuous dark night. There does not seem to be a glimmer of light or a ray of hope, just continuous, clinging torture surrounding the individual, who is unable to escape it. He falls into trouble, aware of just how bad it is, but he has lost his spirit of resistance, closing his eyes and mouth, submitting to the circumstances. Let the days do what they want.

I wake early, while the stars are in the sky. The room echoes back the reverberation of the sound of my bones. The birds agitate my suffering. I drag myself to wash my face, covered in sweat. Then, I put on old clothes and hard shoes suitable for the work that I have to do. Then I go on an empty stomach

171. Although Sāmī said in his entry dated 4 November 1943 that there would be protective glasses at his welding job, apparently his eyes were still affected by the dangers of the job.

172. One can assume that he is directing his speech to the diary, although it is unusual that Sāmī would speak of the diary's "feelings" when he poured out his life's joys and sorrows.

until I reach my workplace where I go to the restaurant to eat a quick breakfast. Then I go to work where the temperature is oppressively hot and where the noise is too loud, where I am slowly, slowly losing my vision. My sweat flows heavily, drenching my body and my clothes, and I wait for the break.

I lie down underneath a tree like a wounded man and my thoughts wander in this huge world that causes problems. My eyelids give in to a deep sleep.

We return to work, to the heat and to the clamor of noise until the evening when I go to my room. I do not leave it without reading a book or studying my lessons. I will not go to Hebron this month until the *ʿid*.[173] I will stay here, far and alone, for I have no hope that I will see the one for whom I have taken to thinking of.

---

30 October 1944
[Untitled]

I am incapable of hiding how I take delight in you and admire your body, or the wonderful euphoria that goes through my heart when I am struck by the flow of your magic.

You were very simply dressed with basic features that makeup and powders cannot distort, for you have an ideal beauty, one of the marvels of natural feminine beauty. I was uncertain what I would talk to you about, and I got up from my chair hoping that you would sit and I would have a space of time during which to remember the thoughts that had flown from my mind and slipped out of my consciousness.

But, unfortunately, you did not grant me more than half a minute's time. You greeted me and departed like a gazelle running from the hunter who has trapped it.

I return to myself and to my troubles, whose source has no end to it, and to the worries pouring over my head like a downpour. My heart is about to be shattered and my soul feels subjugated and broken.

I try to fly in the palaces of imagination and its effect on the world of hopes and dreams, but the material shackles wake me from my sleep and hit me with a cruel, dirty hand. I am in dire financial straits and I hope that it will not

173. This would be *ʿId al-adhḥā,* which falls about two months after *ʿId al-fiṭr* on the Islamic calendar.

affect my relationship with you, as we are, in these days, slaves of despicable materialism and are its obedient servants.

For when I look toward the future I see darkness, and when I look to the present, I find it equal to misfortune. Whenever I convey my troubles to friends, they reassure me and it gives me hope for the future and for the happiness that awaits me. I accept their words, but with a feeble, fake smile that carries both despair and hope.

God said in His great book: "Do not be discouraged from the mercy of God, for God does not like desperate people."[174]

Your dear mother's illness makes me very sad and my heart is beating with concern that her unblemished pure youth shall wither away and that her good heart will be harmed.

Interview on Monday
26 December 1944

I sat next to the bed of my uncle's wife [Ratība] to cheer her up from the weariness of illness which has shown her no mercy at all during the last two months.[175] As we were talking a few women from the family entered to visit my uncle's wife and I stood up and excused myself. I said goodbye to my uncle's wife and left her room.

But, as-Sayyida "N" refused to let me go as it was raining heavily outside.[176] She reminded me that I am sick and that it would only make my illness

174. Qurʾān 39:53. The line Sāmī writes, "for God does not like desperate people," seems to be incorrect. Qurʾān 39:53, rather continues with "for God forgives all sins, for He is Oft-Forgiving, Most Merciful." Another verse, Qurʾān 15:55, continues, "Be not then in despair," which may be what Sāmī meant to have said.

175. At this point, Ratība was in congestive heart failure. As there was no cardiac surgery in those days to correct damaged heart valves, she died when she was about thirty-eight years old. She was unable to attend the wedding of her daughter, Suhayla, to Sāmī. Suhayla's oldest sister (a half-sister from the first wife of Abdullah Bashīr), named Hanafīyya, delegated by Ratība, took care of Suhayla on her wedding day. Samīr, a physician, confirmed the stages of Ratība's disease; correspondence from Samīr, 2 February 2007 and 20 January 2008.

176. With the "N" that appears as is in this entry, Sāmī refers to Naʿomeh, Suhayla's younger sister, who served as a go-between for the engaged couple. He should have used *al-Ānisa* here, as she was not yet married.

worse. I went in and she directed me to the reception room and I sat there, at first bowing my head in silence and after playing with the radio. "N" entered bringing a glass of tea and I asked here where "S" was.[177] She asked me if I wanted to see her and I told her "of course! I am dying to see her." She left for a bit then came back laughing a little, saying that she is coming.

As I stood my heart was palpitating and my emotions became heightened, at which time the frightened gazelle entered the room. I hastened to her and I clasped her hand, taking it in my hand, and I sat her down next to me. We began to draw each other into the details of conversation with a kind of timidity, although each of us enjoyed each other's company. We both became reassured about the other and felt comfortable with the other, certain that this would be our forever soulmate in the life of this world.[178] She rose, frightened, and I grabbed her and asked her to pledge that she would remain by my side, as it was the best opportunity [to ask her to do so]. She blinked her beautiful eyelids and said, "Wait, for perhaps I am coming back." She left for a few moments, which I calculated as years, then she entered and sat next to me, and here I cannot describe my feelings because I felt like I was in a delightful trance in which she held me. Those lovely words that she uttered, as if they were gentle breezes hitting my face softly . . .

As these days pass, it is impossible that they will come back, and we try to keep them and hold them tightly, but they pass anyway, not caring about anything.

That first pure kiss I placed on her forehead when she was standing, powerless, without resistance. I turned my shoulder and left, tripping on the hem of my coat, and I became half-dazed. I dragged myself home, step by step, with the moon rising directly from behind the clouds sometimes and hidden by them at other times. I arrived home and lay down in my bed and gave in to the memory that returned me to her very quickly, to tell her what I did not tell her during our conversation. O days, pass slowly, slowly.

177. Here Sāmī refers to Suhayla.

178. Sāmī and Suhayla—soulmates, as Sāmī writes here—married on 19 May 1945 and were together for fifty-three and a half years, until Sāmī passed away on 11 December 1998.

25 January 1945[179]
This is the will of God; Man has no control of himself, whether for the good or for the bad.[180]

And in this, I accept this new life, of which I had no knowledge; this is Nature repeating its eternal cycles, its violent tragedies and perhaps its quick path. Five years ago, I was an adolescent, not more than fifteen years old, and I was still in school and I was still dependent on others. I did not bear the burdens of life and thought did not weigh heavily on my head with its drudgery.

Now I have begun to think about the house and what follows with regard to expenses and the kitchen and how to furnish it and about the wife and her needs, essential and nonessential things. Yes, I had some money, but I spent all of it on my fiancée—from the *mlak* to the house furnishings to the dowry to the trousseau.[181] Now I do not have a red cent. From time to time I am threatened with being fired from work. I wish I knew what I was going to work at![182] And I have chained myself to the engagement of my cousin, whom I must make happy. As-Sayyida Ratība wants for her daughter a wedding dress that costs thirty pounds and other things double that sum—what shall I do?[183] I cannot upset her while she is ill, but where do I have the money to buy what she wants?

179. In fact, Sāmī wrote this date as 25 January 1944, but it is undoubtedly incorrect and should be 25 January 1945. By this point in the diary, Sāmī consistently listed the dates in chronological order. Here Sāmī speaks of the requirements of marriage, which he would not have spoken of one year prior, as the engagement began in May 1944. When Sāmī's siblings raised the issue of his betrothal to Suhayla in December 1943, he flatly refused, saying he was too young for that. The content of this entry makes it unlikely that he wrote this within a month of his original refusal to get engaged to Suhayla. However, in the diary, the date indeed appears as 25 January 1944, a common mistake at the beginning of a new year.

180. This is a paraphrase of a Qurʾānic verse. The verse, *la yamliku li-nafsihi durran wa-la nafʿan,* appears in a number of Qurʾānic verses in somewhat different forms. What seems to be the closest to what Sāmī has written here is Qurʾān 25:3, *wa-la yamlikūn li-anfusihim durran wa-la nafʿan,* meaning "they have no control over hurt or good to themselves."

181. When Sāmī said he had money, he was probably referring to the money that he received from the sale of the family shop that he put in the bank.

182. This is probably because he still wanted to leave his job in Ramla and was waiting to hear about the job in Hebron at the district governor's office.

183. Sāmī called the wedding dress *badla* (suit or costume), but the term *fustān mukhmal* (velvet/wedding dress) was also used.

12 March 1945
[Untitled]

Slowly, people, it is enough with your pride and arrogance. Have mercy, O days, enough of pride and betrayal. Let us move toward our goal in peace without satisfying your vengeance with our agony or arousing our attachment to this vain world. I went to their [his uncle's family's] home as night began to fall and the wind blew violently on the strings of the trees,[184] playing a sad melody that flows discontinuously, arousing the nerves, and spreading tremors in the body. I entered her [Ratība's] room and sat; she was surrounded by bed covers and pillows and behind her was Miriam, as if she was supporting her, and in front of her was her mother, who had hidden her face from sadness.[185] They sat most gently,[186] not disturbing the complete silence, broken only by the groans of my uncle's wife and the terrifying rattling in her throat that would emerge from her irritated lungs. I sat there in a chair altering my gaze among the women seated there. I brightened my eyes and I began to make a glance at her [Ratība] and saw, in fact, that the illness had become more pronounced in her. The pain harassed her and made her breathing labored and she could not raise her head from exhaustion.

Do you not see her, O God, in need of Your mercy and Your help? How many smiling days this woman has passed through, overflowing with beauty and youthfulness and charm. How she went out and about, how much she laughed, how she delighted all and how happy she was. How often she received gifts and jewelry. How well she dressed in superb clothing and hosted and sent invitations to banquet halls. How this woman comforted the weak and paid condolences to those who had lost loved ones. But here she is today, withering fast like a fresh flower that has been burned by the rays of the sun, then wilts and drops its head, determined to fall from the harsh tree of life.

184. "Strings" is a metaphor here for the wind making sounds as if playing music on the leaves.

185. Miriam was the stepmother of Abdullah Bashīr, the fifth wife of his father, Bashīr Yaḥyā ʿAmr. The mother is a reference to Ratība's mother, Amīna al-Agha (wife of ʿAbbās Yaḥyā ʿAmr), Suhayla's grandmother; interview with Suhayla, 19 January 2006; correspondence from Samīr, 13 February 2008.

186. Sāmī again uses the expression "as if birds were on their heads" to show how quietly and gently these women sat by the sick Ratība.

Can one who sees this scene think about marriage or feel happiness or joy? In addition to feelings of pity and sadness, her sight stirs the soul with a feeling of disdain for this life, while imposing on the individual a passage through black days and nerve-wracking hours like these. "O those who believe, let not then this present life deceive you, nor let the Chief Deceiver [the Power of Evil] deceive you about God."[187]

I told Abdullah that I wanted the wedding before any misfortune happens to his wife. "Give me two weeks," he said. "She [Suhayla] cannot leave her [Ratība] today, but maybe she [Ratība] will improve during the course of the week."[188]

---

17 April 1945
[Untitled]

I have begun to smell the bad odors of this life and I have begun to hear its loud, repugnant sound, and then its deformed, frightened ghostlike image appeared to me.

I have come to have complete faith that I was not created to be happy in this life, rather I will be an example of eternal sadness and misfortune. This world will delight in my appearance of sadness and rejoice in hearing my groans.

The days increased in their desire and exaggerated their gloating of me. They have plunged me in more than one dilemma, inspiring in me bewildering desires of this love and that money and this happiness. These different

187. Qur'ān 31:33. In the Qur'ān, the verse does not include "O those who believe," although Sāmī writes it in the quotation marks as if it did.

188. According to Ruqayya, Abdullah Bashīr said this because Suhayla took care of her mother when she was ill, and the father did not want his daughter to leave her sick mother; interview with Ruqayya, 23 December 2005. Being so ill, Ratība did not make it to the wedding of Sāmī and Suhayla. In fact, Suhayla recalled that her father married again, just before Sāmī and Suhayla did, and before Ratība died. Ratība died about four months later, and Suhayla thought her father's marriage hastened her mother's death; interview with Suhayla, 19 January 2006. Samīr said Abdullah Bashīr's marriage to a girl younger than Suhayla, from the ʿAmr family from the village of Dūra, devastated Ratība and as a result, she left his house and stayed with her brother, Yūsuf ʿAbbās ʿAmr until her death; correspondence from Samīr, 20 January 2008.

Figure 5. Wedding photo of Sāmī and Suhayla, May 1945. Courtesy of Samīr ʿAmr.

paths began to push me and opened my eyes to see ignorance rather than love, greed rather than wealth, and misfortune rather than happiness.[189]

The human soul weakens in front of faith and hope and destroys the will of the imagination.

---

1 May 1945[190]
Marriage

On 24 April 1945 I was called to Hebron by telephone.

189. Suhayla explained this sadness as being due to the expensive demands on Sāmī by her mother and herself; interview with Suhayla, 15 January 2006.

190. It seems that Sāmī sat down to write on the first of May that he had been called to Hebron several days earlier. He wrote nothing else. The wedding took place on 19 May 1945. Suhayla gave 17 May as the date of the wedding, but Samīr stated with certainty that it was on 19 May. He added that she was probably referring to the date of the signing of the Islamic legal contract at which the Shariʿa court official would come to the house to make the marriage a legally binding affair. The actual wedding night could be the same day or within a couple of days of the signing. Sāmī and Suhayla's wedding celebration took place on 19 May 1945; interview with Suhayla, 15 January 2006; correspondence from Samīr, 20 January 2008.

APPENDIX 1 | GENEALOGY OF THE ʿAMR FAMILY

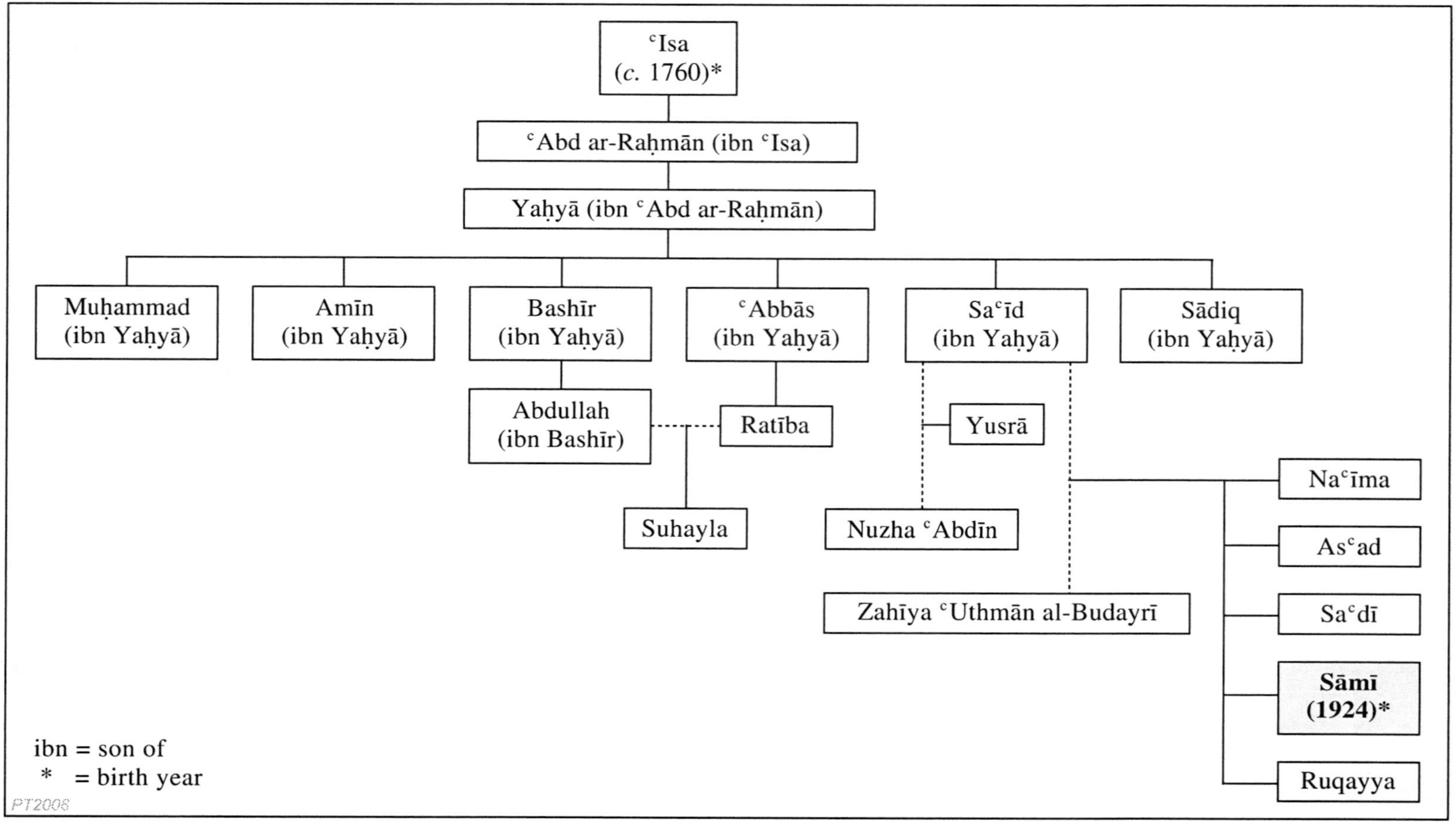

ᶜIsa (c. 1760)*
ᶜAbd ar-Raḥmān (ibn ᶜIsa)
Yaḥyā (ibn ᶜAbd ar-Raḥmān)
Muḥammad (ibn Yaḥyā)
Amīn (ibn Yaḥyā)
Bashīr (ibn Yaḥyā)
ᶜAbbās (ibn Yaḥyā)
Saᶜīd (ibn Yaḥyā)
Sādiq (ibn Yaḥyā)
Abdullah (ibn Bashīr)
Ratība
Suhayla
Yusrā
Nuzha ᶜAbdīn
Zahīya ᶜUthmān al-Budayrī
Naᶜīma
Asᶜad
Saᶜdī
Sāmī (1924)*
Ruqayya
ibn = son of
* = birth year
PT2006

APPENDIX 2 | PEOPLE MENTIONED IN THE DIARY

1. Sāmī's Siblings (Eldest to Youngest) and In-Laws

Yusrā
  ʿUthmān Amīn al-Ḥammūrī—Yusrā's husband
Naʿīma
  Rashad al-Bakri—Naʿīma's second husband
Asʿad
  Hanīyya—Asʿad's wife
Saʿdī (unmarried)
(Sāmī, married to Suhayla)
Ruqayya
  ʿIzzat al-ʿAṭāwna—Ruqayya's husband

2. People Associated with Sāmī's Work at the NAAFI

Abū Sawwān—male co-worker
Ayyūb—owner of a restaurant near the NAAFI office
Captain Pudrell—presumably an official at the NAAFI
Hannā Yaghnam—male co-worker
Ilyās Habbash—male co-worker
Lorenziadis—Sāmī's boss, a Greek man
Lūbā—female co-worker and fleeting love interest
Barbara—Lūbā's sister
Major Tate—presumably a high-ranking official at the NAAFI
Marīkā—female co-worker
Marīttā and Rudaynā—presumably co-workers, girls with whom Sāmī apparently exchanged English for French lessons
Marjarīt—female co-worker
Mary—female co-worker
Nikōlā—female co-worker
Tsibūra—Jewish female co-worker, once Sāmī's love interest

3. Sāmī's Maternal Relatives, from the al-Budayrī Side of His Family

Ḥāfiẓ Kamāl—Hind al-Budayrī's husband
Jamāl al-Budayrī—Sāmī's uncle

ʿAbd al-Karīm, ʿAlyya, Fakhrī, Faṭṭūm (or Faṭṭūmah), Hind, Muḥammad, Saʿīd—Jamāl al-Budayrī's children, Sāmī's cousins, of unknown chronological order

Sulaymān Budayrī—incorrectly noted by Sāmī; his real name was Sulaymān al-Khālidī, as his mother, Sāmī's maternal aunt, married into the al-Khālidī family

4. Sāmī's Paternal Relatives, from the ʿAmr Side of His Family

ʿAbd ad-Dīk—nickname of a man married to a woman from the wider ʿAmr family

Abdullah [*ibn*] Bashīr—Suhayla's father, Sāmī's eventual father-in-law and his first cousin on his father's side

Ḥusayn ʿAmr—not well identified but related to Muḥammad Salīm

Maḥmūd Muḥammad ʿIsa—probably a cousin

Miriam—stepmother of Abdullah Bashīr, fifth wife of his father, Bashīr Yaḥyā ʿAmr

Muḥammad Salīm—not well identified but related to Ḥusayn ʿAmr

Ratība—Suhayla's mother, Abdullah Bashīr's wife

as-Sayyida "N"—Naʿomeh, Suhayla's younger sister

Suhayla—Sāmī's eventual wife, his first cousin once removed

Ṭalab ʿAbd al-Majīd—probably a cousin

ʿUthmān—Sāmī's cousin

Yūsuf ʿAbd al-Ḥamīd—Sāmī's second or third cousin and *mukhtār* of Dūra

4. Roommate, Landlord, and Landladies

ʿAwdat al-Māliḥī—landlord

Muḥammad—a roommate of Sāmī, not clear in which apartment

Umm Aldū—Sāmī's Italian female landlady in the al-Baqʿa neighborhood of Jerusalem who took a strong liking to him

Umm Mikhāʾīl—landlady

5. Other, Less Well-Described Individuals

Bishāra Saḥḥār—Sāmī's classmate at welding school who remained in touch with Sāmī through the 1950s

Fāʾīda—Lebanese girl on whom Sāmī had a crush and to whom he wrote a love letter in the diary

Ḥasan Abū ʿAysha—member of the Palestinian Arab Workers Society in Jerusalem

Hāshim Abū ʿAysha—Sāmī's classmate at welding school and lifelong friend

Jiryis Yūsuf—Palestinian employed in the Department of Labor Affairs
Jones Nather—Supervisor of Provisions in British Mandate government
Mr. Shadley—British Director of Labor Affairs, Jerusalem
Muḥammad ash-Sharabati—mentioned without further identification
Mūsā al-ʿAṭāwna—brother of the husband of Sāmī's sister Ruqayya
An-Natsha family—relatives of the al-ʿAṭāwna family of Sāmī's brother-in-law ʿIzzat
Shafīq Musallam—Palestinian Christian clerk in the governor's office, presumably in Hebron

BIBLIOGRAPHY

ʿAbd al-Hādī, ʿAwni. *Mudhakkirāt ʿAwni ʿAbd al-Hādī* (Memoirs of ʿAwni ʿAbd al-Hādī). Beirut: Markaz Dirāsāt al-Waḥdah al-ʿArabiyya, 2002.

Abu-Bakr, Amīn Masʿud. *Qaḍaʾ al-Khalīl, 1864–1917.* ʿAmman: Manshūrāt Lajnat Taʾrīkh Bilād ash-Shām, 1994.

Abu-Ghazaleh, Adnan. "Arab Cultural Nationalism in Palestine during the British Mandate." *Journal of Palestine Studies* 1, no. 3 (1973): 37–63.

Abū Sabayh, Abdullah Waḥbah. *Min dhākirat al-jihād al-filasṭīnī: Baldat al-ʿAbbāsīyya, taʾrīkuha wa-jihāduha* (From the Memoirs of a Palestinian Struggle: al-ʿAbbāsīyya, Its History and Struggle). Jordan: Matbaʿ al-Jazīra, 2001.

al-ʿAmla, Muḥammad Yūsuf ʿAmr. *ʿAshīrat Āl al-ʿAmla "al-ʿAmr"* (The Clan of Āl al-ʿAmla "al-ʿAmr"). ʿAmman: al-Eiman Printing Press, 1990.

al-ʿArif, ʿArif. *Al-Mufaṣṣal fī taʾrīkh al-Quds* (Detailed History of Jerusalem). 5th edition. Jerusalem: Maṭbaʿat al-Maʿārif, 1999.

ʿAlqām, Nabīl. *Al-Intidāb Al-barīṭānī fī dhākirat ash-shaʿb al-filasṭīnī* (The British Mandate in the Memory of the Palestinian People). ʿAkka: Muʾassasat al-Aswar, 2002.

Armbrust, Walter. *Mass Culture and Modernism in Egypt.* Cambridge Studies in Social and Cultural Anthropology. Cambridge, England: Cambridge University Press, 2001.

al-Ashhab, ʿAwdat. *Mudhakkirāt ʿAwdat al-Ashhab* (Memoirs of ʿAwdat al-Ashhab). Supervised by Sulaymān Rabadi; introduction by ʿAbd ar-Raḥīm al-Mudawwar. *Ṣafaḥāt min adh-dhākira al-filasṭīnīyya* (Pages from Palestinian Memory) Series, no. 8. Bir Zeit: Center for the Study and Documentation of Palestinian Society, Bir Zeit University, 1999.

Ayalon, Ami. *Reading Palestine: Printing and Literacy, 1900–1948.* Austin: University of Texas Press, 2004.

Bein, Alex, ed. *Arthur Ruppin: Memoirs, Diaries, Letters.* Introduction by Alex Bein; translation by Karen Gershon; afterword by Moshe Dayan. London: Weidenfeld and Nicolson, 1971.

Berlin, Howard M. *The Coins and Banknotes of Palestine Under the British Mandate, 1927–1947.* North Carolina: McFarland, 2001.

Chapple, John. "Jewish Land Settlement in Palestine." In *From Haven to Con-*

quest: Readings in Zionism and the Palestine Problem Until 1948, edited by Walid Khalidi. Washington, DC: Institute for Palestine Studies, 1987.

Christison, Kathleen. *Perceptions of Palestine: Their Influence on U.S. Middle East Policy.* Los Angeles: University of California Press, 1999.

Cohen, Amnon, and Gabriel Baer, eds. *Egypt and Palestine: A Millennium of Association (868–1948).* New York: St. Martin's Press, 1984.

Constable, Giles. *Letters and Letter-Collections.* Turnhout, Belgium: Brepols, 1976.

Courtney, Roger. *Palestine Policeman: An Account of Eighteen Dramatic Months in the Palestine Police Force During the Great Jew-Arab Troubles.* London: H. Jenkins, 1939.

Dabbāgh, Muṣṭafā Murād. *Bilādunā filasṭīn: Fī diyār al-Khalīl* (Our Country, Palestine: In the Region of Hebron). Volume 5 (of 10), part 2: *Kafr Qaraʿ: Dār al-huda li-ṭ-ṭibāʿa wa-n-nashr,* 2002.

Darwaza, Muḥammad ʿIzzat. *Mudhakkirāt: Sijill ḥāfil bī-masīrat al-ḥaraka al-ʿarabiyya wa-l-qadīyya al-filasṭīnīyya khilāl qarn min az-zaman, 1305–1404h/1887–1984m* (Memoirs: A Celebratory Record of the Journey of the Arab Movement and the Palestinian Issue over a Century, 1887–1984). Beirut: Dār al-Gharb al-Islāmī, 2003.

Davis, Rochelle. "Al-Kutub at-tidhkarīyya al-filasṭīnīyya wa-s-siyar adh-dhātīyya al-jumāʿīyya" (Palestinian Memorial Books and Collective Autobiographies). In *Dirāsāt fī-t-taʾrīkh al-ijtimāʿī li-bilād ash-shām: qirāʾāt fī-s-siyar wa-s-siyar al-dhātīyya* (Studies in the Social History of Bilad al-Sham: Readings In Biographies And Autobiographies), edited by Issam Nassar and Salim Tamari. Beirut: Institute for Palestine Studies, 2007.

———. "Commemorating Education: Recollections of the Arab College in Jerusalem, 1918–1948." *Comparative Studies of South Asia, Africa, and the Middle East* 23, no. 1/2 (2003): 190–204.

———. "The Growth of the Western Communities, 1917–1948." In *Jerusalem 1948: The Arab Neighbourhoods and their Fate in the War,* edited by Salim Tamari. 2d edition, revised and expanded. Jerusalem: Institute of Jerusalem Studies, and Bethlehem: Badil Resource Center, 2002.

———. "Mapping the Past, Re-creating the Homeland: Memories of Village Places in Pre-1948 Palestine." In *Nakba: Palestine, 1948, and the Claims of Memory,* edited by Ahmad Saʿdi and Laila Abu-Lughod. New York: Columbia University Press, 2007.

Davis, Ronald. "Jewish Military Recruitment in Palestine, 1940–1943." *Journal of Palestine Studies* 8, no. 2 (1979): 55–76.

Dīwān al-Mutanabbī. Beirut: Dār Bayrut li-ṭ-ṭibāʿa wa-n-nashr, 1983.

Doumani, Beshara. "Rediscovering Ottoman Palestine: Writing Palestinians into History." *Journal of Palestine Studies* 21, no. 2 (Winter 1992): 5–28.

———. *Rediscovering Palestine: Merchants and Peasants in Jabal Nablus, 1700–1900.* Berkeley: University of California Press, 1995.

Eisenman, Robert H. *Islamic Law in Palestine and Israel: A History of the Survival of Tanzimat and Shariʿa in the British Mandate and the Jewish State.* Leiden: E. J. Brill, 1978.

Farsoun, Samih, and Aruri, Naseer. *Palestine and the Palestinians: A Social and Political History.* Boulder, CO: Westview Press, 2006.

Garbarini, Alexandra. *Numbered Days: Diaries and the Holocaust.* New Haven, CT: Yale University Press, 2006.

Gelvin, James L. "The Ironic Legacy of the King-Crane Commission." In *The Middle East and the United States: A Historical and Political Reassessment,* ed. David W. Lesch. 4th edition. Boulder, CO: Westview, 1999.

George, Alan. "'Making the Desert Bloom': A Myth Examined." *Journal of Palestine Studies* 8, no. 2 (1979): 88–100.

Gershoni, Israel, Hakan Erdem, and Ursula Woköck, eds. *Histories of the Modern Middle East: New Directions.* Boulder, CO: Lynne Rienner, 2002.

Haydār, Rustum. *Mudhakkirāt Rustum Haydār* (Memoirs of Rustum Haydār). Beirut: ad-Dār al-ʿarabīyya li-l-mawsūʿāt, 1988.

Horne, Edward. *A Job Well Done: Being a History of the Palestine Police Force, 1920–1948.* Sussex, England: Book Guild, 2003.

Howard, Harry N. *The King-Crane Commission: An American Inquiry into the Middle East.* Beirut: Khayat, 1963.

Hurewitz, J. C., ed. *Diplomacy in the Near and Middle East: A Documentary Record.* New York: Octagon Books, 1972.

———. *The Struggle for Palestine.* New York: First Greenwood, 1968.

Ḥusayn, Taha. *The Days: His Autobiography in Three Parts.* Trans. E. H. Paxton, Hilary Wayment, and Kenneth Cragg. Cairo: American University in Cairo Press, 1997.

Inert-Gas Arc Welding: History and Fundamentals. London: Institute of Welding, 1966.

Jackson, Ashley. *The British Empire and the Second World War.* London: Hambledon and London, 2005.

Jiryis, Sabri, and Salah Qallab. "The Palestine Research Center." *Journal of Palestine Studies* 14, no. 4, (Summer 1985): 185–187.

Khalaf, Issa. *Politics in Palestine: Arab Factionalism and Social Disintegration, 1939–1948.* New York: Albany State University Press, 1991.

Khalidi, Rashid. *The Iron Cage: The Story of the Palestinian Struggle for Statehood.* Boston: Beacon Press, 2006.

Khalidi, Tarif. "Palestinian Historiography: 1900–1948." *Journal of Palestine Studies* 10, no. 3 (1981): 59–76.

Khalidi, Walid. *All That Remains: The Palestinian Villages Occupied and Depopulated by Israel in 1948.* Washington, DC: Institute for Palestine Studies, 1992.

———. *Before Their Diaspora: A Photographic History of the Palestinians, 1876–1948.* Baltimore, MD: Institute for Palestine Studies, 1984.

———, ed. *From Haven to Conquest: Readings in Zionism and the Palestine Problem Until 1948.* Washington, DC: Institute for Palestine Studies, 1987.

Khater, Akram Fouad, ed. *Sources in the History of the Modern Middle East.* New York: Houghton Mifflin, 2004.

al-Khaṭīb, Amīn. *Tadhakkurāt Amīn al-Khaṭīb* (Recollections of Amīn al-Khaṭīb). Supervised by ʿAlī Jarbāwī, introduction by Muʿāwīya Tahbūb. *Ṣafaḥāt min adh-dhākira al-filasṭīnīyya* (Pages from Palestinian Memory) Series, no. 2. Bir Zeit: Center for the Study and Documentation of Palestinian Society, Bir Zeit University. 1992.

Khouri, Fred J. *The Arab-Israeli Dilemma.* 2d edition. Syracuse, NY: Syracuse University Press, 1976.

Klieman, Aaron S. *Foundations of British Policy in the Arab World: The Cairo Conference of 1921.* Baltimore, MD: Johns Hopkins Press, 1970.

Kolinsky, Martin. *Britain's War in the Middle East: Strategy and Diplomacy, 1936–1942.* New York: St. Martin's Press, 1999.

Langford, Rachel, and Russell West, eds. *Marginal Voices, Marginal Forms: Diaries in European Literature and History.* Atlanta, GA: Rodopi, 1999.

Lejeune, Philippe. "The Practice of the Private Journal: Chronicle of an Investigation (1986–1998)." In *Marginal Voices, Marginal Forms: Diaries in European Literature and History,* edited by Rachel Langford and Russell West. Atlanta, GA: Rodopi, 1999.

Leleu, Michèle. *Les journaux intimes.* Paris: Presses Universitaires de France, 1952.

Lesch, Ann Mosely. *Arab Politics in Palestine, 1917–1939: The Frustration of a Nationalist Movement.* Ithaca, NY: Cornell University Press, 1979.

Lesch, David W., ed. *The Middle East and the United States: A Historical and Political Reassessment.* 4th edition. Boulder, CO: Westview, 1999.

Lindenberg, Sidney. "The Cultural Life of Arabs." *Journal of Educational Sociology* 22, no. 3 (1948): 232–239. Translated from Hebrew and adapted from a chapter in J. Shimoni, *The Arabs of Palestine*; Tel Aviv: N.p., 1947.

Little, Douglas. *American Orientalism: The United States and the Middle East Since 1945*. Chapel Hill: University of North Carolina Press, 2002.

Lockman, Zachary. *Comrades and Enemies: Arab and Jewish Workers in Palestine, 1906–1948*. Berkeley: University of California Press, 1996.

Mackintosh-Smith, Tim. *Yemen: The Unknown Arabia*. New York: Overlook Press, 2000.

Makdisi, George. “The Diary in Islamic Historiography: Some Notes.” *History and Theory* 25, no. 2 (May 1986): 173–185.

Malti-Douglas, Fedwa. *Blindness and Autobiography: al-Ayyam of Taha Husayn*. Princeton, NJ: Princeton University Press, 1988.

Mannāʿ, Adel. “Between Jerusalem and Damascus: The End of Ottoman Rule as Seen by a Palestinian Modernist.” *Jerusalem Quarterly* 22–23 (2006): 109–125.

Mattar, Philip. *The Mufti of Jerusalem: al-Hajj Amin al-Husayni and the Palestinian National Movement*. New York: Columbia University Press, 1992.

McAlister, Melanie. *Epic Encounters: Culture, Media, and U.S. Interests in the Middle East, 1945–2000*. Revised edition. Berkeley: University of California Press, 2005.

Miller, Ylana. *Government and Society in Rural Palestine, 1900–1948*. Austin: University of Texas Press, 1985.

Morris, Benny. *The Birth of the Palestinian Refugee Problem Revisited*. Cambridge, England: Cambridge University Press, 2004.

Morris, Colin. *The Discovery of the Individual, 1050–1200*. New York: Harper and Row, 1972.

Muslih, Muhammad Y. *The Origins of Palestinian Nationalism*. New York: Columbia University Press, 1988.

Naafi Up!: The Official History of NAAFI Commemorating 75 years of Serving the Services. Cornwall, England: AQ&DJ Publications, 1996.

Nashef, Khaled. “Tawfiq Canaan: His Life and Works.” *Jerusalem Quarterly File*, issue 16 (November 2002): 12–26.

Nassar, Issam, and Salim Tamari, eds. *Al-Quds al-ʿuthmānīyya fī-l-mudhakkirāt al-Jawhariyya: al-kitāb al-awwal min mudhakkirāt al-musīqi Wāṣif Jawhariyya (1904–1917)* (Ottoman Jerusalem in the Jawhariyya Memoirs: The First Book of the Memoirs of Musician Wāṣif Jawhariyya [1904–1917]). Jerusalem: Institute for Palestine Studies, 2003.

———, eds. *Al-Quds al-intidābīyya fī-l-mudhakkirāt al-Jawhariyya: al-kitāb al-thānī min mudhakkirāt al-musīqi Wāṣif Jawhariyya (1918–1948)* (British Mandate Jerusalem in the Jawhariyya Memoirs: The Second Book of the Memoirs of Musician Wāṣif Jawhariyya [1918–1948]). Jerusalem: Institute for Palestine Studies, 2005.

———, eds. *Dirāsāt fī-t-ta'rīkh al-ijtimā'ī li-bilād ash-shām: qirā'āt fī-s-siyar wa-s-siyar adh-dhātīyya* (Studies in the Social History of Bilad al-Sham: Readings in Biographies and Autobiographies). Beirut: Institute for Palestine Studies, 2007.

Obenzinger, Hilton. *American Palestine: Melville, Twain, and Holy Land Mania.* Princeton, NJ: Princeton University Press, 1999.

Pappe, Ilan. *A History of Modern Palestine: One Land, Two Peoples.* 2d edition. Cambridge, England: Cambridge University Press, 2006.

———. *The Making of the Arab-Israeli Conflict, 1947–1951.* New York: I. B. Tauris, 2001.

Partner, Nancy, ed. *Writing Medieval History.* London: Arnold, 2005.

Porath, Yehoshua. "Palestinian Historiography." *Jerusalem Quarterly,* no. 5 (Fall 1977): 95–104.

al-Qāḍi, Maḥmūd. *Shay' min adh-dhākira.* Damascus: Dār Kan'ān Li-d-dirasāt Wa-n-nashr, 1995.

al-Qawuqjī, Fawzī. *Mudhakkirāt Fawzī al-Qawuqjī, 1912–1932* (Memoirs of Fawzī al-Qawuqjī, 1912–1932). Beirut: Dār al-Quds, 1975.

Reynolds, Dwight, ed. *Interpreting the Self: Autobiography in the Arabic Literary Tradition.* Berkeley: University of California Press, 2001.

Rubenstein, Jay. "Biography and Autobiography in the Middle Ages." In *Writing Medieval History,* edited by Nancy Partner. London: Arnold, 2005.

Sa'di, Ahmad, and Laila Abu-Lughod, eds. *Nakba: Palestine, 1948, and the Claims of Memory.* New York: Columbia University Press, 2007.

as-Sakākīnī, Khalīl. *Yawmīyyāt Khalīl as-Sakākīnī: Yawmīyyāt, risā'il, ta'mulāt* (The Diary of Khalīl Sakākīnī: Diaries, Letters, Reflections), ed. Akram Musallam. 6 volumes. Ramallah: Khalīl Sakākīnī Cultural Center and Institute for Jerusalem Studies, 2003–2006.

Schlaeger, Jürgen. "Self-Exploration in Early Modern English Diaries." In *Marginal Voices, Marginal Forms: Diaries in European Literature and History,* edited by Rachel Langford and Russell West. Atlanta, GA: Rodopi, 1999.

Seikaly, Sherene. "Meatless Days: Consumption and Capitalism in Wartime Palestine, 1939–1948." Ph.D. diss., New York University, 2007.

Shamir, Shimon. "Egyptian Rule (1832–1840) and the Beginning of the Modern Period in the History of Palestine." In *Egypt and Palestine: A Millennium of Association (868–1948),* ed. Amnon Cohen and Gabriel Baer. New York: St. Martin's Press, 1984.

Sherman, A. J. *Mandate Days: British Lives in Palestine, 1918–1948.* New York: Thames and Hudson, 1998.

Sidqī, Najātī. *Mudhakkirāt Najātī Sidqī* (Memoirs of Najātī Sidqī). Beirut: Mu'assasat ad-Dirāsāt al-Filasṭīnīyya, 2001.

Simonson, R. D. *The History of Welding.* Morton Grove, IL: Monticello Books, 1969.

Simpson, John Hope. *Palestine, Report on Immigration, Land Settlement and Development.* London: His Majesty's Stationery Office, 1930.

A Survey of Palestine Prepared for the Anglo-Arab Committee of Inquiry. London: His Majesty's Stationery Office, 1946.

Swedenburg, Ted. *Memories of Revolt: The 1936–1939 Rebellion and the Palestinian National Past.* Minneapolis: University of Minnesota Press, 1995.

Tamari, Salim. *ʿĀm al-jarād: al-ḥarb al-ʿuẓma wa-maḥu al-māḍī al-ʿuthmānī min filasṭīn* (Year of the Locust: The Great War and the Erasure of Palestine's Ottoman Past). Beirut: Institute for Palestine Studies, 2008. Draft in English furnished by Tamari, 2007.

———, ed. *Jerusalem 1948: The Arab Neighbourhoods and their Fate in the War.* 2d edition, revised and expanded. Jerusalem: Institute of Jerusalem Studies, and Bethlehem: Badil Resource Center, 2002.

———. "Jerusalem's Ottoman Modernity: The Times and Lives of Wasif Jawhariyyeh." *Jerusalem Quarterly,* issue 9 (Summer 2000): 5–27.

Tibawi, A. L. *Arab Education in Mandatory Palestine: A Study of Three Decades of British Administration.* London: Luzac, 1956.

———. "Educational Policy and Arab Nationalism in Mandatory Palestine." *Die Welt des Islams* 4, no. 1 (1955): 15–29.

Vester, Bertha Spafford. *Our Jerusalem: An American Family in the Holy City, 1881–1949.* London: Evans Brothers Limited, 1951.

Zumthor, Paul. "The Medieval Travel Narrative." *New Literary History: A Journal of Theory and Interpretation* 25, no. 4 (1994): 809–824.

INDEX

Page numbers in boldface indicate a map or photo.

CPSIA information can be obtained at www.ICGtesting.com
Printed in the USA
LVOW080143080213

319053LV00002B/166/P

9 780292 723559